D0812050

GETTING BY

Rural America

Hal S. Barron

David L. Brown

Kathleen Neils Conzen

Carville Earle

Cornelia Butler Flora

Donald Worster

Series Editors

GETTING BY

WOMEN HOMEWORKERS AND RURAL ECONOMIC DEVELOPMENT

Christina E. Gringeri

 *University Press of Kansas*

To Yolanda and Anthony Gringeri
for their faith, love, and support
and to Armando and Jesse
for their patience, inspiration, and sense of humor

© 1994 by the University Press of Kansas
All rights reserved

Published by the University Press of Kansas (Lawrence, Kansas 66049), which was organized by the Kansas Board of Regents and is operated and funded by Emporia State University, Fort Hays State University, Kansas State University, Pittsburg State University, the University of Kansas, and Wichita State University

Library of Congress Cataloging-in-Publication Data

Gringeri, Christina E.
    Getting by : women homeworkers and rural economic development /
Christina E. Gringeri.
        p. cm. — (Rural America)
    Includes bibliographical references and index.
    ISBN 0-7006-0640-8
    1. Home labor—Middle West—Case studies. 2. Rural development—
Middle West—Case studies. 3. Rural women—Employment—Middle
West—Case studies. I. Title. II. Series: Rural America
(Lawrence, Kans.)
    HD2336.U5G74   1994
    331.4'0977—dc20   94-13557

British Library Cataloguing in Publication Data is available.
Printed in the United States of America
10 9 8 7 6 5 4 3 2 1

The paper used in this publication meets the minimum requirements of the American National Standard for Permanence of Paper for Printed Library Materials Z39.48–1984.

Contents

Acknowledgments

Learning is a social endeavor, and the products of learning, such as this book, are the result of many people working together and contributing their time and knowledge. Many people gave their time, shared their experiences and knowledge with me, and opened their homes to me during the process of the research and writing that formed this project. I am enriched by their contributions to my work.

I am deeply indebted to the people in Riverton and Prairie Hills who participated in this study and who opened their homes and their lives to me. They taught me a great deal about work, families, and life in general simply through their willingness to share. Two very special couples took me into their homes for several weeks: Arlene and Ralph extended great hospitality and showed me a good time around town, too; Ruby and Floyd not only let me stay very comfortably in their home but also became my "adopted" family. They introduced me to many fine people in the community, taught me to play cards, and welcomed me on several later occasions into their family. These generous people will always have a special place in my heart; this book is one small way of saying thank you.

The Woodrow Wilson Foundation generously supported the research and fieldwork for this project with a Rural Policy Fellowship from 1988 to 1990. Gene Summers and Naomi Farber have been wonderful advisers and critical supporters throughout this project. As colleagues and friends, they have enriched this work and my academic work in general. Eileen Boris and Carolyn Sachs carefully read earlier versions of the manuscript and provided thoughtful and insightful suggestions for revisions to strengthen it. Cynthia Miller at the University Press of Kansas certainly embodies my ideal for editors: patient, humorous, and always confident that the project will reach completion.

My parents, Anthony and Yolanda, contributed to this book by instilling in me an early appreciation for the written word and through their unwavering belief that I would finish the project. Armando has generously read and reread drafts of various chapters, kindly pointing out the rough spots and making helpful suggestions. Both he and Jesse have tolerated my absences on weekends and evenings as I finished writing and revising. I appreciate their contributions and inspiration immeasurably.

Introduction

Industrial homework in the United States has long been portrayed by observers as the working province of the very poor, the economically and politically disadvantaged, and usually, the urban immigrant woman worker. When a fellow student and researcher returned from her fieldwork and mentioned that a rural community had implemented home assembly work as part of a development strategy, I became interested for two reasons.[1] A rural midwestern setting implied that the workers would not be similar in social or cultural background to the typical urban immigrant homeworker and the use of homework as development suggested the intriguing aspect of involvement and approval of the local and perhaps the subnational state. Such were the beginnings of this study: a curiosity on my part to learn about assembly homework from the homeworkers and an interest in understanding state involvement in its local, rural resurgence.

Soon after hearing about the workers in Riverton, I carried out a small pilot project to better understand the local context and the topics that would inform a later agenda for interviews. During the pilot project I learned that the same company had established home assembly jobs in Prairie Hills and decided to carry out case studies of the work in both communities.

Gaining access to all the homeworkers was a challenge because The Middle Company (TMC), as it will be called here, exerts enough influence in each of these communities that such access could not be granted by any local person. Given the control and influence of the company in the community, few workers would have participated without company approval for fear of endangering their livelihood. If I had used the snowball technique, I would not have known if I had contacted everyone; thus I undertook the study with the goal of gaining permission from TMC to contact and interview all the homeworkers.

Company managers were open enough to the project that they invited me to the headquarters for a daylong meeting, during which they "wanted to get to know me, hear about the project, and tell me about the cottage industry work." They seemed to have a few major points of concern, mostly relating to my political views about unions, women workers, and homeworking. What would I do, they asked, if someone refused to participate? I assured them that the workers could be interviewed only on a voluntary basis. If possible, I would try to learn the reason for their refusal. Was I in favor of homeworking? What did I think of unions? Was I trying to bring "women's lib" to these rural areas? Various managers assured me that rural women "don't want or need that women's lib stuff." We talked at length that day, and the managers were informative, even taking me through the factory. I left with permission to contact and interview all the homeworkers in each community.

Although I gained access to all the homeworkers, the process did affect the study and the data collected. TMC's permission meant that the project was carefully watched for the duration of the fieldwork. For example, midway through the interviewing in Prairie Hills, TMC managers telephoned me and asked me a few hours' worth of questions about the research and were especially concerned about my questions regarding Social Security. They almost called the research to a halt but by the end of the conversation had somewhat reluctantly decided to allow me to finish. I did finish the fieldwork although not without a short-lived sense of walking on eggshells.

The company connection to this research affected the response rate and the information shared in the interviews, too. The response rate averaged 90 percent between the two communities, partly because the workers felt comfortable participating since TMC approved. No one reported feeling obligated to participate because of TMC's approval although a few workers said they would not have consented had the company not approved. It is possible that the TMC connection tended to make workers less likely to share negative information about the working conditions, perhaps because of a concern that it would get back to the company. Yet most workers did not have difficulty pointing out aspects of the work that they thought were not right or that could easily be improved. Even workers who expressed great satisfaction with the employment situation were able to make comments about improving the pay, the lack of benefits, or the instability of the work. Taken together, the workers' interviews seem to give a realistic, balanced portrait of homework even in this context of the company's approval.

Beginning in November 1988 I conducted personal interviews with homeworkers in Riverton, staying with a local family for about six weeks and working from their home. TMC's local manager, with permission from the main headquarters, had given me a list of forty homeworkers. First I contacted each homeworking family by letter and then with a phone call in which I asked workers to participate in a personal interview at their convenience. Among the forty homeworkers, thirty-seven (92.5 percent), agreed to participate. Each interview was conducted in the participant's home and lasted from an hour to an hour and a half; all the interviews were audiotaped and transcribed for use in content analysis.

In Prairie Hills I used the same method, staying with a local family for six weeks and contacting the homeworkers by letter first and then by a phone call to request their participation. Forty-three of the forty-eight homeworkers (89.5 percent) were interviewed. Six former homeworkers also were referred to me by current workers; I contacted them for interviews, and four in Riverton and two in Prairie Hills participated.

To all respondents I presented myself as a student who was interested in learning about their work from their perspective. Most of the workers did not ask for more than basic information about the study although a few asked what I was going to write about and what sort of "story" I would tell about them and their work. At that time I was not at all sure about the final product, so I explained generally that the story depended greatly upon the content of the interviews. A few people refused to participate. In at least three of these cases, the workers declined because another family member, usually the homeworker's husband, objected to the interview. The other people who did not want to be interviewed would not give their reasons.

The homeworkers in both communities are fairly similar demographically. Of the thirty-six workers in Riverton, the women's average age was about thirty-nine years, the men's forty-six. Eleven of the thirty-six households, or about one-third, were farming households. Almost all the workers had completed high school, a few had a little postsecondary education, and thirty-two were married at the time of the interview. In Prairie Hills, the women workers' average age was forty, the men's about forty-three. Two-thirds of the homeworkers lived in farming households, and only two of the workers interviewed were not married. Most workers had finished high school, three had finished four years of college, and several more had had some postsecondary education. I designed three approaches to explore how industrial homework has become an integral facet of economic development in these two rural midwestern communities. The first focuses on the local development process that brought industrial homework jobs to Riverton and Prairie Hills, both of which are located in the corn and dairy belts of the Midwest, in order in order to provide an in-depth description and analysis of how two economically depressed rural communities defined an economic development strategy in which industrial homework became a key component. Given the lack of job security and low wages common to industrial homework, it is important to examine the community-development goals that homework was intended to fulfill to ascertain how the community weighed the costs and benefits.

To examine the community-development process, I used content analysis of minutes from council and open town meetings and data from twelve interviews with elected and private-sector leaders in each community. I also examined the company's agreements or contracts that pertained to the employment of homeworkers and analyzed local newspaper pieces on the topic. The reality of fieldwork revealed the somewhat unrealistic nature of these methods, however, since minutes of meetings were notoriously devoid of any record of discussion about industrial development. Usually the notes from both communities listed only motions made and seconded. More helpful were the records from the state-level departments of development that detailed state financial support for the development of cottage-industry jobs.

In each community there was a private community-development corporation made up of influential local citizens such as the mayor, one or two local bankers, the city lawyer, and one or two prominent businessmen. In Riverton, the group was well organized and kept a detailed log of their meetings. As a private group, however, they exercised the right to deny access to this material, as they reportedly had done in the past with other researchers, although the president of this group did grant me an informative interview. In Prairie Hills, the development corporation did give me access to their records, but unfortunately they were on a par with the minutes of council meetings: brief and relatively without substance. In both cases, community leaders openly stated that the materials were kept in such a way as to protect the privacy of industry, both new and potential.

The newspapers in both communities are fairly typical of small town periodicals: bits of local news, lots of articles about social clubs and students' achievements, and a healthy dose of high school sports news. Press releases regarding the implementation of subcontracting were controlled by TMC. In Riverton, the publisher had about two years of back issues available for purchase, which I obtained; in contrast, the publisher in Prairie Hills did not have back issues even for the previous month.

I also gathered information from the respective state-level departments of Development, relying on both printed materials and interviews with officials. Officials on the local and regional state levels agreed to be interviewed, allowed me to audiotape record sessions when I requested, and offered me whatever printed information was available and accessible to the public. From the interviews I hoped to gather a variety of perspectives on the development goals associated with homeworking. The officials, however, shared the opinion that development is equivalent to job creation: Since homeworking is a job, it therefore is development.

For the interviews I chose subareas designed to examine how local and state leaders defined the development problem, how they chose homeworking as one strategy, and what objectives they thought homeworking jobs could accomplish:

1. How did local leaders define the need or problem in the community?
2. Which development goals would be met by developing industrial homeworking? Which costs and benefits were considered?
3. Which nonofficial local residents were involved in deciding to develop homework jobs?
4. What incentives were used to attract a homework-employer?
5. What was the manufacturer's involvement in initiating homework jobs in these communities?

My second objective was to examine workers' experiences with industrial homework, both as a job and as a development strategy. This approach included an exploration of their homeworking experiences, its consequences for home and family life, and their perceptions of how homework fits into the local economy.

The personal and in-depth interviews were based on a semistructured, open-ended topic agenda that focused on the worker's descriptions of various aspects of work, home, and family tasks and relationships. Included were specific questions about working conditions such as pay, hours, schedules, others who helped with the homework, and where the work was performed. I also asked questions about housework and about who was responsible for various chores around the home and farm.

The interviews with the homeworkers were designed to allow conversation to flow freely, to a certain extent. I would ask questions or raise topics for conversation, but within that structure, workers were free to talk as much or as little as they chose and free to deviate from the topic at hand. Thus respondents had some control over the content of their interviews. Moreover, this style offered me information that I had not specifically asked for but that was helpful in understanding the individual and her or his work.

I analyzed the interviews for major themes and categories relating to workers' descriptions of the interaction of homework and other aspects of their lives, beginning this process by reading through all the transcripts a couple of times without categorizing any of the material into themes. While I read I kept an informal list of ideas, questions, and possible themes and categories for analysis. Once I had excerpted material from all the interviews, I read the excerpts with the goal of seeing what "story" could be told.

Interview data were examined in relation to the themes of wages, criteria for work deadlines, quality-assurance criteria, and other working conditions. Most of the themes analyzed were generated from preconceived topics or categories, such as the themes on working conditions and housework. Some of the themes emerged from the interviews during several intensive readings of the transcripts. For example, I was interested in how workers developed and maintained their work spaces. The interview data contained material about these topics since spatial separation for work at home was an item I had asked about. Some workers had family concerns about work space, and women and men experienced this issue differently. I was interested in learning how these workers understand the concept of a work ethic, but it was not until I had completed several interviews that I found a way to ask about it, based on earlier discussions with respondents. People seemed to understand when I asked them generally, "Some folks say industries relocate to rural areas because of the people's work ethic here. What does that mean to you?" Respondents would talk about hard work, good family values, anti-union attitudes, and, quite directly, about industrial firms' searching for cheap labor. Often, their answers gave me more than I asked for, and I learned more than I set out to learn from these people.

During each interview I asked the homeworker to describe

1. the effects of homework on sharing of home and farm tasks
2. the effects of homework on child/dependent-care responsibilities
3. homework as a job—its strengths and weaknesses such as working conditions, deadlines, criteria for quality assessment, and wages
4. workers' involvement in the process to bring homework jobs into the community
5. homework as community development
6. the place of homework in the local economy on a short- and long-term basis

The names of homeworkers have been changed, and quotations from their interviews are not given sources in order to ensure the workers' anonymity.

These interviews covered homeworkers in two locales who worked for one company and who performed small assembly work. I analyzed the data comparatively with existing case-study data on urban homeworkers in the United States, Mexico, and Great Britain in chapter 6. Comparing homeworkers and their experiences across regions and types of work reveals similarities that enhance the generalization of findings regarding working conditions.

My third objective was to determine the extent to which industrial homework has achieved the community's development goals. The analysis of the policy process and of the data on the workers' perspectives on homeworking is synthesized to assess how industrial homeworking fits into the local development strategy. The analysis examines data on the intentions of the development strategy and the consequences experienced by the workers in order to evaluate industrial homework in a rural context.

The framework of uneven development suggests that the relationship between the local state and capital investment is integral to understanding the process of development. Thus, the analysis must also focus on the interaction between internal and external structures shaping development. The emphasis here is on the relationship between industrial restructuring and the labor and development policies of the state as the external structures that support the use of industrial homework as local development. The internal conditions examined include the histories of local economic development in these communities and the role of the household unit in the process of contemporary development projects. This approach will aid in the "identification of those sectors tapped as sources of support for development and of those 'made to pay' its costs."[2]

1

Industrial Homework as Rural Development

In the early 1840s Mary and Harriet Nutting, sisters in rural Massachusetts, wrote of the work activities that made up their days. "Last week Mother wove . . . carpet I sewed for Doria Cook, the girls braided. This week we have took up the carpets and cleand house and made soap and cut five dresses and made two or three sun bonnets. Amelia has been to the Academy one day . . . all this besides braiding [which] we wont say anything about." Some time later, when Harriet was the only woman at home, she wrote, "I have to be Hannah and mother in the house and John at the barn, besides braiding double rimmed hats when there is 'nothing else to do.'"[1] The Nutting sisters were rural outworkers, taking home palm-leaf hat-braiding from a local merchant. Their letters depict the weaving of paid and unpaid work in and around the home that occupied rural women's days and evenings in the nineteenth century, exposing the notion of homeworking as a spare-time activity as mere illusion in their case. Anna Rea, a rural homeworker in Danvers, bound shoes for over nine years during the 1830s in an effort to keep the farm going and to support herself, her sister, and her mother.[2] She earned little, however, because the piecerates changed minimally over those nine years.

Harriet Nutting and Anna Rea may seem fairly typical for the nineteenth century, but though the activities may have changed, the combination of paid homework, paid child care, and unpaid family work and housework continues in rural areas today. For example,

Gail, a young woman in rural Riverton, Wisconsin, assembles small screws and washers in her home for a subcontractor of General Motors. She spoke about how she started homeworking:

> Yes, it's no fun. 'Cause when we were first married, they were my dreams to move, to live on the farm and raise a family and help with the farm work, but it didn't work out like that. We really started out from scratch and when farming went down, we went down. So our best decision was to get out or be in debt forever, and never ever make it. So, we went out, and he started workin' for this farmer, and we moved into Riverton, and I started babysitting and then I started, just started my homeworking job, and I work part-time at the county hospital.

Gail's experience portrays the human face of the farm crisis beyond the dismal economic indicators of high debt load and low farm prices. Like Anna Rea, Gail takes in piecework to add to the family economy; like Harriet Nutting, Gail's work schedule shows that homeworking is not done in her spare time but is fit in and around several other work activities. Over a span of more than 150 years, these women's experiences highlight a common response of rural people to economic need: They juggle as many jobs as possible in an effort "to make it." Gail babysits for three other children, assembles bolts at home, and works part-time outside the home. Her husband, no longer operating their family farm, is a wage laborer for a local farmer. A typical day for Gail shows that "making it" is hard work.

> Well, I get up at 5:30 in the morning and start working on my bolts. I work four hours in the morning. I try to get four hours in the afternoon, but I work, start working at the hospital at 6:00 P.M., so I usually get just about two hours in and then I have time to get ready and get my kids ready, get my house picked up before I go to work, and then, I get done working at the hospital at 9:00. Then I come home and fix supper for my husband and my little girl, and then I get her to bed, if I can. And I put her to bed and then my husband goes to bed and I work three more hours on the bolts. So I usually get, try to get in seven hours a day, unless there are days that I got to take her to the doctor, to the dentist, or if I hafta run out and that puts me behind. But I hafta put seven hours a day in on my bolts, because the weekends I usually try to save for my husband, 'cause I never see him very much.

Gail's job as a home assembler is woven throughout the day and evening hours with her responsibilities as a wife, parent, and wage worker outside the home. Her work responsibilities are organized around the assumptions that the home is her sphere and that her wage work is secondary for her and her family. Thus gender is central to the organization of home-based production because such production depends on the sexual division of labor in the home and in the wage-labor market. Incorporating homework jobs into local development serves to weave the same assumptions through the process of job recruitment and community development.

In the 1980s, when the farm crisis meant that many people began seeking off-farm wage work, job creation became the byword of rural development groups trying to stem the tide of local decline. Private and public development officials worked together to develop assembly homeworking jobs in two midwestern rural communities, Prairie Hills, Iowa, and Riverton, Wisconsin, with the cooperation and financing of the two states. Since 1986 more than eighty families have worked as home-based contractors in the two towns, putting together a variety of small auto parts for TMC, a Fortune 500 manufacturer and subcontractor of General Motors (GM). This company established warehouses in Prairie Hills and Riverton to distribute the automotive assembly work that people could do at home. One homeworker recalled TMC managers saying that they had picked these locations because they could "feel the total agricultural distress" in "our small communities."

Decentralized economic development policies allow local states to finance homework as rural development, thus supporting the creation and mobility of deskilled, non-unionized jobs largely carried out by women. Economic development, then, is a tool of the private industrial sector and the public sector that achieves, in the case of homework, the maintenance of inequalities based primarily on sex and secondly on class. Industrial homework incorporates women into the labor process as "secondary" workers, which justifies the low pay, job insecurity, and lack of insurance benefits characteristic of informal-sector work. These strategies undergird industrial efforts to weaken the position of both urban and rural labor because they support the creation of non-union, low-paying, insecure jobs.

State financing of homework as development not only indicates public support for gender as an organizing principle in private and public divisions of labor but also state support of restructured jobs. These rural homeworking jobs resulted from the fragmentation of one labor process in the Detroit GM plant. Once fragmented, parts of the labor process were easily moved to other locations, such as Prairie Hills and Riverton, where workers were subcontracted to perform the repetitive and deskilled jobs at home. TMC created these jobs with financial support from the local communities, in addition to state-level economic development funds. One homeworker observed:

> That building out there. See, TMC doesn't own that. Small communities, in order to lure big businesses and stuff have free incentives for X number of years. They [TMC] don't have to pay any property tax. That building out there is not owned by TMC. It's owned by a group of investors in Prairie Hills, and then TMC rents it from them. They just strictly rent it. Those big companies get some advantages that a small business person wouldn't.

Public- and private-sector support for informal jobs as development raises questions about the nature and process of development, such as who bears the costs and enjoys the benefits.[3]

Development groups and local states cooperate to attract industrial jobs to their areas. In the case of state support for industrial homework, the development process is undergirded by a particular understanding about how households are organized, who does what work, and how that work is valued. In order to understand how two rural locales incorporated homework as economic development, then, it is necessary to examine the relationships between rural households and the work they do, the local development group and the state, and industry.

Industrial homework as rural development exemplifies the common ground between local development officials trying to recruit employers and business managers seeking to restructure and relocate production. The importance of industrial relocation to local development converges with the industrial sector's ongoing efforts to restructure production and to regain a competitive position in the world market. The trend toward decentralized production, including the resurgence of informal labor, the separation of larger plants into smaller dispersed factories, and the deskilling and relocation of jobs to low-wage zones such as rural areas are all aspects of this process.[4] Industrial firms are in a favorable market for relocation as rural areas and states are giving high priority to industrial development.

Rural development has often meant industrial recruitment, but the most recent and severe decline in the agricultural economy has lent a desperate and competitive edge to the process. As farm insolvency becomes increasingly likely, the need for immediate cash flow is greater, so that more rural people, notably women, are looking for wage labor. Local development groups form with the intention of bringing in industries that will create new jobs for residents. Competition between communities is strong, and the community that acquires an industry often does so at the cost of offering a benefit package that may include absorbing the costs of building a factory or warehouse, connecting public utilities, and offering discounted utility rates and tax incentives.

How did industrial homework became an integral facet of economic development in these two rural communities in the Midwest? Because of the location and working conditions of industrial homework, it is important to consider how household structure and the division of labor shape and support informal labor as economic development. Homework as rural development in Prairie Hills and Riverton is analyzed from the perspectives of the participating households as well as from those of the local leadership and the state development agencies. First, through the examination of the process of development on the local and subnational state levels, we shall explore the ways in which the states absorb risks and costs for TMC (in this regard, the state is seen as subsidizing industrial homework as development).[5] Second, through a detailed portrait of the experiences and the working conditions of the homeworkers, we shall examine the ways in which they, as women and as contract employees, are subsidizing the costs and risks of homework as development. The workers' experiences and the organization of home assembly work illustrate the centrality of gender to homeworking. Thus, the state subsidizes homework as development, and in doing so subsidizes the creation of jobs that depend on workers who are defined as secondary, namely women.

This general pattern of development fits the cases of Riverton and Prairie Hills: economic decline, followed by the use of state funds for industrial recruitment, and the development of local jobs taken from the urban, unionized factory and dispersed into rural homes. Uneven development theory is the lens through which I present the pattern and process of development in these two communities. Four themes provide a background for this portrait: industrial restructuring, the role of the subnational and local state in development, the rural context of work, and the importance of integrating the household unit into the analysis.

THEORETICAL BACKGROUND

Theories of regional development tend to represent two schools of thought. Modernization theory emphasizes the importance of economic and industrial development as a means to achieve a higher standard of living. Thus, generating industrial wage labor should result in a "trickle down" of new wealth that improves living conditions and well-being within the locale. Modernization theory grew from attempts to promote and explain industrial development and economic growth in less developed societies, especially during the nineteenth and early twentieth centuries. Critics of this theory argue that the framework does not adequately account for the processes of growth and development or for the outcomes of development that are unevenly and inequitably experienced throughout societies. Based on this critique, theories of uneven development focus on the specific sociopolitical, economic, and historic context in which processes and outcomes of development occur in a given locale. Neither school of thought explicitly considers the household central to an understanding of economic development, yet it is ultimately household members who experience the benefits or burdens of homework as local development. Yet uneven development theory, with its focus on examining the structural rather than on the cultural aspects of development, is more appropriate to incorporation of the household as a unit of analysis.

This second theory emphasizes development as a dynamic nonlinear process that occurs in a specific historical and interactional context. It focuses on studying the structural contradictions that arise from economic development, including why economic growth occurs with increasing social inequalities and why local strategies for autonomy result in greater local subordination. In her study applying uneven development to the Deep South of the United States, Glenna Colclough writes that this framework supports examining processes of uneven industrialization among or across groups of workers.[6] The development processes in Riverton and Prairie Hills incorporated women as secondary workers and supplemental earners and, as such, reinforced the unequal position of women as low-wage workers within the local division of labor.

Industrial relocation to rural areas has often meant that the industry controlled "investment capital and commercial technology which allowed it to follow a strategy of corporate profitability and ignore issues" of community autonomy in development.[7] Local and state decisionmakers establish a pattern in which the locale relies increasingly on external loans that underwrite further industrial relocation or expansion; thus accentuating further loss of autonomy. Policymaking is gradually tied to the loan institutions and their requirements rather than to local needs. Development under such conditions becomes uneven because of constraints from external structures.

Within this framework it is important to study the relationship between the internal conditions of the local community and the external structures that influence the process of development. Thus the emphasis here is on the roles of industrial restructuring and the labor and development policies of the state as the external structures that support the use of industrial homework as local development. The internal conditions include the processes of local economic development in the two communities and the role of the household unit in contemporary development projects. This approach will aid in the "identification of those sectors tapped as sources of support for development and of those 'made to pay' its costs."[8]

Uneven development theory posits that the state is a regulator and mediator of capital investment. Specifically, the national, regional, or local state develops policies that either favor the activities of a particular branch of industry or deter the development of those activities that are not congruent with the interests of the state at a given time. The mechanisms used by the state most often are tax exemptions and incentives, political or financial concessions, and regulation of the labor force to ensure participation. Often, such industrial development generates and supports an increased bureaucratic structure that includes a local elite who financially and politically manage development as well as a larger number of people who engage in wage labor and reap fewer benefits. Because the structural processes of industrialization strongly influence the well-being of the workers and the level of local development, state policies and programs are examined for the ways in which they support capital mobility and regulate labor. Most important, external constraints interact with internal conditions to generate particular forms of development in a specific historical and social context. Thus this framework highlights how decentralized economic-development policies and state financing supported the creation of gender-specific jobs as part of the development strategy in Prairie Hills and Riverton.

As a framework, however, uneven development does not directly incorporate gender or the household as analytical categories. Although the framework reveals that the state is not a neutral arbiter between capital interests and workers' interests, it does not specify that the state is not gender neutral. For example, by defining farm operators as males, state monies for training displaced farmers help channel men into new jobs and restrict the access women as displaced farm operators have to such resources. The result is frequently that women workers are channeled into the secondary labor-market jobs or, in this case, into informal-sector work.

Moreover, uneven development theory accepts the separation of the market economy as the public sphere and the home as the private sphere, implicitly accepting that production for the market takes place only in the public sphere. The productive and reproductive labor that occurs in the private sphere, largely done by women, becomes invisible. This framework thus misses the possible roles of gender and class-related dynamics on the microlevel that are integral to the processes of development and production.[9] Such is the case with homeworking, where both the government and the market interact in the private sphere, where women are both productive and reproductive workers and yet are outside the realm of the public structures considered analytically important for uneven development. In homeworking as development, however, the local structure is involved in the gendered processes of recruiting, funding, and developing this work to create secondary jobs for rural women. Industrial homework as development illustrates the need to modify uneven development to include the structures of the private sphere, such as the household, and to see the public and private spheres as points on a continuum rather than as dichotomous concepts.[10]

The household as a unit is important in its effects on the organization of and participation in economic activities by its individual members. Thus it is necessary to incorporate the household into the analysis as a means of examining industrial homework as a facet of rural development. Uneven development provides a way to discuss the meaning of gender and its intersection with labor in the household and in the market, with development and the state, and with industrial firms in the midst of restructuring. The case of homeworking as development allows for an emphasis on the importance of the household theoretically within the framework of uneven development because both the state and capital use its gendered structure to establish homeworking as local development. Focusing on the activity of the state in development helps to clarify its contradictory position: The state uses funds to reinforce traditional roles and division of labor while still insisting on the rhetoric of formal equality. Under the rubric of development the state is supporting women as waged workers in a restricted and segregated labor market even as it contributes to trends that weaken labor.

An analysis of the interaction of the household unit with the local and regional state and with private industry will help to delineate how certain kinds of development occur and how the benefits or burdens or both are distributed among the participants. This approach includes not only an examination of the local and state policies that support the implementation of industrial homework as economic development but also a consideration of the local and household dynamics that support and are reinforced by such development.

INDUSTRIAL RESTRUCTURING AND INFORMALIZED LABOR

"The informal economy is, at the same time, flexibility and exploitation, productivity and abuse, aggressive entrepreneurs and defenseless workers, libertarianism and greediness. And, above all, disenfranchisement of the institutionalized power conquered by labor, with much suffering, in a two-century old struggle."[11] The resurgence of informalized labor is not confined to the United States but is an international development. While Saskia Sassen-Koob has examined informal labor and homework in New York City, and Naomi Katz and David Kemnitzer have studied homework in Silicon Valley, many other researchers have investigated homework abroad. For example, Lourdes Benería and Martha Roldán document the use of homework in Mexico City, Alejandro Portes and Lauren Benton in Latin America generally, and Cynthia Truelove in rural Colombia. María Fernández-Kelly examines informal economic activity in the Border Industrialization Program situated on the U.S.–Mexican border. Manuel Castells and Portes further the comparative perspective by focusing on informal activities in developed economies such as Italy and Spain as well as within the United States. Their studies show that the resurgence of homeworking and other informal activities is not the result of random cases of profit-seeking or vestiges of our preindustrial past but a response to a more fundamental and global process.[12]

An examination of industrial homework in the context of industrial restructuring in the United States and internationally shows that the homework taking place in Prairie Hills and Riverton is not an isolated occurrence but part of an international pattern of fragmented, deskilled, and mobile jobs across many industrial sectors. This type of work is not a historical anomaly within the United States or merely within rural areas. After looking at a brief historical sketch of industrial homework, we shall explore the international context and conditions of the resurgence in homeworking and labor informalization, with a particular focus on the social and economic effects of these work processes.

HISTORICAL CONTEXT

Industrial homework has its roots in the putting-out or outwork system that emerged in England during the transition from the feudal economy to the early capitalist economy in the late seventeenth century.[13] Outworking started in rural areas and was organized by merchants seeking to avoid the restrictions, especially the wage levels, of the town-based craft guilds. In eighteenth-century Great Britain agricultural underemployment meant that large numbers of rural people were looking for additional income-earning opportunities; concurrently, merchants, distributors, and manufacturers involved in the production and selling of clothing, lace, stockings, and buttons were seeking low-wage workers and "saw in the material circumstances of the countryside the possibility of profit to themselves."[14] Manufacturers fragmented production processes and distributed the work among households to achieve greater control and efficiency than they exercised over the self-sufficient craft guilds. Carding, spinning, and weaving of linen and wool were the earliest examples of outwork.

In the late eighteenth and early nineteenth centuries rural households in the United States processed raw materials such as cotton, linen, and wool as well as manufactured goods such as shirts, cloth, gloves, and other articles of clothing and supplied them to local merchants, mill owners. or store owners.[15] Although textile production appeared first, soon the division of labor made other manufacturing activities suitable for homework: straw-braiding, knitting, sewing, button-making, broom-making, cigar-rolling, and stitching shoes. By the early nineteenth century merchants often depended upon outworkers for products as varied as hats, bonnets, chairs, shingles, shoes, paper, and woodenware as well as for edible items such as butter, grain products, and other farm produce.[16]

In the regional economies of the Northeast, rural homeworkers were numerous and contributed significantly, although major contributions were limited to certain areas of production such as button-making and hat-braiding. Massachusetts homeworkers produced 3.3 million straw-braided hats in 1837, worth about $700,000; 2 million of those hats were made in Worcester County by 5,000 or more homeworkers. By comparison, there were 5,700 textile workers in the Lowell mills at the same time. Statewide, there were 33,000 palm-leaf outworkers and about 20,000 textile-mill workers during 1837.[17] Throughout New England, there were 13,311 workers employed at home braiding palm-leaf hats in 1837, and the total value of their product was $1,659,496.[18] In Easthampton, Massachusetts, one storeowner put out button-making to as many as 1,000 families in the area and also sent work to distant merchants who further subcontracted the button-making in their areas. During this stage of industrialization, outwork coexisted with factory work and was an integral part of the organization of production.

Shoe-binding, hat-braiding, and button-making were the main areas of outsourced production in the early to mid-nineteenth century in the rural Northeast, and merchants exercised control over the process in a number of ways. First, the materials they put out to home-workers were not widely available in the local economy, such as the imported palm leaf for hat-braiding or the various materials for button-making. Second, they contracted out production at levels that far exceeded any need for the item in the household so that the outworkers were dependent on the local merchant for marketing and distribution. Often, merchants kept store accounts for outworkers and paid them in goods from the store, a practice that helped maintain the contractual relationship between merchant and worker. Finally, over time, merchants came to control ownership of the tools and machinery needed to do outwork, which workers would then rent from them for a set fee; moreover, merchants started to require "furnishing," meaning that workers had to supply necessary materials such as thread to complete the work.

Most of the steady rural homeworkers were women living in households of economic need. Single women often did homework to contribute to their own support while living with family members; widows took in work to support children and other dependents, married women to augment meager household incomes. Christopher Clark notes that in rural areas, 50 percent of the hat-braiding families were farm operators and that on average they were poorer than families not engaged in that work. Among nineteenth-century contractors in Essex County, Mary Blewett found that the merchants relied on a fairly small number of outworkers who "kept production going out of economic necessity and personal circumstance." Yet a dominant view of the times promoted the notion that homework was a spare-time activity that women undertook to occupy otherwise idle hours. One commentator wrote that "hatmaking is, with many, a work of odd moments which would otherwise be unimproved, so the frugal housewife will include in her day's work a stent of so much braiding to be done."[19]

By the late nineteenth century family-based industry was unable to meet rising market demands for manufactured goods. Production moved increasingly from the home to the factory as wages for homework declined and mechanization grew. Mechanization and centralization of production increased the use of male workers and diminished the use of female workers, pushing higher the wages of the former to the detriment of women's wages. Not only were there dual wage levels for men and women working in factories but also another—and lower—tier of wages for work done at home, usually by women. Lower wages spurred a decline in homeworking that was usually reversed only during economic recessions.[20]

Homework, however, was not eliminated by the expansion of factory production; the factory system instead incorporated it into production in two ways. In some cases, manufacturers used outworking until they succeeded in persuading women to work for wages outside the home and then allowed the practice to decline. In other cases, manufacturers capitalized upon the resistance to women working in factories, using it to reinforce the outworking system. As part of the factory system, managers would subcontract work to women, often the wives and daughters of inside workers; the managers paid them by the piece or unit of production, offering a wage far below that earned by the factory employees. Outwork was not simply a protoindustrial form of production but was integral to the development and expansion of capitalist industrialization, hence its incorporation into factory production.[21]

In the late nineteenth century, the garment or apparel industry emerged as a giant employer of homeworkers. Industrial homework became a fundamental part of the sweated-labor system. Garment manufacturers ("jobbers") would employ only the cutters and examiners (usually males) in the factory, contracting out all stitching and finishing to contractors ("sweaters"), who competed among themselves to get these contracts by underbidding each other. The low bids that won contracts were based upon the low piecerate the contractor paid to the homeworker. Low piecerates induced homeworkers not only to work long hours in order to earn subsistence income but also to incorporate child labor into the process to finish rush orders on time and to try to increase their wages.[22]

Industrial homework had several advantages for the manufacturer, especially in the garment industry. Homeworkers provided a reserve labor pool for the manufacturer who offered no job protection or security; they could be hired or fired at the whim of the contractor. The cost savings of using informal, sweated labor were attractive to the manufacturer: overhead costs of rent, transportation, machinery, and utilities were passed on to the homeworker. The existence of the homeworking labor force allowed the industrialists to keep inside-factory wages low and to stave off unionization. And as one more advantage, in contemporary markets production can be adjusted to variable consumer demand without the risk and cost factor of maintaining unused facilities.[23]

It is crucial to understand that most of these economic advantages depend upon the different use and valuation of women's and men's labor within manufacturing. The emergence of the outwork system was tied to the household economy, and as such, incorporated the sexual division of labor in the household. Outworking later served to divide the work force into a sex-based hierarchy that bestowed greater rewards upon male workers. The factory system developed, inheriting the mostly male craft system of production and the predominantly female outwork system. As Alice Kessler-Harris points out, the "effect of this process was insidious." Men could enter the factories as skilled craftworkers; women, having labored as outworkers on the piecerate system, were limited to less skilled, partial assembly work within the factory. Thus the emergence of women as secondary wage workers was brought about by the incorporation of a productive system based on the household's hierarchical sexual division of labor.[24]

Through the 1930s, homework was an important part of the productive labor force in the garment and related apparel industries. Social reformers began to campaign against homework out of a concern for the living and working conditions of the families involved in it. They collected and presented documentation showing that industrial homework violated accepted labor standards such as minimum-wage, maximum-hour, and health and safety standards. Moreover, homework, by its very organization, was impossible to regulate in order to enforce reasonable standards. Reformers called for a complete ban on industrial homework, claiming that it was "commercializing the home, degrading motherhood, childhood and family life."[25]

The Fair Labor Standards Act (FLSA) was signed into law in 1938 at a time when organized labor was strong and was also demanding the regulation, if not the elimination, of outwork. In part, the FLSA prohibited the use of homeworkers in seven apparel-related industries and set up mechanisms for the regulation of homeworkers where allowed. Social reformers claimed a victory and assumed the end of homework had arrived. Yet it never completely disappeared even in the regulated industries and recently has emerged in several areas of work unregulated by the act.

Industrial homework reappeared in the public view in the early 1980s as homeworkers in New York, Wisconsin, and Vermont spoke out to defend their jobs in the knitted-outerwear industry.[26] Public hearings followed on the state and federal levels as elected officials rediscovered homeworking and sweatshops in much the same way earlier leaders had rediscovered poverty in the early 1960s.[27] The surprise, however, lay not only in the existence of homeworking but in the variety of occupations that people performed in their homes for pay. In addition to garment construction, researchers have found electronics and computer-chip assembly work,[28] automotive assembly work,[29] shoemaking,[30] clerical work,[31] computer programming,[32] insurance claim filing,[33] craft work, toy assembly, and production of jewelry and jewelry boxes.[34] The majority of home-based wage workers today are women,[35] with the exception of professional, or white-collar homeworkers, who seem to be fairly evenly divided between men and women.[36]

It has been challenging for researchers to attempt to enumerate home-based wage workers in the United States using available aggregate data sets. Robert Kraut used the 1980 Census data to estimate 750,00 white-collar, non-farm homeworkers; using Bureau of Labor statistics data for 1985 Kathleen Christensen and Hilary Silver estimate 1.9 million homeworkers, of whom 953,000 were full-time.[37] Using the same data Silver estimates 501,151 of the 1.9 million homeworkers were rural, non-farm residents. These data sets have limitations, such as not counting second jobs that are home-based or undercounting workers engaged in illegal forms of homework; the latter category includes 50,000 workers in New York City and 40,000 workers in Los Angeles alone.[38] Silver concludes that the number of homeworkers of all types in the United States remained fairly constant during the 1980s, with small increases in the rural, non-farm, home-based work force.

It is interesting that a relatively small proportion of the work force has commanded so much public and academic attention. Industrial homework has long been viewed sociologically, albeit incorrectly, as an obsolete form of production that was eliminated by more efficient forms of standardized mass production. Yet the diversity of firms that subcontract labor and other production seems to be increasing. Christensen reports that a 1986 Bureau of National Affairs survey of 441 firms found two-thirds of those firms using subcontracts for production or administrative work and 13 percent of them reporting an increase in such contracts between 1980 and 1985.[39] In research in rural New York, Jamie Dangler found sixty-seven firms located between Rochester and Utica that employed homeworkers; the rural homeworkers were subcontracted by major companies such as IBM, Ford, Magnavox, Kodak, and Squibb.[40]

The historical and contemporary contexts, then, indicate that homeworking has been a persistent and normative aspect of production in rural areas, one that has ebbed and flowed with variations in the organization of production, availability of labor, particularly women's labor, and the overall health of the regional and national economies. Rural industrial homework in the United States is embedded currently in the national and international contexts that show employers' growing use of informal labor and decentralized production and include increasing use of contingent labor such as temporary and part-time workers.

INFORMALIZATION AND DECENTRALIZED PRODUCTION

"What is *new* in the current historical context is that the informal sector grows, even in highly institutionalized economies, at the expense of already formalized work relationships."[41] One can hardly imagine more formalized work relationships than those in the automotive industry. The control of management over the entire work process, the oversight of the union over the relations between management and workers, the organization of production, and the compensation packages have yielded almost institutionalized work relationships over time. A series of changes in the automotive industry, however, that are often packaged together as industrial restructuring have served to break down the institutionalized character of automotive production. James Rubenstein distinguishes three types of restructuring that typify the industry's reorganization during the 1980s. First, intensification involves an increase in labor productivity without greater investment, new technology, or greater demand for labor; that is, the same number of workers produce more than before. A second strategy is rationalization, whereby firms reduce productive capacity through closure and often standardize components so that many more can be used interchangeably across models. Relocating reduced production to low-wage regions or subcontracting work to independent producers serve as examples of this strategy. Finally, firms may choose to invest in technology as a means of reorganization. Use of new technology is often accompanied by the retraining of workers, many of them for a variety of jobs, yielding a more flexible work force. Other jobs are restructured from full-time to part-time, temporary, or subcontracted positions. Any one of these strategies or a combination of them results in greater control over the work force by the management.[42]

Thus, the process of restructuring production in various ways is one indicator of the tendency toward informalization. Current terminology also suggests the growing presence of informal economic production in the United States: the electronic cottage, sweatshops, industrial homework, clerical homework, home-based businesses, telecommuting, temporary workers, and contingent workers. That we have so many accepted labels to describe the consequences of industrial restructuring indicates the extent to which we experience, observe, and perhaps even promote these changes in our working lives.

Informalization is a dynamic process of production rather than a static event and is described as being: "unregulated by the institutions of society, in a legal and social environment in which similar activities are regulated."[43] Although the product is usually an item legitimately sold in the market, the terms of the work relationship are often not within the legal bounds of labor law (or are within gray areas) and usually involve lack of protection, underpayment, insecurity, and the dependence of the worker as well as a disregard for zoning laws and safety and health standards. Homework is defined as income-generating activity done in one's domicile for an outside employer or an intermediary; usually referred to as industrial homework, it has its roots in various forms of historical outwork.[44] The homework performed in Prairie Hills and Riverton exemplifies such informalization.

The impact of international competition in all industries has resulted in a contest to decrease labor costs, resulting in the growth of informal economic activity. Industrial capital is increasingly integrated internationally, and thus managers and employers in developed economies find themselves searching for ways to compete with low-wage sectors of workers in the Third World. Michael Piore and Charles Sabel argue that "flexible specialization" is an important strategy that industrial managers use more and more as a means to reduce labor costs, increase capital productivity, and thus sharpen international economic competition. Under this strategy, workers develop a variety of skills that allow them to adapt rapidly to constant innovation. A flexible, multiskilled work force enables a given industry to adjust to the frequent changes required by small-batch production without the expenditures of retraining and retooling. Moreover, they argue that workers benefit from this revised "craft-oriented" organization because the basis of their value to a firm will be the skills they accumulate. Piore and Sabel believe these shifts will result in greater worker autonomy and control over the work process.[45]

Not all scholars in this area share their enthusiasm, however. The benefits of increased skills and autonomy are seen as the harvest of a small proportion of white-collar workers, and the work force in general will experience greater segmentation as a larger proportion of blue-collar workers enter downgraded jobs in the secondary labor sector. Just as technology allows for greater skill accumulation for some workers, new technology allows jobs to be deskilled by breaking down the labor process into basic components that are then dispersed among workers. Since these jobs require less skill, the production process gains both mobility and dispersion, often at the expense of workers.[46]

Most observers agree that the resurgence of informal economic activity is a response to global restructuring initiated to overcome the structural crisis in capitalism that occurred during the 1970s.[47] An alternate explanation suggested in the neoclassical economic literature is that the increasing availability of pools of immigrant labor, which readily absorb informal labor, is contributing to its growth in the United States, especially in major urban areas. Yet the available evidence refutes this position by noting that homework is performed for U.S. electronics firms by white, native-born women in New York and California, for Italian shoe and cycle firms by nonimmigrant women, and for Spanish garment and footwear industries by native Spanish women. In Mexico a great deal of homework is performed by domestic migrants, who often move from rural to urban areas. It is apparent from many of these case studies, including my own, that the industrial restructuring underlying the increasing informalization of labor has relied heavily on the employment of women workers.[48]

The U.S. electronics industry has received a fair amount of attention regarding the use of homeworkers and other informal workers. The Silicon Valley in California is well known for the concentration of electronics firms located there, many of which use informal labor, mostly for small assembly work that has at times required workers to heat toxic chemicals on their kitchen stoves. Castells and Portes write that "the significance of these reports is that they indicate that the underground economy is not limited to services and traditional manufacturing, but has leaped to sectors at the forefront of technology." These reports also suggest that advancing technology and standardized production do not automatically wipe out supposedly earlier or more fragmented forms or relations of production. Katz and Kemnitzer examined the use of informal labor among the electronics firms in

California and found several instances similar to practices in Italy. For example, researchers found that migrant and immigrant labor were important, that informalization was an integrated and significant part of technologically advanced areas and industries, and that independent small firms and contractors were not truly autonomous but were in relationships of disguised dependence on larger firms. In both Italy and California, there is a marked disintegration of workers' hard-won benefits. "We are witnessing not a recapitulation of earlier forms of capitalist development in a new industry but the further development of contemporary capitalism as part of capital's efforts to deal with current economic conditions."[49]

This point is well illustrated by Beverly Lozano's case study of thirty-five home-based computer programmers, word processors, and electronics assemblers in the Bay Area of San Francisco. Most of these workers considered themselves self-employed, independent contractors though through the interview process Lozano realized that they were more often disguised employees of major firms. Lozano notes that many of these informal computer programmers had been employees of the companies who are now their clients; these companies reported substantial savings from using professional services on an informal basis. Informal work relations "are integral features of a single system of competitive production in which firm and informal worker are complementary parts growing out of the antagonisms fostered by capitalist competition."[50]

In New York City, Sassen-Koob observed that there was a proliferation of small producers and that the labor market was economically polarized between high-income and low-wage jobs. This pattern contrasts with the post–World War II pattern of a strong middle-income sector of mass consumers that necessitates standardized production on a large scale. The shrinking middle class, further economic polarization of the work force, and competition lead to changes in consumption patterns that support small-scale, nonstandardized, informal production. The greater polarization of jobs lends support to the critique that small-scale production is not necessarily leading to skilled employment but that it is contributing to the increase in relatively unskilled, low-wage work. Industrial growth trends in New York City show substantial downgrading and deskilling in various industries and a concomitant growth of the service sector. Part of the process of industrial downgrading is increased informalization of labor as seen in the use of homework and the establishment of sweatshops. In the field component for her study Sassen-Koob documented the use of homework or other informal labor practices in construction, garment-finishing, footwear, furniture, retail activity, electronics, and transportation ("gypsy cabs").[51]

Homework has a notable presence in almost every country, regardless of the stage of industrial development. The garment industry is the largest employer of homeworkers globally because the work is labor intensive and easily decentralized and because the technological and tool requirements are low. Other industries that use homeworkers in several countries include electronics and optical businesses, paper and cardboard processing plants, packing and sorting operations, clerical and computer-work firms, and equipment-assembly businesses. In several developing nations homeworkers process various agricultural products, rolling cigarettes, peeling shrimp, or sorting and packing different products. The variety of industrial sectors that use homeworkers internationally indicates that many processes of production can be easily fragmented and decentralized, that homework is easily incorporated regardless of industry, and that despite current technology, unskilled portions of a process are outsourced to homeworkers for very low pay.[52]

Several underlying causes contribute to the increase in informalization on the international level and also apply to rural and urban informal activity. Most often mentioned is industry's reaction to the increased working-class strength that occurred during the 1960s. Unions impeded capital accumulation by organizing workers' demands for insurance, health and safety standards, and higher wage and benefit packages. Informalization is a way to decentralize and to isolate the labor force, weakening organized labor and allowing employers to avoid the costs of unionization. Thus, although union strength impedes capital accumulation, it also motivates managers to reorganize production in ways that weaken organized labor; weak unions in the United States have cleared the way for an increase in the use of informal workers. In Italy the powerful and developed informal sector of the 1980s has followed on the heels of strong labor gains in the 1960s; Fiat, for example, slowed production in the 1970s, moved toward an informal labor force, and has resurfaced in a strong financial position in the 1980s.[53]

Sassen-Koob links informalization with the growth of the service sector in the United States, which is an indicator of manufacturing downgrading. She notes that areas experiencing sharp declines in unionization are also experiencing rapid growth in high-technology and service industries, industries that are prime contributors to the trend of informalization. Union weakness opens the door to increasing informalization. A good example is in the city of Miami, where use of union labor dropped from 90 percent in 1960 to 10 percent in 1980 and where informal contracting abounds.[54]

A second aspect of global restructuring that leads to increased informalization concerns employers' reactions to increased state regulation of the economy, especially in areas of labor legislation. Informalization becomes a means to reduce production costs involved in taxes, social insurance, and maintenance of health and safety standards. "The rise of the welfare state promoted subsequent informalization, directly, by stimulating companies' efforts to escape its reach and, indirectly, by weakening the resistance of the working class to new forms of labor organization."[55]

A third underlying cause of increased informal labor is traced to the process of industrial development in previously undeveloped areas, where countries respond to international industrial competition by informalizing their labor force to attract foreign investment. Finally, Castells and Portes cite informal labor as a response to increasingly harsh living conditions resulting from economic crisis. People may choose informal types of labor not only as a means of survival but also because it represents more personalized working conditions. "The informal economy is both the mirage of individual economic opportunity and the means for personalized survival out of the crisis."[56]

Castells and Portes and Sassen-Koob note several economic effects of the trend toward informalization: decentralization of the work force and of production, flexible production, delays in the trend toward full automation, decreased labor productivity, increased capital productivity, decreased labor costs, and an undermining of the social wage produced by the welfare state.[57] Fernández-Kelly also notes that informalization allows industry to diversify its economic and political risks and that it brings married women, their unmarried daughters, and single mothers in Mexico into the wage-labor force.[58] Carla Lipsig-Mummé and Sheila Allen point out that fragmentation of the labor force stimulates competition among homeworkers and between home and factory workers, weakens the potential for unionization, contributes to the growth of contracting and subcontracting, and undermines full-time factory jobs.[59]

Portes and Benton summarize the causes:

Higher labor costs and lower flexibility in labor use in modern firms result in large part from the regulations enforced by the state, including the setting of minimum wage levels, protection from arbitrary firing, and social insurance programs. The activities of labor unions impose further restrictions on the ability of employers to vary the size of the work force in response to market fluctuations and longer term economic cycles. One would expect to find that the importance of the informal sector varies in relation to three factors: costs imposed by the state on formal enterprises, the degree of enforcement of labor legislation, and the relative strength of organized labor.[60]

Although these general reasons apply to developed and to developing nations, some differences in conditions in Third World countries seem to add to the explanation of the flourishing informal economy there. That is, in newly industrializing or reindustrializing Third World countries, such as Mexico and Brazil, workplace regulation was established early in the industrialization process. In the United States and other industrial nations in Western Europe, by contrast, workers won labor legislation at a more advanced stage of industrial development, beginning in the late nineteenth and early twentieth centuries. These nations enacted regulation during a period of labor scarcity and strong working-class mobilization. Newly industrializing countries impose workplace regulation at a time of labor abundance, low union activity, and incipient industrial development. The result is that informal activity in the Third World is normative and is a continuation of earlier nonindustrial practices; thus it has an ideological legitimacy that facilitates its perpetuation in Latin America. Similarly, in rural areas of the United States, many types of informal household production have a long tradition that lends support to contemporary development of homeworking and other informal work.

Two other general aspects of informal labor deserve mention. First, the informal sector is not isolated or marginalized relative to the formal sector but is an integrated and significant component. The regional economy of Miami relies extensively on informal contracting and subcontracting in major industries, and the ethnic subeconomies in the city are based on intricate networks of informal labor in areas such as food production and car repair.[61] Italy's economic recovery has been credited largely to the increasing use of informal labor in the last decade. The second and related point is that the informal sector often develops and flourishes under the knowing tolerance of the national state.[62] In Latin America, "governments tolerate or even stimulate informal economic activities as a way to resolve potential social conflicts or to promote political patronage."[63] In Europe the governments of developed industrial nations have come to depend on informalization for reducing unemployment and for stimulating economies out of recessionary periods. In the United States deregulation of homework-

ing laws during the 1980s indicates federal support for globally competitive, informal labor practices. Prairie Hills and Riverton are good
examples of local governments actively encouraging the implementation of homeworking as part of a general development strategy.

Industrial homeworking in rural and urban America is closely
tied to this process of increasing informalization and is an indicator of
industrial restructuring in response to the economic crises of the
1970s and 1980s. Homework in the United States is increasing precisely when unionization is diminishing and in rural areas where unions never have been dominant. Industrial relocation thus avoids the
potential for unionization in urban areas and flourishes in rural areas
almost outside the unions' reach. The depressed agricultural and
manufacturing economies, with high unemployment and underemployment, generate an expanded reserve labor force, many of whom
are more than willing to accept low piecerates, job insecurity, and no
benefits in exchange for a somewhat increased household cash flow.
Especially when the final product is destined for the domestic market,
industrial homework in local areas increasingly makes good sense to
industrial managers. One can hardly avoid noting the recurrent patterns in rural employment over the last 200 years or so: agricultural
underemployment, a rising need for increased cash, and the subsequent increase in the employment of mostly rural women in various
forms of informal labor.

THE ROLE OF THE STATE

The reemergence of industrial homeworking in developed or postin-
dustrial capitalist societies such as the United States raises interesting
questions about the role of the state in regulation and enforcement,
people's "right to work," and the role and influence of organized labor.[64] For example, how do the various branches or agencies of the
state determine who is an employee? Understanding this issue requires an examination of federal labor policy, specifically the Fair Labor Standards Act and the various public hearings and attempts to
amend it in the last decade. The matter of employment status further
requires that we look at the tax code, in which the definition of employee differs from that of labor policy. These differences and ambigu-
ities in the laws create gray areas that allow employers (and indeed
some workers) to construe the status of some workers as independent
or self-employed; one set of policies from the state may support that
status while another contradicts it. Part of our task is to understand

the meaning of these contradictory policies for the federal state's role in the context of informal-sector growth.

Regional development policy is another arena that bespeaks state action in the growth of informal work relations vis-à-vis job development, employer recruitment, and development incentive packages. What kinds of jobs and employers are supported by the state for specific areas? Who does the employer recruit for the new jobs? What kinds of tax, utility, and property incentives does the local state offer to the employer? Such questions indicate the importance of examining not only the outcomes of state-supported development, but also the process of development: Who makes the decisions, and what are the contexts for those decisions?

Development Policies

Subnational state policies regarding development generally aim to attract capital investment in local areas, especially during difficult times in rural locales. The assumptions of the modernization framework often support these development policies since the multiplier effects of new wages and services are presupposed to benefit everyone in the locale. Economic progress and expanding industrialization should bring the recipients into fuller participation in the process.

Within the framework of uneven development, however, these same policies are examined for their potential to facilitate capital mobility and to influence the outcomes of development. For example, the federal government offers business incentives through the tax code, through special depreciation of business capital, through salary or wage support for employing disadvantaged workers, and by offering financing through industrial revenue bonds.[65] Local governments offer further incentives through tax concessions, discounted public-utility rates, and low-interest loans. These are not neutral policies based upon assumptions of a free market; instead, they are policies that in practice have varying effects on different social groups and locales and thus must be considered.

Under the Manpower Development and Training Act (MDTA) the federal government provides support for a variety of training and employment programs. The expenditures have varied greatly from urban programs to rural programs: Forty-seven dollars per capita in metropolitan areas and eighteen dollars per capita in nonmetro areas.[66] Yet rural unemployment rates have been consistently higher than in urban areas, and the cost is greater to implement programs of comparable quality in rural areas. One reason for the cost differential is the likely underestimation of rural unemployment, which the General Accounting Office (GAO) estimates may have cost small communities about $129 million in Jobs Training Partnership Act (JTPA) funds during 1984. Moreover, within the unemployment estimates, rural women are seriously undercounted.[67]

The JTPA provides for a decentralized, state-run program funded by MDTA that focuses on employment training, largely for disadvantaged workers. Under this act, twenty states have implemented displaced-farmer programs that pay wages during the training period of any displaced farmer hired by an industrial firm. In practice, when a farm files bankruptcy, it is often the man who is defined as the displaced farmer, not his wife, even if she operated the farm with him over a period of time. Thus, the program supports industrial retraining for unemployed rural men, ignoring the displacement and unemployment of many rural women. The men are more likely to be retrained into skilled jobs, but the women tend to enter the job market in entry-level assembly work.

Financial support for rural infrastructure is usually available at the local or state level and is offered as an incentive to attract industry, but these improvement costs are high, given the low tax-base of most rural communities. Some communities finance infrastructure development through industrial revenue bonds; others, such as Riverton, use tax incremental financing. The pattern that emerges among these policies is one of encouraging capital mobility at the expense of community absorption of capital risk.

Labor Policies

The Fair Labor Standards Act of 1938 is a prime example of state intervention to regulate both the labor force and the working conditions desired by industry. The federal government enacted the act to legislate acceptable minimum working standards for all covered workers, including minimum wage and maximum hours. Under the FLSA, "employee" is defined as "any individual employed by an employer"; an "employer" is any person "acting directly or indirectly in the interest of an employer in relation to an employee"; "employ" is "to suffer or permit to work." Such broad definitions are inclusive of all workers but the self-employed entrepreneur or the independent contractor, a distinction that offers an easy loophole to employers. Since the passage of the act, homeworkers have been considered covered employees by the Department of Labor though rarely classified as such by employers.[68]

To implement the requirements of the FLSA, the Wage and Hour division of the Department of Labor set up investigative committees in various branches of industry to determine acceptable minimum-wage standards. These investigations documented the problem of enforcing FLSA requirements for homeworkers, principally among the seven garment-related industries, as the committees summarized five major difficulties in policing homework employers for compliance. First, homeworkers were difficult to find since employers often did not have them listed on the payroll. Second, the number of hours worked was impossible to establish with much accuracy because homeworkers feared reprisals from employers and often underestimated the number of hours worked or the time required to complete one piece. Third, payment by piecerate made it difficult to find out if the worker was remunerated for the time actually spent working, such as setting up, packing, and finishing; the determination of the piecerate often did not include these tasks. Fourth, the investigation concluded that it was impossible to know who actually did the work at home since several workers may have participated but only one was compensated.[69]

The fifth problem concerned the misclassification of employees as independent contractors: By failing or refusing to recognize workers as employees, the employer no longer has to comply with fair-labor practices. The judicial system generally applies a test of "economic reality" to determine whether a worker is an employee or an independent contractor based on five criteria: independent control over one's business life, control over profits and losses, investment of risk capital, control over permanency of contracts, and the extent of skill contributed by the individual to the business.[70] According to the test of economic reality very few homeworkers are determined to be independent contractors, yet the employer clearly benefits by such misclassification. Indeed, a survey of clerical homeworkers showed that the majority wished to be considered employees and to be treated as such in terms of benefits and other conditions.[71] Legally many homeworkers are employees, but they accept the employment misclassification because they fear losing their jobs if they complain about violations.

The problem of state regulation is important beyond the question of its capacity to enforce adequate working standards. As several observers point out, increased state regulation serves to clarify the boundaries between formal contractual labor and informal, unstable work. State regulation also may act as an incentive to informalize production and distribution in manufacturing by increasing costs of labor and operation within firms.[72]

Tax Policies

Two main areas of tax policy affect people working at home, and both depend on whether a worker qualifies as a self-employed independent contractor. Under the income tax structure, workers who are self-employed and use their primary residence as a workplace are allowed to deduct work-related expenses involving the cost of space, utilities, and capital depreciation; such deductions can be a major savings for the worker. Under Social Security tax policies, the self-employed worker is responsible for paying the full 15 percent tax on gross income; an employee contributes half, which is matched by the employer's contribution. Homeworkers misclassified as self-employed bear two tax burdens: they cannot take the tax deductions because they do not pass the test of "economic reality," yet they pay the full contribution to Social Security because the employer is not obligated to contribute.

The Internal Revenue Service (IRS) contributes to employers' potential to misclassify workers by defining two different employer-employee relationships: common-law employee and statutory employee. If the employer has the legal authority to control the process and outcome of the worker's services, then the IRS recognizes that person as a common-law employee and requires the employer to withhold taxes and contribute to federal unemployment taxes. Under the category of statutory employee the IRS includes "homeworkers who work by the guidelines of the person for whom the work is done, with materials furnished by and returned to that person or to someone that person designates."[73] There are no obligations for employers to withhold taxes or to contribute to unemployment taxes for statutory workers. Thus, the IRS guidelines make it profitable for employers to classify workers as statutory employees even if they are called independent contractors; the guidelines also create a loophole through which employers may outsource work to homeworkers.

Two patterns emerge from this overview of the state's role in development and labor. First, the state is an active participant in the resurgence of informal labor through explicit deregulation of homework as well as through selective enforcement of existing regulation. Second, the state is actively absorbing risks for capital development and mobility while allowing employers to pass those risks to the workers. In the case of rural development, this second pattern involves passing those risks to women who are entering a rural job market dominated by low-wage entry-level positions in increasing numbers.

THE RURAL CONTEXT OF WORK

The conditions present in rural labor-market areas, such as high unemployment and an increase in unskilled jobs and service-sector jobs, have contributed to making homeworking an accepted development strategy in Prairie Hills and Riverton. The changing structure and constraints of the local labor market suggest the kinds of employment experiences rural residents are likely to have and the kinds of development that will probably continue.

Historically, nonmetropolitan unemployment rates have been lower than those of urban areas through both recession and recovery periods. This circumstance held until the recession of the 1970s, when nonmetro unemployment rates increased more quickly, peaked at a higher level, and stayed above metro-unemployment rates throughout the 1980s.[74] Moreover, nonmetro areas also have higher rates of both discouraged and underemployed workers.

The recessionary period of the 1970s resulted in broad economic restructuring, with particular outcomes for rural labor-market areas. The major economic change has been a shift from manufacturing jobs and a marked increase toward service-sector jobs. In 1980 there were almost 34 million more people in the labor force than in 1960; 29.4 million were working in the service sector, and manufacturing provided jobs for an additional 4 million workers.[75] These trends are more accentuated in rural labor-market areas. Nonmetropolitan service-sector growth doubled between 1960 and 1970, constituting about 75 percent of employment growth during the 1970s while the contribution of manufacturing to rural employment growth was about 17 percent.[76] The relative contributions of these two sectors to total nonmetro employment show an increase in the service sector from 50 percent in 1960 to 69 percent in 1984; manufacturing, however, contributed 22.6 percent in 1960, peaked at 25.5 percent in 1970, and decreased to 20 percent by 1984.[77]

Compared to the rate in metropolitan areas, the employment growth in the rural service sector was greater between 1969 and 1976, but after 1976 this pattern was reversed, with service-sector growth greater in the metro labor markets. Within the manufacturing sector, metro growth was three times faster than nonmetro growth from 1970 to 1985. The significance of economic restructuring for rural areas is noteworthy when one considers that 40 percent of non-metropolitan residents live in counties that are dependent upon the manufacturing sector for employment.[78]

An examination of the distribution of occupations within both the service and the manufacturing sectors in rural labor-market areas shows another pattern emerging. Within the service sector 18.2 percent of the employed held skilled white-collar jobs, and 24.2 percent were engaged in semiskilled white-collar work in 1980. Among blue-collar manufacturing jobs, 22.7 percent were low-skill positions and 14.5 percent were highly skilled jobs.[79] Of the employment growth that occurred, rural areas attracted a disproportionate number of unskilled low-wage jobs.[80] As the manufacturing sector declines, it is precisely these unskilled jobs that are lost, leaving rural areas at an even greater disadvantage.

David McGranahan describes four aspects of this "rural disadvantage." First, the primary industries of mining and agriculture are experiencing long periods of decline that are not projected to end soon; these businesses had provided the main economic base of most rural communities. Second, the manufacturing firms typically found in rural areas are the older industries no longer experiencing strong demand and thus provided 12 percent fewer jobs in 1986 than in 1979. Third, the manufacturing decline of the 1980s almost entirely reflects a decline in the less-skilled jobs that are disproportionally located in rural labor-market areas. In 1986 about 57 percent of nonmetropolitan jobs were in the less-skilled job category; only 37 percent of metro jobs were classified as such. Fourth, rural areas experience disadvantage in that these manufacturing jobs are more susceptible to fluctuations in the business cycle.[81]

In analyzing the rural manufacturing sector, Leonard Bloomquist applies the product cycle model, which divides the organization of production into "top-of-cycle" and "bottom-of-cycle" phases. Firms engaged in top-of-cycle production are involved in product innovation, conception, and prototype production. At this stage, firms rely heavily on skilled white-collar workers and provide better working conditions and wages. As production becomes standardized, firms enter bottom-of-cycle production, where the labor demand is for less technically skilled workers and the conditions and pay decline. Bloomquist notes that in many cases as production becomes more routine it is moved into the nonmetropolitan periphery, and the urban core maintains its advantage in the proportion of skilled to unskilled workers. General Motors exemplified this process when it fragmented and relocated production; less-skilled work that did not involve heavy components, such as electronics, was moved to the South, and assembly of heavy components that also required relatively unskilled labor was relocated to the rural Midwest.[82] Thus, the rural areas gained low-paying unskilled jobs, and the more skilled work remained in urban areas.[83]

Bloomquist observes that although rural areas provide certain advantages to industry, such as lower labor costs, lower taxes and land values, and local financial concessions, these factors are important only to locational decisions insofar as they are relevant to the organization of production. For example, firms in the top-of-cycle phase place a high priority on a pool of skilled professional workers and ready access to communications, and thus local concessions are not as important. These firms, often high-tech, are considered to be more desirable since they are internationally more competitive, providing greater job stability and growth as well as better salary and working conditions. Indeed, most of the job expansion in manufacturing is attributable to growth in highly skilled, top-of-cycle firms. The rural disadvantage can be seen not only in terms of job decline, then, but also in the failure to share in the benefits of an increase in stable, high-wage jobs.

These trends in the rural labor market suggest an inequality of industrial mix between rural and urban areas, and the results are made clear in a comparison of employment and unemployment rates, earnings, and poverty rates. Since the mid-1970s rural areas have had higher rates of unemployment than urban areas, and this gap has steadily increased. When the unemployment rate is adjusted to include discouraged workers and involuntary part-time workers, the situation of the rural areas is notably worse. In 1973 both metro and nonmetro adjusted rates were 7.1 percent; by 1988 the metro rate had settled at an annual average of 7.9 percent, but that of the nonmetro areas was hovering around 10.1 percent.[84] The adjusted metro rate was showing signs of recovery as a result of job creation nationally, yet the nonmetro rate remained high, indicating the limits of recovery.

Even when nonmetro workers are employed, their earnings are less than the earnings of their metro counterparts, and this gap is also widening. In 1980 median income for nonmetro families was 78.5 percent of that of metro families, and by 1987 this ratio had decreased to 73.1 percent. The ratio remains about the same if households are used in place of families. Poverty rates are also higher in nonmetropolitan areas; in 1985 the relative poverty rate was 13.2 percent, compared to 9.3 percent for metropolitan America. Despite higher poverty and unemployment rates, nonmetro areas have a higher proportion of working poor families; more than 66 percent of nonmetro poor families had one employed member and over 25 percent had two.[85]

These trends in general indicate that labor-market entry is competitive and that successful entrance does not necessarily bring sufficient means for self-support. They also suggest that most workers entering the rural labor market will start at entry-level, unskilled, low-wage jobs and that very few will advance beyond that point within the rural job market. Rural workers are typically less educated and less skilled than those in urban areas, and the local job market offers little incentive to procure advanced training. Workers generally need to leave their locale and enter a metropolitan labor-market area to reap the potential rewards of further training.

As a low-paying, unskilled job, homeworking can be viewed as a good fit in the rural labor-market context, and evidence shows that the conditions of the rural labor market attracted developers of home-based work. The lack of competition from better-paying jobs, the high-unemployment and farm-insolvency rates, and the numbers of geographically dispersed women seeking any employment indicated to the manufacturers of TMC that homeworking could be successful in such a locale.

It was more than structural conditions in the local labor markets that attracted the developers of home-based work; they were also drawn by what they perceived as the traditional division of labor in the home and the communities. TMC managers saw greater chances for success with homeworking if the people in the communities supported norms of women staying at home to care for family members as a primary responsibility. Thus TMC and the private development corporations in the communities developed homework jobs with a specific group of workers in mind: women who were at home to care for children and maintain the home and whose earned income would be considered secondary, at least in the abstract.

Homework presents a challenging case for analysis because the public sphere of the market economy becomes invisibly embedded in the private sphere of the home. Unlike most other wage work, homework merges with housework, and the organization of paid production takes on the characteristics of unremunerated housework. Homework, like housework and child care, becomes typed as women's work and is woven throughout the day and evening with these family responsibilities. Furthermore, these family responsibilities shape and condition the worker's experiences in production, often determining the extent of her control over work space, schedule, and workload. The work of the public sphere enters the private sphere, and the work of both are changed.

The location and organization of industrial homework make a household-based analysis imperative. Only within the household can one document the relationships that support homeworking, the dynamics that are reinforced by it, and the conditions under which it is performed. Then by extending the analysis from the household, it is possible to examine the interaction of household dynamics and the macrostructural supports for homeworking.

The importance of the household unit in structuring women's participation in paid and unpaid work suggests that the household also shapes women's roles in and experience of economic development strategies. The score of studies examining a variety of topics from the view of the household reveals the inadequacy of analyzing broader social concerns separately from the microlevel relationships that support them and the need to continue the "effort to view women's role in the development process as conditioned by dynamics set up at the household level."[86]

As part of this effort it is also important to examine and understand how household dynamics filter into the process of development, into the priorities and goals of local community-development officials. These aspects of the processes of development in Prairie Hills and Riverton lend support to examining household structures and relationships and their contributions to local considerations about industrial recruitment. The relationship between development processes and household structures is dynamic, embedded in local historical, social, political, and economic conditions. Thus, examining development through the household involves viewing household relationships within the web of local conditions and observing how these interactions are understood and incorporated into processes at various levels.

2

Restructured Production:
Homework as Rural Development

In autumn 1986 a group of ten people in rural Prairie Hills began assembling suspension bolts in their homes for TMC; the following
summer about twelve people in Riverton started pounding small
screws and washers together in their homes for the same GM subcontractor. By 1990 about forty-five homeworkers were assembling bolts
in Prairie Hills and about forty in Riverton. In both communities these
jobs are part of state-supported rural economic development strategies, and because of the number of jobs created, local and state officials judge homeworking to be quite successful. The story of how
these jobs came to Prairie Hills and Riverton reveals the process of
finding common ground between local development efforts and firms
seeking to restructure and relocate production.

Economic conditions in Prairie Hills and Riverton during the
1980s provided fertile ground for almost any kind of job creation. Both
communities are county seats in agriculturally dependent counties
and suffered in the early 1980s from the concomitant declines in the
agricultural and manufacturing sectors of the local and national economies. Farm insolvency increased rapidly as did rural and farm unemployment. In the southern district of Iowa, which includes Prairie
Hills, the farm-insolvency rate more than quadrupled between 1982
and 1985.[1] As a result of economic decline and decreased personal income, the retail sectors of each community shrank, and Main Street
businesses often followed farms into insolvency. At the same time,

economic leaders in rural communities developed strip malls and re-cruited major discount stores, which only served to cement the de-cline of the small, local retail businesses by siphoning away local pur-chasing power.[2] Mark Friedberger wrote of the broad impact the agricultural decline had on small, agriculturally dependent communi-ties:

> Tax bases eroded, conservation was neglected, and support for community institutions dissipated. Nowhere was the impact felt more than in the service communities of the Midwest, which de-pended on farming for their livelihood. The welfare of agribusi-ness suppliers, the local retail trade, and social institutions such as schools and churches, was directly linked to the prosperity and numbers of farmers.[3]

Economic development in these communities meant increasing the number of jobs, with little consideration for the quality of those jobs. Off-farm employment for any member of a farming household became an important survival strategy to increase cash flow during the agricultural crisis, but with the economic decline, finding such employment was difficult: "Where off-farm jobs were scarce in the av-erage small farming community and the downturn had eliminated many of the employment opportunities in agricultural machinery manufacturing and meat packing, such a strategy seemed dubious."[4] The economic conditions during this decade supported the develop-ment of any jobs. These conditions, however, combined with local norms and values concerning the differences in women's and men's work, made possible the successful development of industrial home-working jobs.

Indeed, homeworking in each of these communities has as much to do with local norms and values about women and work as it does with local economic need. Economic development policies and the funding to support development projects are decentralized to the sub-national and local states, in practice.[5] Local communities, within the guidelines and requirements of their particular state, are able to act in-dependently and to compete for resources to support development activities, whether that involves refurbishing Main Street or attracting and expanding employment. Economic development, then, can be seen as a process that partly incorporates and expresses the norms and values of a given locale. Industrial homeworking, in particular, il-lustrates local values and beliefs about women, families, and women's work in Prairie Hills and Riverton; local officials speak of homeworking as "good secondary jobs for women."

Yet if homeworking as development reveals an aspect of local values, homeworking as reorganized production also reveals managerial values about women as workers. When production was relocated from GM's Detroit factory to the rural communities of the Midwest, the new workers, instead of being unionized, paid by the hour, and largely male, were non-unionized, paid by the piece, and largely female. Restructuring production allowed TMC and General Motors to profit from cheaper female labor and the greatly lowered overhead costs associated with homeworking.

Managers of industrial firms and local development officials meet on common, albeit unequal, bargaining grounds. The former seek those factors that the latter advertise as community strengths: an abundant supply of low-cost, non-union labor, the presence of traditional family and gender roles, and local financial subsidies for job creation. In return, firms generally offer to create a certain number of jobs. Both Prairie Hills and Riverton offered cheap labor, traditional gender roles, and financial subsidies; TMC promised to create one salaried warehouse job and approximately two dozen home assembly positions in each community. Within two years, the company was able to exceed its promises and had expanded to employ almost twice as many homeworkers as planned. By local development standards, which rely on the number of jobs created, both communities scored a success with homeworking.

How did this success come about? The answers lie in an examination of the local contexts and the processes used to bring homeworking into each community, the types of funding used, the values and beliefs shared by TMC and the communities, and the implications of decentralization for development and job creation.

COMMUNITY BACKGROUND

Prairie Hills is a small county seat of fewer than 1,700 people in the hilly grasslands of Iowa. The entire county has a population of less than 18,000, with only three cities having over 1,000 people. Agriculture is the dominant, and certainly preferred, way of making a living. As of 1980 more than two-thirds of Prairie County's labor force was engaged in only four types of labor: agriculture, professional and related jobs, retail, and manufacturing.[6]

The disparity between poverty rates for the state and for the county or the farm population increased, however, when the values of farmland and products plummeted. Between 1981 and 1985, "land lost 55 percent of its value" in Iowa, and from 1984 to 1985, "the average worth of an [Iowa] farm fell 25 percent, or $114,000."[7] An older woman who assembled bolts at home while her husband did road repair recalled that "the land that was bought for $700 or $800 [per acre] went to $200 to $300. We had no buying power." The massive loss in equity deeply affected the emotional, physical, and financial well-being of people in farming communities such as Prairie Hills and Riverton and continues to affect them because of the debt load.[8] Financing the debt drained most farmers of any ability to generate income for the household. One homeworker considered the problem:

I suppose in the late seventies . . . when the interest rates weren't high, we probably paid forty or fifty thousand dollars interest. And when it got, up into '82 and '83, when it really got high, we were spending about ninety thousand dollars on interest. It just ate us up. . . . It was just unbelievable. I mean, we knew what was happening. But how do you get ahead of it? You just couldn't generate enough money.

In some cases, one off-farm job was not enough to cover basic household expenses. Of the forty-three homeworking families interviewed, eighteen of them had more than two sources of earned income in their households, including the home assembly work. Another homeworker described the situation:

Well, the farm income was not, was just barely covering the farm expenses and the debt load. And so in order to have any kind of a living at all, we had to have some kind of income. And her wages just wouldn't cover it. . . . It was either something like this [homework], or I was gonna end up at an eight-to-five job somewhere in order to have any kind of a standard of living at all above the poverty. That's basically what it amounts to. You're either gonna live in poverty, or put yourself out and do something.

By early 1989 downtown Prairie Hills still exhibited signs of economic decline. There were several empty storefronts on Main Street, and many building exteriors were in need of repair. Prairie Hills supported one small grocery, albeit with difficulty since many people purchased food from nearby larger stores that offered greater choices and lower prices. There were two drinking and eating establishments, only one of which was patronized regularly by local residents. Prairie Hills also had a variety store, one menswear shop, a pizzaria, two banks, a parcel service, and a county hospital and manor for the elderly. Although there was much talk about supporting local businesses and services, limited retail choices and higher local prices forced most people to make purchases outside the county.

Other indicators show that the mid-1980s were difficult times for Prairie County. Public assistance programs, such as distribution of food stamps, Aid to Families with Dependent Children (AFDC), and Reduced or Free Lunch programs, peaked in the mid-1980s in the county relative to the remainder of the decade. The Food Stamp program had its highest enrollment in 1986, with almost 10 percent of Prairie County families receiving assistance. The number of county recipients of AFDC peaked in 1987; moreover, the number of AFDC–Unemployed Parent recipients was highest in 1984 and 1986. Peak enrollment in the Free Lunch program occurred in 1986 and 1987 and in the Reduced Price program in 1985 and 1986. In 1989 median household income in Prairie County was $23,356, yet more than 25 percent of county households had incomes below $15,000.[9] The toll of farm indebtedness, closing businesses, and generally low wages in the early 1980s was experienced by many Prairie County residents by the middle of the decade, occurring at the same time as aggressive economic development efforts and the recruitment of homeworkers by TMC.

Prairie Hills is surrounded by open country, vast areas of land rather sparsely populated. Small villages, townships, and unincorporated areas are connected by miles of straight, hilly, and often unpaved and seemingly unnamed roads. Dilapidated barns and homes needing paint dot the small towns and the countryside, and yards often contain rusting machinery and auto parts. On one bright winter day as I photographed Main Street, an elderly resident watched me with amusement and asked, "Taking pictures of our town falling apart?" The decline so evident to an outsider was simply accepted, perhaps taken for granted, by this resident.

Such decline struck a favorable note with visiting industrial managers, however. When TMC came to Iowa to pick a site for relocation, the managers visited Prairie Hills and a larger community in an adjacent county to the north. As one manager observed,

> The northern community had a very professional development team, but the area was too prosperous and didn't seem to us to need homeworking enough to support the operation. The soil was very black, the land flat for miles, the homes recently sided,

and there was new model farm equipment. There just wouldn't be enough demand for the work. Then we went to Prairie Hills, and they have an aggressive development team there, too. But Prairie Hills is built on rolling hills, it's full of red and yellow clay, has lower bushel-per-acre yields, smaller homes, less recent farm machinery. We knew the demand for work was there, and we were right.[10]

Most homeworkers agreed with the manager's assessment of the local demand for work and the general economic conditions, particularly one farm operator and homeworker:

I think everybody was concerned about the farm economy and we knew we needed some jobs in this area, or we were gonna have more and more people moving off of the farm and leaving the small towns. And everybody was afraid that these small towns were just gonna dry up and be ghost towns if we didn't do something pretty soon. . . . 'Cause there were a lot of farm families that couldn't even buy groceries, you know, that were really destitute for some income.

The decline in the agricultural, manufacturing and retail economies resulted in a greater need to increase cash income and in a growing number of farm residents seeking off-farm work. Local officials were motivated by the economic conditions to apply for state monies for development of the homeworking jobs. In a 1986 application for funding they described their community as "depressed, both financially and physically. We have had several business closings along with many farm sales and bankruptcies. Our unemployment rate is about 10 percent." This situation was evident to visiting industrial managers who selected Prairie Hills as the first of two homeworking sites established by TMC.

Riverton is the county seat in River County, Wisconsin. It is a little larger than Prairie Hills, with a population slightly under 2,500 in a county of about 20,000. River County is one of the most agriculturally dependent counties of Wisconsin, with fully 30 percent of its labor force engaged in agriculture.[11] Seventy-five percent of the county's labor force is engaged in agriculture, manufacturing, professional and related jobs, and retail services. Although its labor profile is quite similar to Prairie County's, the manufacturing sector in River County accounts for about 20 percent of the total labor-force activity, in contrast to 10 percent in Prairie County. Historically, the manufacturing sector in River County has been larger and more diverse than in Prairie County. Riverton itself has experienced the opening and closing of several industrial firms; the efforts to recruit industry there during the 1980s were designed in part to fill empty industrial sites. Prairie Hills entered the 1980s with a small manufacturing base, and development was a new effort to industrialize rather than to reindustrialize the economic base.

Riverton is an attractive small community, with a downtown four blocks long. It is occupied by ten eating and drinking establishments, three clothing stores, a jewelry store, a leather and crafts store, a new grocery store, and two banks, one old, the other new and stately. Unlike Main Street in Prairie Hills, Riverton's downtown seems active and lively, especially at noontime and suppertime and even more so on weekends. Riverton also supports a variety store, a fast-food establishment, and a convenience store, recruited in the past few years as part of the overall community-development strategy. River County maintains its own hospital and manor for the elderly. In this setting it is a little easier to imagine a successful local campaign designed to encourage residents to purchase locally.

Helping to make the Riverton area attractive is the careful attention to building exteriors on Main Street, in particular the restoration of historic homes and storefronts. The surrounding area in River County is open country, dotted by dairy farms with white houses, red barns, and blue Harvestors. Towns and villages are connected by a web of paved, two-lane highways that wind around hills and farms like the local river. The difficulties produced by the manufacturing and agricultural declines are not as readily visible here as they are in Prairie Hills.

TMC's managers did not describe Riverton in the same terms as they did Prairie Hills; rather, they had had positive experiences relocating two small factories to other rural areas of Wisconsin and had considered Riverton for a third factory. That factory did not materialize, but the managers had become acquainted with Riverton and, more important, with the mayor. It was the mayor who had described the community as "desperate, because we were having all these people gonna commit suicide," at the peak of the farm crisis, and who had informally suggested to the managers that "it was a shame work was going to those developing countries when it was needed right here in Riverton." Within a few weeks of that suggestion, TMC announced its plans to establish their second homeworking site.

It was not merely the mayor's suggestion that brought the homeworking jobs to Riverton. As in the case of Prairie Hills, economic decline had produced greater numbers of people seeking jobs. A local development official noted that increased numbers of job seekers were not always reflected in the official unemployment rate. In the mid-1980s, when local unemployment was officially hovering around 6.5 percent, approximately 2,000 people (10 percent of county residents) responded to a county labor survey as needing or seeking work. Immediately before this, however, in 1982 and 1983, River County's unemployment rate was at 9.5 percent, the highest rate experienced between 1978 and 1992. Moreover, 1985 and 1986 were years in which other indicators of economic decline peaked: AFDC, AFDC–UP, food stamps and free school lunch recipiency rates were highest in these years.[12] In 1988 and 1989, when median household income was $24,479, approximately 25 percent of River County households had incomes below $15,000.

One homeworker offered her perspective on the conditions that had attracted TMC to Riverton:

> Because this is the poorest . . . they went a lotta places. They didn't just come here and decide we're comin' here. They looked at a lotta places, but I think they needed to find people who needed money bad enough to work for the little wages that they're paying, and boy, they found the right area. This is one of the poorer counties, especially with the way farmers been going. It's one of the poorest communities around, and they could see that, knew they would get plenty of help. Some people don't stay with it long, but they knew there's plenty of people here lookin' for work that they'd always have somebody to do it, and I think they're right. I mean, it isn't good pay, it's just a little extra income. The pay is not real good. . . . So they needed a place where we'd take those little wages and still work, and we do.

The pay may not be considered "real good," but as a retired woman homeworker said, "People were real excited about it, in the fact that at that time the unemployment was so high. They just was wanting most anything they could get for a job." Although the visual cues prompting industrial managers were not as obvious in Riverton as they had been in Prairie Hills, the abundant labor supply reassured them that the operation could be as successful in the former as it was in the latter.

THE DEVELOPMENT PROCESS

In the face of fierce competition from Japanese manufacturers and the loss of market shares during the late 1970s, General Motors was pushed to restructure production and increase profitability. Restructuring took different forms, including fragmenting various processes of production and relocating them to the South or to rural areas. Less skilled production, particularly assembling electronic components, was moved to the South; small towns and rural areas there and throughout the Midwest were attractive spots for new factories because GM sought to avoid concentrations of organized labor.[13]

Production of various parts from GM's suppliers was not immune to restructuring efforts, and suppliers had to compete in terms of cost and quality in order to obtain and then maintain contracts with the company. GM also instituted "just-in-time" delivery systems for most parts suppliers, including TMC, shifting the burden of inventory and storage to them and thus freeing some of GM's working capital. Under this system suppliers had schedules of needed components about ten days in advance and then received more detailed schedules of the precise hour the components would be needed on the final assembly line during the next five days. Suppliers were responsible for ensuring the precise arrival of the exact quantity of their product on the assembly line. Moreover, reduced inventory was not the only advantage for General Motors under the just-in-time system. Because components were used immediately any problems with quality also showed up at once, and improvements could be made quickly and efficiently. Some observers believed that the advantages of quality control outweighed those of reduced inventory because of the speed with which quality problems could be corrected.[14]

From the suppliers' perspective, however, the just-in-time system was challenging to manage until the wrinkles could be ironed out. Changes in GM's demand for components could mean that a batch of parts would be flown to the final assembly plant rather than hauled by truck or it could mean that the workers suddenly had to produce more than usual, resulting in rush orders for factory employees or homeworkers. Or it could mean a sudden decrease in the components needed so that the supplier temporarily needed fewer workers. General Motors enjoyed the advantage of not having to deal with shifts in workers or inventories since the suppliers were responsible for delivering only those parts needed exactly when they were needed. Thus GM gained lower-cost, higher-quality parts on demand, and the suppliers absorbed these costs by structuring production in the most flexible ways possible, increasing the potential for employing part-time and temporary workers, subcontractors, and homeworkers.

It was in this context of restructured production that TMC gained a contract to produce various small automotive parts for GM. The company manufactures various industrial and automotive components, including metal fasteners, plastic carriers, measuring tools, and other precision equipment; by 1986 it employed roughly 8,000 people worldwide, in twenty-five domestic and twenty foreign plants that were non-union shops. In the early 1980s TMC was also restructuring production and began to look for rural sites in the Midwest in which to develop smaller plants, making a concerted and successful effort to move jobs from one central location in an urban setting to several locations in small cities and towns. One of TMC's managers described the company's attitude underlying the organization of production: "It is our philosophy once a product line reaches a certain level, to spin off and start a new manufacturing or assembly operation. We believe this approach helps maintain the entrepreneurial spirit." Wisconsin managed to attract six of these smaller spin-off factories into several rural communities over five years. The mayor of Riverton spoke directly about the motivations behind industrial relocations:

A lotta these companies chose to come out to the rural areas because they felt they could get by with paying lower wages, which they did. . . . And of course, the companies came out here to get away from the unions and the union wages. I understood that the companies were in a crunch because of offshore competitiveness. . . . [This company believes] they can carry on a good enough relationship with their employees, that they don't need unions. . . . They said the fastest way that they'd pull out of Riverton would be if they unionized. [The manager] told me in no uncertain terms they were not anti-union, they were pro-people.

The importance of avoiding unions figures prominently in local officials' understanding of the motivation behind industrial relocations as another development official observed:

That's why you're seeing a lot more companies branch out, into different areas. With smaller branches. There are two reasons. One is for distribution. The distribution cost is much less. Plus if they stay small, the risk of a union coming in is less. We've been in contact with a number of companies that are expanding, but they'll never get more than say fifty people. If they have, if demand grows where they need more than fifty, they'll locate some-place else to add that fifty people on. 'Cause for fifty people, the union is not going to bother.

During this same period of relocation, TMC was developing the cottage-industry plan. The idea came from one of the executives who had recently visited Japan and had observed rural people assembling a wide variety of products, including automotive parts, in their homes. The company was enthusiastic about the idea, and a few managers were directed to implement it. Finding the right product for people to assemble at home, selling General Motors on the concept, and getting it approved by the leaders of the powerful United Auto Workers (UAW) took about two years of persistent work by GM and TMC managers and engineers.[15] They were successful in redesigning a variety of small auto parts so that the subcomponents could be shipped to rural families for assembly and then returned to General Motors for final assembly on cars and trucks.

The cottage-industry concept served two major company interests. First, it fragmented the process of production used at the GM factory in Detroit so that production could be removed from the factory. Second, this decentralization of production increased its mobility, making it easier to relocate to a lower wage, non-union zone. The mayor of Riverton recognized these structural changes as influential in TMC's relocation efforts:

> Industries nowadays like to be mobile. They want a good work force, cheap. And they weren't getting that in Detroit, Chicago, and those places anymore. The people weren't dependable, didn't have good work ethics. . . . That's what brought 'em to the rural areas in the first place. . . . It's hard to find cheap labor.

Having accomplished the reorganization of the work process, two managers from TMC went to Iowa to look for a site. They met with various state development officials in order to discuss possible locations and to present the officials with TMC's cottage-industry proposal. The plan described the operation as assembly work to be done on the farm in existing buildings; the parts would be centrally located in a warehouse, where they would be "staged into kits" for the workers to take home. A kit, or one-week's-worth of work, was designed to fit easily into the back of a pickup truck: "The farmer will pick up the kits on a scheduled basis at the warehouse and be debited accordingly. The farmer will return the assembled parts to the warehouse as scheduled and be credited accordingly." TMC managers described company involvement as including marketing, engineering and design, and shipping of all parts. They would also design the basic modules and any necessary machines or equipment, provide all training, repair machinery, carry the costs of inventory, and "pay the farmer for assembly." TMC wanted the state of Iowa to select the site and the "farm families" for employment, provide a building to be used as a warehouse, and "provide assistance to the farmer by subsidizing the cost of assembly machines and any other specific equipment required."[16] The proposal further detailed the kind of assembly work the people would do and the projected earnings. Development officials from the state decided the cottage-industry concept was "good and worth pursuing" and committed the state to assisting in the development of these jobs in the rural community selected by the company.

FINANCING THE DEVELOPMENT OF HOMEWORKING

TMC selected Prairie Hills for the first homeworking site. The company's expectation that the state of Iowa would provide or subsidize the cost of the warehouse in practice meant that Prairie Hills, and later Riverton, would be responsible for seeking the necessary funds. Thus local officials in Prairie Hills had to find ways to finance the building of a 7,200-square-foot warehouse to the exact specifications of TMC's managers and to do so on a very tight budget: TMC did not want the price per square foot in rent to exceed ten dollars. Prairie Hills met the stringent budget requirements with a variety of financial offerings: $50,000 loaned by investors through the local bank over ten years at 0 percent interest, $55,000 loaned by the state at no interest for ten years, tax abatements during the first five years with property taxes and insurance costs subsidized locally, and local provision of water, electric, and telephone lines. In addition, TMC received small amounts of training monies through JTPA, distributed regionally to employers hiring and training the unemployed, the physically and economically disadvantaged, and displaced workers. Most of the start-up costs were either paid for or subsidized by the community or the state. TMC's financial contribution at the beginning was in the form of inventory and equipment.

Prairie Hills development officials, the bankers in particular, screened people for the local managerial position and for the home assembly jobs; applications and interviews were at the local bank, which was instrumental in providing financial support. In order for TMC to use JTPA funding, workers had to be classified as displaced workers or farmers, long-term unemployed, or economically or physically disadvantaged. Through the application process the bank helped TMC's personnel manager to identify individuals who would be eligible. The local warehouse manager was a displaced farmer, and JTPA disbursed $1,461 for his on-the-job training, the equivalent of about one month's salary. The first ten home contractors, nine men and one woman, qualified as economically disadvantaged workers, meaning their household income over the past twelve months was at or below the federal poverty line. JTPA contributed about thirty-five dollars per contractor for "preemployment training," which, according to the TMC proposal, lasted about twenty-two hours. Subsequent contractors were not screened for JTPA eligibility, thus ending the small subsidies for training in Prairie Hills.[17]

Within less than one year TMC established a second warehouse to distribute parts to home assemblers, this time in Riverton. The process of financing this warehouse differed slightly because TMC had an established relationship with Wisconsin and also because of the variations that exist in funding sources and mechanisms in different locales. Riverton had hired a professional development consultant who knew an executive at TMC and who was instrumental in suggesting Riverton as one of the sites to be visited by company managers when the opportunity for the warehouse came up. The consultant also assisted Riverton in procuring the funds necessary to close the deal with TMC.

Wisconsin is one of thirty-five states using a development tool known as tax incremental financing (TIF), a process that allows local communities to invest in the development of property for the purposes of attracting industry, improving blighted areas, or establishing commercial districts.[18] The hope is that such improvements will result in development that increases the property value, thus increasing tax revenues in that district. The community is allowed to collect the difference in taxes between the old valuation and the new one until the costs of such improvements have been paid; then the various entities supported by property taxes receive the amount based on the higher valuation. The law restrains the use of tax incremental financing in Wisconsin to a small percentage of the total valuation of the locale.

Riverton used tax incremental financing to fund the purchase and development of the property for the TMC warehouse. The site required grading, water, and electric and telephone lines, the immediate costs of which were borne by the community. In addition, the Riverton Area Development Commission (RADC) financed a loan of $100,000 at 6 percent interest for ten years in order to construct the warehouse. The design and construction of the warehouse in Riverton were as tightly managed and budgeted by TMC as they had been in Prairie Hills, with the requirement that the average price per square foot not exceed ten dollars. One local development official described the effort:

> They [TMC] came and told us what they would pay for lease-rent. And we had to come up with a package that would fall into that bracket. . . . That was very challenging. I mean you have to cut about every corner you can to meet it. . . . That's where you have to get into your TIF districts and use every means that you have available to keep the cost down. And the banks were a tremendous help [in getting] favorable interest rates.

Labor, however, was one cost not subsidized through community or regional funds in Riverton. Because of the absence of training for the home contractors and because of TMC's use of temporary agency workers in the warehouse, homeworkers were ineligible for funds from JTPA.

The financing of homeworking in these two communities reveals a pattern: The community and local state bear the costs and risks involved in supporting new industry. TMC generally assumed little or no risk since most of their capital investment was in small machinery and inventory that could be moved easily. The costs of purchasing property and developing it for industry and the costs of warehouse construction were absorbed by Prairie Hills and Riverton; TMC leased the warehouses and was not responsible for them after occupancy. As one local development official put it, "The industry is not at risk whatsoever other than their lease." The company entered each community without having invested initially in property or development and could leave each community without the financial burden of property ownership. The initial risks and costs of industrial development thus are largely borne by each locale, which, concluded the same official, "decreases the cost to make it more appealing to the industry."

TMC-CONTRACTOR RELATIONSHIP AND COMPENSATION

Several of the initial investments in industrial development are financed by each of the local states, a process suggesting that in the relationship between TMC and the local state, the latter absorbs risks for the former. Distribution of the relative costs also can be examined in the labor relationship between the contractors and TMC. Home-based assemblers work under a weekly contract that sets forth the terms of their employment and compensation; it thus provides a basis for a look at labor costs.

TMC requires all contractors to sign an agreement specifying the terms of the labor relationship that, as one TMC manager says, "establishes the subcontractor status" of the homeworkers. The document states that the contractor is "interested in providing assembly services" to TMC on "an independent contractor basis." The terms stipulate that TMC will make parts available for the contractor to pick up using her own transportation. The parts must be assembled in "accordance with specifications" provided by TMC, and pickup of unassembled parts and delivery of completed work must be done according to schedule. "Failure to meet such delivery schedules shall be grounds for termination of this agreement." The contractor agrees to use her own facilities to complete the assembly work and further agrees to allow inspections of such facilities "upon reasonable notice to contractor" by TMC. Quality control is the responsibility of the contractor who agrees that all work will "meet or exceed quality standards relating to workmanship established by" TMC. The final stipulation states that "as an independent contractor" the worker "shall not be eligible for any TMC employee benefits."

This agreement defines the homeworker as an independent contractor, which allows TMC to avoid certain labor costs and to pass other costs to the workers. Whether the homeworkers are independent contractors is questionable. Although definitions of independent contractors vary somewhat from one state to another and between the IRS and the federal government, five criteria commonly are used to determine employment status and can be applied to the specific agreement between TMC and the homeworkers.

The first characteristic of an independent contractor is the ability to control a substantial part of her own business life. According to the guidelines used by the state of Wisconsin to determine unemployment compensation, the worker's ability to control means she must be free from "the employer's direction or control over the performance of the services both under contract and in fact." General indicators of direction and control include deadlines, the requirement that the work be done by the individual, an ongoing relationship between worker and company, the mode of compensation (hourly, weekly, monthly, or piecerate instead of by the job), and the furnishing of necessary materials. TMC's agreement with a homeworker sets deadlines for pickup and delivery and stipulates that the failure of the contractor to meet these deadlines is reason for termination. The agreement also requires the contractor to "assemble the parts in accordance with specifications" provided by TMC. Both requirements suggest that TMC has the right to control and direct the work of the home contractors, at least on paper. The guidelines require that the company control labor "in fact" as well as on paper. Such control is exerted on the homeworkers through the inspection of all parts returned and through the use of set quality standards. If returned work does not meet the quality standard, the contractor must redo the assembly work at the warehouse and is not paid for extra time or work.

Second, the opportunity for profit or loss must exist in the business venture. An independent contractor is in control of the major factors that determine profit or loss, such as price, location, advertising, and volume; the homeworkers clearly lack control over any of these. TMC controls the piecerate for the assembly work, the location of the warehouses, and the quantity and availability of work.

Capital investment is a third criterion for determination of employment status. An independent contractor has risk capital invested in the business; the homeworkers lack entrepreneurial risk in the assembly business. If TMC should declare bankruptcy, the homeworkers would be laid off but would not suffer loss as a result of any investment in TMC as an enterprise. Another way of assessing this risk factor is to determine if the worker has a proprietary interest in the firm and is able to sell or give away such interest; if so, the individual is an independent contractor. Although homeworkers informally share their subcontracted work with others, they are not able to sell or give away the contract itself.

The fourth criterion of an independent contractor is the ability to terminate the contract with the firm and to move the operation to a new location. Clearly, only TMC has this option to relocate and thus might be considered an independent contractor of General Motors. The ability to terminate the contract must rest solely with independent contractors rather than with the employing unit; in the case of TMC, a contract may be terminated by the company as well as by the worker.

Finally, the worker's contribution of business skills and management is a measure in the determination of independent contractor status. Control of daily operations, distribution of work and specifications, hiring and firing, and the implementation of new initiatives are factors that contribute to some aspects of business skill that define the independent contractor. The point here is not only to determine who has those skills but also to determine who controls and directs the use of those skills. Each TMC warehouse is controlled centrally by managers at TMC headquarters who determine inventory and standards and send the specifications to the local managers. Any skill the homeworker contributes is usually limited to improvements on the assembly process itself and not to the management of the business operation.

Some states also specify conditions of economic dependence in determining employment status. For example, in Wisconsin, the state supreme court wrote that because independent contractors "are not dependent on the employer, the risk of their unemployment must be borne by themselves and not another. This class of persons cannot have employment terminated at the will of the employing unit." An independent contractor, by this ruling, should not be economically dependent upon the employer and should have the sole right to terminate the contract and to determine the conditions of the contract. The TMC agreement does not allow the home contractor the sole right to terminate the contract, nor is the contractor allowed to set the terms of the contract.

Other factors are considered in the twenty criteria that the Internal Revenue Service uses to determine employment status. For example, under the guidelines of direction and control, the IRS includes the presence of training as an indicator of employee status. If a person must devote full time to the business of the employing unit, the person is an employee because the firm implicitly restricts other activities for income. An independent contractor "is free to work when, and for whom, he or she chooses." The homeworkers are trained by TMC, and many do find they must work full-time to complete the work. The assembly work is not an activity the homeworker can market as a service to other firms in the area, and thus she is not free to work when or for whom she chooses. A homeworker cannot refuse work for a few weeks and then start the assembly work again as may be convenient. TMC controls those aspects of the labor process.

Based on these criteria it seems that the homeworkers are employees of TMC rather than independent contractors, an important distinction for the purposes of compensation, social insurances, and taxes. Even if challenged, TMC could redefine the homeworkers as statutory employees according to the IRS regulations, justifying the company's lack of contribution to social insurances and taxes. Labor classification is also central to a discussion of how the risks and costs of labor are shared or distributed by TMC. By defining the workers as independent contractors, the company writes into the contract that the workers "shall not be eligible for any employee benefits" and thus avoids paying for benefits such as health and life insurance and any pension plans, realizing a major cost savings. Moreover, TMC is able to avoid paying unemployment tax at the state and federal levels and does not contribute to workers' compensation or disability insurance. Social Security contributions are made in such a way that suggests the workers are employees since TMC deducts the employee rate and contributes a matching amount of Social Security for each Prairie Hills worker; Riverton workers have the self-employed amount deducted from their gross payments.

Labor status as an independent contractor rather than as an employee contributes to the definition of these jobs as secondary and of the income as supplemental. If these assembly jobs were defined as employee positions and if they offered some benefits and stability, they would be considered closer to the idea of a primary job, which often would employ more men. But status as a contractor allows TMC to organize production in a cheaper manner, acceptable within the confines of a secondary job suitable for women as workers. Defining the homeworkers as independent contractors even though the labor relations and process of production indicate that they are probably employees allows TMC to pass risks and costs to the workers. The pattern observed at the community level, with TMC entering at little or no risk to the firm, is the same pattern found with respect to the workers. They bear the risks of self-employment, such as intermittent work stoppages and responsibility for unemployment, with none of the benefits of independence, such as control over the labor process, the wages, or the investment of profits. They are subject to the controls of the company as though they were employees, but they share none of the employees' benefits, such as guarantees of minimum wages and maximum hours. In the same way that the communities subsidized and supported TMC's local development at greater risk to themselves than to the company, the workers subsidize TMC's production with greater benefits and costs savings to the company than to themselves. Because the local state, embodied in local capital and development officials, approves and subsidizes the development of job creation in which workers also subsidize the labor process, it acts as a conduit for the interests of TMC; that is, the local state indirectly passes costs and risks to workers by financing homeworking under these conditions as job creation. In TMC's relationship with the local states and the workers, the company passes costs to workers and to the locales and the state also indirectly passes costs to workers. The reasons that communities, and especially workers, enter such an unequal relationship with the firm have a great deal to do with the local context and the lack of employment options available.

DECENTRALIZATION AND THE LOCAL STATE

Decentralization by the federal government is intended to increase not only local autonomy over the development process and its outcomes but also local responsibility for financing development activities. Through decentralization, development becomes infused with local priorities and values and, it is hoped, meets some local needs. The results of development in each community can be an indicator of local values and the role those values can play in the development process. In Prairie Hills and Riverton, what does industrial homeworking reveal about local values and norms and about their importance in development?

In each community, a small group of about three persons was actively involved in the recruitment of TMC and in the development of homeworking jobs. Homeworking impressed these development officials in general as a good opportunity for economic and sociocultural reasons. The former are fairly straightforward and are usually expressed in terms of the agricultural decline, the loss of retail business, and the need to increase cash flow in households struggling to make ends meet. For example, Prairie Hills applied for state funds claiming "dire need" for this project

> to maintain our county seat town, and give our townspeople additional income for their physical and mental stability. We feel the impact of this new business will place the dollars of income in the hands of our financially strapped citizens and area farmers. We need the financial assistance that a project like this will provide. . . . This would increase tax rolls at both county and state levels. There would be less unemployment paid in the state. It would take some off unemployment and not allow additional recipients.[19]

A Riverton development official said the local committee was very receptive to the cottage-industry jobs because "it was only for farmers, because they were the people that seemed to be most traumatized at the time. . . . If we could get some cash flow back into the hands of these farmers, the businesses in town were going to be better off, too." Economically, the cottage-industry concept made sense to local officials, who saw job creation simply as increasing the cash flow in households.

Homeworking made sense socioculturally in these locales, too. Development officials were just as clear about the "who" of homeworking as they were about the "why." At first, said a Riverton official, "we were not real excited" about the cottage-industry work, mainly because TMC was not going to pay any benefits. But then the Development Committee members "talked to some of the people that were interested in that type of work and they thought it was wonderful. They just wanted to jump at the chance. [Who?] Well, the women that are doing it. The farm wives, that don't have to hire babysitters, they don't have to leave their homes every day." Another development official agreed that although the jobs paid no benefits, "that wasn't what the people needed at this time. What they needed was cash flow." This official described the ideal homeworker:

> The farm wives that take an active part in their farming operation, when they weren't there [because of off-farm jobs], it was having a bad impact on the farming operations, and it was separating families and creating just bad human type emotion. And so this way, they could take the work home, be with their kids, be on the farm, rainy days both husband and wife would work on 'em, and, y'know, it was bringing families that were getting separated, together.

Congruent with local norms and values, the officials speak of a farm crisis, about the farmers (men) being traumatized, and of the need to increase cash flow. In the same breath, the officials speak of the solution as being one of employing farmers' wives; homeworking was strongly gender-typed in the perceptions of officials and workers. In "desperate" times or on "rainy days" men might help with women's work, but women were the workers. The use of off-farm work as a survival strategy during and after the farm crisis is a plan that relies heavily on women as wage laborers.

Women were pictured as the homeworkers by the officials and indeed are the majority of those doing the assembly work. Homework is portrayed clearly as women's work in both communities largely because the work is done at home, which is seen as the woman's sphere; because the wages earned are low and are defined as supplemental or secondary income; and because popular perceptions of the advantages of homeworking are often tied to responsibilities defined as primarily female. And these perceptions of homework were common to workers and their families, not only to the officials.

"Supplemental" and "secondary" are frequently used to describe the home-based assembly jobs, especially when local officials are discussing the work. Supplemental income was also a term of importance to TMC managers who stressed that homework was meant only as a supplement rather than as providing a living wage. On the basis of interview data, the term seems to have different meanings for the company than it has in the community. For TMC it is important that the income from homeworking be considered supplemental because it relates to the requirement that independent contractors pass a "test of economic dependence." A worker who is dependent upon a sole employing unit for income is considered an employee, rather than an independent contractor. If homeworkers are not solely dependent upon TMC for income, they more closely approximate independent contractors, as desired by the company.

In the view of local development officials the TMC homeworking jobs were secondary, the income definitely supplemental:

> It was another form of employment. It was never mentioned or introduced in this community as being a primary employer. I don't think that that type of labor is a primary employer. I don't know anybody that could live on that. It was intended as a supplemental employment. . . . The intent being that it was not intended to take the place of primary employment.

Secondary employment, continued this official, is "low-paying employment." Once they knew TMC wanted to establish a warehouse, the officials informally surveyed local women, especially farm women, to see if there was enough interest. Homeworking was the kind of job one takes to provide a second income in a household, and, observed one committee member, a second income is "what buys a lot of the frills and the goodies, you know, of a family. That the wife comes in with her pay check and buys the new furniture or buys new carpeting, the new dress, or food, or something that isn't an absolute necessity. It's that extra income coming in." These new jobs created under the auspices of economic development clearly were seen as being performed by women and as providing supplemental income that "added to the family kitty," but they did not take the place of "primary employment."

The advantages of homeworking perceived by both officials and workers reveal further how people associate the work with the work-

er's gender. Homeworking would allow "farm wives" to participate in
the farm operation and earn money while "staying home with their
children." Several people mentioned that working at home allowed a
savings by not "spending on the wife's new wardrobe" for a job outside the home. Many of the women workers saw an advantage in being able to combine wage work with house and farm responsibilities
and with child care. In interviews with local officials, homeworkers,
and their families, these advantages clearly accrued to women workers, not to men. The perceived advantages of homework are tied to
the accepted definition of home and family as the primary responsibilities of women, with which homeworking interferes less than
would working outside the home. Homeworking as economic development incorporates these accepted norms and values.

In approving TMC's cottage-industry jobs as development the local communities shouldered the responsibility of procuring funds to
subsidize the new industrial plants. Decentralization of funding for
development in Prairie Hills and Riverton supported the creation of
particular jobs, that from the outset were defined as advantageous for
women. In contrast, other jobs in both communities that were created
with local and state subsidies, both by TMC and by other firms, and
that required training and offered better pay and advancement were
filled by men. In fact, one development official and local businessman
described a second TMC machining plant as "the first primary employment" in his community in over thirty years. This plant is "predominantly male" because "it's heavy work, hard work. Noisy, terrible noisy. Women can't talk when they're working." The use of JTPA
funds to train the local manager of the TMC warehouse is another example of financing a stable, relatively well-paying or primary job,
which is then seen as a man's job. Further, the use of JTPA funds for
preemployment training of contractors in Prairie Hills shows that the
funds were disbursed for "displaced or disadvantaged" workers, nine
out of ten of whom were male, even though the assembly work itself
was done by the women in these households. Decentralized job-train-
ing funds can be used as the locale dictates as long as eligibility criteria are met by the individuals. In practice this can mean, as it does in
Prairie Hills and Riverton, that the funds are often used to retrain men
for primary employment and women for secondary and supplemental
jobs.

Local autonomy is enhanced by decentralization because it allows
officials in local government and managers of capital to subsidize development and job creation in ways that seem congruent with their
own and others' values. Decentralization of the development process

allows that process to be infused with the norms and values of the local communities and the relocating firm. In Prairie Hills and Riverton, the communities and TMC infused the process of development with traditional notions of women's primary responsibilities as home and family and paid work as secondary, seeing it as natural that the slots of low-paid, less stable work were filled with women. Such work reinforces the definition of women's primary responsibilities and in effect, reproduces traditional gender socialization. Development, or job creation through homeworking in these two communities, supports the reproduction of gender roles that maintains and reproduces the labor supply for those jobs as well as for similar kinds of jobs.

LOCAL DEVELOPMENT GOALS

In written documents and in interviews local officials clearly expressed economic goals as the only ones met by supporting homeworking. Simply put, any job means an increase in cash flow, which in their view meets the objectives of economic development as the chair of the Development Board in Riverton pointed out on two occasions:

> [Homeworking] is still putting money into the community. So that's what our main purpose was. How they do that is immaterial, as long as we have the flow of money.

> When you first think of it, of a company coming in, not willing to pay any benefits out. You just get the impression that it's the workers are going to suffer from it. [The company is] not going to benefit your area, or your community that much by it. And actually we are gaining the same results.

Such is the classic justification for local "smokestack chasing" or supply-side development, as Peter Eisinger calls it.[20] As long as the number of jobs increases and workers receive some compensation, the goals of development have been met; the local leadership justifies the means, such as subsidizing secondary jobs, by the end result of increasing the numbers of jobs. The means are "immaterial" as long as the outcome is an increase in cash flow in individual households and in the community. Encouraging a philosophy of development that narrowly defines a successful outcome by the number of jobs created is in itself an indicator of the local state's role in supporting capital mobility; the corresponding lack of concern for the quality of jobs suggests the state's unwillingness to promote workers' interests.

If one uses a ledgerbook approach to evaluate new jobs under development, the means are indeed "immaterial." One could account for so many people now working, or working additionally, and for the increase in household income and its local multiplier effects as results. With this view of development the ledger would show numerically that the goals of economic development were met, illustrating what the official means by "gaining the same results."

Although the ledgerbook may reveal the same results regardless of the organization or the type of work, it is questionable whether those effects are the same when viewed from the worker's perspectives. To a worker, a job with health insurance is clearly not the same as one without, income being equal. A stronger case can be made for the provision of unemployment insurance, which would make a significant difference to a worker who is only intermittently employed, as are these homeworkers. The material conditions and the context in which the work is performed can contribute as much to the worker's experience as does the income earned and are as important in considering the results of development.

THE ROLE OF THE LOCAL STATE IN DEVELOPMENT

Three main groups are involved in the creation and support of home-working jobs as rural economic development in these two communities: TMC, the workers, and the local development officials in each community. Cheaper labor costs and the avoidance of unions are among the primary motivations of the company in organizing home-based production and in relocating it to rural areas. The local states actively recruited and financially supported TMC's reorganization and relocation of production, actions that reveal not only the local states' relationship to TMC but also their relationship to the workers. The local states are working in behalf of private industry's interests in mobility and cheap labor, serving essentially as a conduit for capital to enter the community on its own terms.[21]

In doing so the local states allow capital development, through the creation of homeworking jobs, to take advantage of the local labor force, leaving workers unprotected by the social insurances and other provisions of the Fair Labor Standards Act, such as minimum-wage and maximum-hours laws. Supporting tactics for union evasion suggests lack of state support for the workers' right to choose collective representation or other methods to ensure that fair labor practices are upheld and denies the workers' needs to exert control over their working lives.

Because women are the majority of the homeworkers, state support for these jobs suggests particular assumptions about women as workers, primarily that there must be other income earners in the homeworker's household and that members pool all income and other resources. Thus it is acceptable for the homeworker not to be covered by health insurance or unemployment compensation because the other earners assumed to be in the home, it is hoped, are covered through their work. If homeworking is meagerly compensated and somewhat unstable, it is acceptable to have the secondary worker thus engaged because of the assumption that she depends upon a male employed in a primary job, with the compensation such a job may entail. In supporting homeworking, the local state sends a strong message of supporting women as secondary workers for whom a low wage is consonant.

Decentralization is the mechanism by which the state allows the local state to promote homeworking as development, or in effect, to promote the interests of private industry in the local community. By promoting the interests of capital development, the local state, and indirectly, the national state, are not promoting the interests and well-being of the workers. Capital mobility, cheap labor, union evasion, and subsidized relocation are necessary supports for successful industrial restructuring of production. The state on various levels is supportive of industrial restructuring through its development and tax policies and finds itself in a contradictory position vis-à-vis workers. Promoting the interests of workers, in the eyes of industry and the state, is antithetical to industrial restructuring.

In this case, development becomes synonymous with development for industry rather than for workers or their communities. The differences are not semantic but are rooted in the experiences of the homeworkers and their relationship with TMC. In the words and experiences of the workers, the means do not seem "immaterial." Indeed, the experience and conditions of working are never immaterial for the worker, and it is crucial in the case of homeworking to understand the daily, concrete experience of home assembly work.

3

Homeworkers in the Heartland

Understanding the material conditions of homeworking requires a household-level view provided by the workers. Through interviews and informal conversations homeworkers in each community presented a detailed description of their work, how it is organized, how they accomplish paid and unpaid work, and how they assess the experience. Their voices do not allow even a casual listener to believe that the process of development is "immaterial."

The home is central to the work and the workers. It is a hub from which extend the spokes of wage work, child care, marital and family relationships, and housework. Women homeworkers oversee this hub, doing whatever seems necessary to keep all the spokes in good working order, and their comments offer perspectives on that experience. First, however, a general description of the groups of homeworkers in each community will provide a context.

In both communities, the overwhelming majority of the homeworkers are married and have at least one young child living at home. In Riverton, twenty-nine of thirty-seven households had children living in them, and all but three of these children were under eighteen. Three homeworking households were headed by a single adult, two of whom had children. Twenty-eight of the thirty-seven households had primary homeworkers between the ages of twenty and fifty; only three households had homeworkers who were over sixty. At the time of their interviews, about one-third of the homeworking households

had more than two sources of earned income, including the home assembly work. Less than one-fourth of the homeworkers rented the
homes in which they lived.

In Prairie Hills, thirty-four of the forty-three homeworking households had children living in them, all but five of whom were under
eighteen. Forty-one of the households were headed by a married couple; only eight of these did not include dependent children. Most of
these households had between one and three children, but seven
households had four or more children at home. More than one-third
of the households reported more than two sources of earned income,
and almost one-fourth, or ten respondents, rented their living quar-
ters. Thus in both communities the typical TMC homeworker is a
white married woman between the ages of thirty-seven and forty-five,
living and working with her spouse and two or three children in a
home they have purchased.

PORTRAIT OF A RIVERTON HOMEWORKER

In the community of Riverton the type of work put out to home contractors by TMC is fairly uniform. The homeworkers are involved in
pressing together nuts, bolts, and washers that vary only in size or in
the combinations of pieces assembled; a manual press and table are
provided by the manufacturer. A typical kit or a week's worth of work
might involve pressing or "pounding" 45,000 pieces into 22,500 bolt
assemblies. In addition to the time required, space is needed to store
as many as twenty-four or more boxes of the piecework. A pickup or
van is helpful for hauling parts.

Rita Kelly rises early before anyone else in her household so she
can start laundry, cook breakfast, and make lunches for her husband
and children who will leave for work and school. Her teenage son and
daughter are the next to rise since they deliver papers before breakfast
each day. Her typical day weaves together two paid jobs, babysitting
and home assembly work, with the major responsibilities of child care
and housework.

> Then I get the next three up, help them get ready to go. I try to
> have them all out the door by quarter to eight, *try*. So then I still
> have one left, . . . try to get her clothes and get her bath done,
> and get her ready to go, and she just plays. I try to do some
> housework then, try to run through and get the beds made and
> get the wash finished and, I try to be done with that by nine. I try

to give myself from 8 to 9 to do whatever I can in the house; everything else gets let go. And then I try to go out and work [on the bolts], but in-between that, I have children [to babysit] coming in and out the door, starting around seven-thirty. Usually about nine I like to go out and start doin' my nuts and bolts. Kids are usually playin'.

But by ten, the babies are ready for a nap, so then I work from nine till about quarter to ten, and then I change diapers and get bottles and whatever and try to get them down for a nap. Some days I have two babies, and some days I have three. So then if I get them down, then I try to work again till eleven and then we hafta start lunch. So I get lunch cooked, so usually by 11:30, ya know, I can sit 'em down and get 'em fed, and then I send the two girls off to kindergarten. So then I try to do the dishes, sweep the floor, ya know, clean up from lunch, so then ya hafta get the next group ready for naps.

Well, then, I gotta feed the babies, acourse. They hafta be hand fed. So it's about 1:00 then, when you have all the, everybody's fed and the dishes are done, and the house is put back together, so about 1:00, then I take the resta the kids and put 'em down for their nap. So that gives me then until 3:00 or 3:30 to work again, and that's it. But the babies . . . don't usually go down until two or two-thirty again, but I can usually just take 'em back there with me, and they'll play with toys, so I can usually work, till 3:30. Then the kids come home from school, so then they've got this and that to show ya, and so then I just kind of spend time with them and look over school papers and, about 4:30 maybe start gettin' things around up. Between 4:30 and 5:00, it's pretty busy with the parents comin' and, ya know, they like to talk to you about how the kids' day went, but I'm usually done at five or five-thirty.

I finish fixing supper and get it on the table, and we eat, and then I usually head back out to work, like I said I let them clean up. . . . I usually work back there till ten-thirty, and try to make it to bed by eleven, which I don't usually make it by then, but I try.

The "work back there" that Rita does usually takes at least forty or more hours per week; she is pounding together the nuts, bolts, and washers of various types and sizes that are used by General Motors on both cars and trucks. She has her press set on an old table in the laundry and tool room behind the kitchen, where she is surrounded by twenty-four to thirty-six boxes of parts each week. A normal workload for Rita is to assemble 21,000 to 35,000 screws, which means she started with at least twice as many unassembled parts.

Housework—"putting the house back together"—is complicated for women who, like Rita, use their homes for babysitting. Cleaning and washing become twice-daily tasks, and caring for children overflows into an eighteen-hour day so that each day is a balance between "doing what I can" and "letting the rest go." Weekends become catch-up time with the children, errands, housework, and home assembly work.

> Sundays is one of the best days to do it, for me. Sunday I go to church, and like I said, I teach, and then when I come home, it's, it's almost the best day, is to sit there and work it. Saturdays I usually have shoppin' . . . there's usually someplace to go on Saturday, but Sunday, I usually work Sunday afternoon, and for a while Sunday night. . . . That's the only disadvantage, there's never a day off. You work, it's an everyday job, you never get time off.

A lot of work can be accomplished on the weekend but it is not without a sense of sacrifice: "A lotta Sundays for people is a day when ya have a big dinner and a lotta company, ya know. Ya go someplace for the day. For us, it's soup and sandwich day, and, ya know, and bolts."

Rita sees her most challenging task each day as achieving a balance among her many responsibilities. Industrial homework, housework, and children form a never-ending cycle of things and people requiring attention. Most often, the unfinished chores were "let go" rather than picked up by another family member: "Well, whatever I don't do that I used to do, if I don't do it, it just plain don't get done. . . . Still, the chores are mine to do, the house chores."

Children are most often given higher priority than other tasks in homeworkers' households, and Rita's home is no exception. She makes time for the children and their needs, fitting her work around the family:

> Oh yeah, housework is really hard ta fit in. Seems like I let it get really messy till I can't stand it anymore, and then I, . . . the day I get my kit done is like "oh, I gotta get this house clean." So I hurry up and get the house all put back together, then I sit down and do bolts and devote the week to bolts. I try to cut out housework instead a cuttin' out time with the kids. I try to make that important, spend time with the kids.

This balancing act sometimes becomes burdensome for Rita as she "never feels caught up" and wonders how she can "manage better."

> It really gets ta me if I get behind in my housework. Then I get a real bad attitude, ya know. And it gets so, by the time ya get to the end a the day's work you're, boy, you're just a-slammin' that old press, ya know, and, um, and every day I think, I gotta do something different. I got to schedule my time better. I hafta get myself more organized. But then when I sit down and think about it, I really can't think of any way that I can . . . that I haven't already, . . . other than just staying up twenty-four hours a day, and ya can't do that either.

Job and income insecurity color the context of Rita's home and working life. Ron, her husband, earns "good money" when he is working, which lately has been rather intermittently. Ron's employer is a local, unionized implement manufacturer, and his job provides good wages and benefits; however, there have been annual layoffs of a few months' duration each over the past several years. "It seemed like every year around the holidays, he'd get laid off, and then maybe get hired back in like February again, . . . but maybe he'd get laid off in like October, every year for the past five years." Ron initially entered factory work because of the economic insecurity involved in farming. When the agricultural economy slumped in the early 1980s, Ron left farming and felt lucky to get a job in a unionized shop with good benefits. Yet job insecurity plagues him in the factory as well since the manufacturing sector experiences reverberations from the depressed local and national economies. By homeworking and babysitting Rita helps to compensate for fluctuations in household income.

Fluctuating household income is not the only reason some people decide to work at home, and Rita's extended family exemplifies how homeworking fits in other households. Her parents-in-law are retired farm operators who share one position as contractors; the employer allows only one contract per household, so they applied together. Rita thinks it must be "less stressful" for them because "that's all they do." A typical work day for Dave and Sarah does indeed look different because of less housework and the absence of children and because the older couple tend to share the assembly work.

> Well, the days that we're gonna work on this stuff, we get up between four and four-thirty. We get more done. We do better in the morning like that. And we do the bolts until breakfast, and then

we take a break. We work until 8:00 A.M. on the bolts, building Buicks, building tractors. We generally do about three boxes. That's—there's 850 pieces in a box. And, we do generally not more than three boxes at a time. Because you do get tired. And so we take a break and do something else.

Cleaning house and preparing meals, however reduced in a smaller household, still need to be done each day and are woven into the schedule with the home assembly work, most often, it seems, into Sarah's sphere. As Dave said, "Well, uh, the days that we're gonna work on this stuff, why, usually we have breakfast, and I go out and start while she finishes up the dishes and stuff, and we usually work all day."

Sarah concurred:

He'll usually be out workin' while I'll run in and get the meals or whatever and then . . . I just rinse everything, put it in the dishwasher, and then at night I do everything for the day together. Lotsa evenings, we'll put the pieces together in the house here, and then he can go out and work, and I can be cleaning.

The day ends much as it began, much as tomorrow will begin: punctuated by work. For Rita and Sarah, ironically, at a time and place marked by external job insecurity and economic fluctuation there is no end of work in the home.

PORTRAIT OF A PRAIRIE HILLS HOMEWORKER

The assembly work put out to the homes in the Prairie Hills area is different from the work done in Riverton and comprises a variety of tasks that are rotated weekly among the home contractors. Most of the workers perform a type of manual bolt assembly, in which an assortment of metal washers, rubber grommets, and a metal spacer are placed on a nine-inch steel bolt to form a link in the suspension system of GM's front-wheel drive cars or trucks. The size of the steel bolt depends upon the model of the vehicle, and thus the kit that is rotated among the workers varies for each vehicle. A few of the workers prepare and glue together metal washers and rubber grommets, parts in the kits sent out to assembly homeworkers. Other contractors use an air-powered press and glue to join nuts, bolts, and washers similar to the parts worked on in Riverton. The tasks of gluing and nut assembly are not rotated among workers.

Liz Schaeffer lives in the open country ten miles outside of Prairie Hills, where she and her husband Dan operate a large hog farm and custom farrow some 300 sows, most of which are sold as feeder pigs although a few are raised to market weight. They have six children, ranging in age from primary school through high school; all of them help with the family businesses. Both Liz and Dan also have jobs in nearby towns in addition to working on the bolt assemblies.

> Oh, we get up between 5:30 and 6:00. Everybody's on their own, pretty much. The kids are all old enough to get themselves ready for school. And I get ready for work. And all of us leave about 7:30, for school and work. Dan kinda runs on his own schedule, whether he has things to do for work, or whether he's here for the day, or what. I'm off to work and they're off to school. The older kids are all out for sports, and so our nights are very, very full. Lots of nights, you know, it's close to 10:00 before we all get home for supper.
>
> We try to fit the bolts in on lots of late nights, and I usually will try to do most of them on weekends. We usually try to do a few every night after we get home from whatever. And a lot of times, I don't work [in town] on Fridays, and so I'll have Friday and Saturday to get a good many of them done. And then we just finish up here and there in between. Lot of nights, if I can work it out, I'll come home, like at 4:30, 5:00 from work and do four to five boxes of bolts [out of sixty to ninety] before we'll take off and go for something at night, you know.

The Schaeffer household's schedule revolves around a variety of jobs that Liz and Dan took on to avoid foreclosure on their farm. In addition to farming, Dan works for a feed company and custom raises hogs and crops. Liz works thirty-five hours a week in town as a secretary and about forty hours or more each week on the bolt assembly. The children help with farm chores and the bolt assembly, but their hours are few and sporadic because of school activities. The bolts are a high priority for Liz, whose name is on the contract, because she knows the kit has to be completed and returned on time. Cooking and housework become catch-as-catch-can with everyone chipping in as needed.

> Things are a lot different than they used to be. I used to have time to keep all the books and keep up with everything. Now it's just

kinda whoever has time. Trying to keep a hold of too many jobs, I think. But, that's the way it's gotta be right now.[1]

The bolts are definitely first for me. I know that I've gotta give them the attention they have to have before I worry about anything else. If I can get them done, if I end up with an extra day a week, after I get them done, that's fine. If not, things just kinda go on a song and a prayer. The house is dirty [chuckles], and we just have to live with it. Everybody kinda fends for themselves, because I know that I've gotta give all, all my extra attention to the bolts.

My house has never been so neglected since I had one. You just have to take your priorities, and realize that things aren't always gonna be that way, and you can live with a dirty house. Or coming home to eating sandwiches and fast food every night.

Fridays and Saturdays, Liz's days off from the office, are usually spent in the bolt shop, a small corner of the barn where all the pieces are stored and assembled. Sometimes several of the children help her complete a kit on a Saturday; although appreciative of their help and company, she was also aware of the extra work involved:

And we'd do a whole kit on a Saturday. And that was nice, although, I'd run in and I'd fix food, and we'd eat and leave that mess, and run back out and finish [the kit]. Then I'd have all that to clean up when we got back in the house. They can always tell on me, 'cause at night they'd say, "Oh-oh. Mom's been in the bolt shop too long!" But they'd still sit down while I did the rest of the stuff in the house. And that would just, I'd be grinding my teeth thinking, I wouldn't mind some help doing this!

Liz and Dan responded to the fluctuations of the agricultural economy and to the insecurity of their own farm-based income by finding extra jobs. When Liz started working in town several years ago, the farm lost a worker and a business partner: "We used to both do farmwork. When I wasn't working in town, I was outside as much as he was. But no time for that anymore." As Dan explained, they were worried that replacing Liz with hired labor would result in a net loss of income:

She said she was concerned about not bein' able ta help me in the field, and that I was gonna hafta hire some help. She said that didn't make sense. Well, I'm just tellin' ya it did make sense, because I went ahead and hired my help and got my fieldwork done, when I only paid approximately $1,000 out in labor to do it, and we turned around and made $8,000 ta $9,000 doin' the bolts, so we gained by doin' it this way, financially.

The insecurity of farm income is a concrete reality for the Schaeffers and their neighbors. No one in the county has escaped the experience of threatening bank letters, notices of repossession from the Land Bank, or the sheer inability to keep up with basic bills for food, shelter, and clothes, whether personally or within their extended family or neighborhood. Outside jobs to help maintain the farm, such as custom grain and livestock work, working in town, or assembling bolts at home are necessary.

Everybody lives off of it. That's where you get your living. Everybody does. It's, it supports the farm, because you can't get income off of your farms. . . . If you took a platt book and put it on the table and went down the families that live in these townships, all the wives work, somehow. They either have a job in town, or you know, they do this, or both. Something. You have to have it.

Outside job options are limited and are equally insecure in many cases, often because such jobs depend on the agricultural economy. People such as Liz and Dan opt for a combination of several jobs, trying to spread the risks of investment and involvement in agriculture, hoping their jobs will not fail at the same time.

The loss of a farm operation in Prairie Hills usually forces a family to consider several options as they attempt to maintain cash flow and to reduce their overall debt load. A neighbor down the road from Liz explains what it was like for her family to pick up the pieces economically after their farm was lost:

We were down to no money at all. We didn't have money ta buy groceries or anything, and so [the bolts] was just a lifesaver for us. . . . We needed the money, the total money coming from the bolts to be able to pay our bills and everything, and then that was getting to be quite a responsibility for me alone, all the time, um, because of trying ta do the doll clothes and all these other [crafts]. And, that money was helping also. . . . I usually try ta work in the evenings also, after the kids are home. Sometimes I feel somewhat guilty about this, because I am here, but I am really not here, because I am downstairs working.

Liz's neighbor had considered off-farm work but had found it to be a rather costly option: "It wasn't very feasible. It was a minimum-wage situation, and by the time we sat down and figured out how much it would've cost me ta go ta work and have a babysitter . . . we'd a lost money for me ta do it." Homeworking, whether it is bolt assembly or craft work, becomes part of the family's effort to maximize the inflow of cash while minimizing the expenses incurred as a result of off-farm work.

HOMEWORKERS AND THEIR WORK

Job creation of any kind in a small rural area is always big news that spreads long before the actual arrival of the company, and homeworking was no exception in Prairie Hills or Riverton. Although most contractors learned of the company and the jobs through the newspaper, few of them identified the application process as the way to get the job. Instead, personal connections of various sorts were perceived as important in being hired, an understandable response in a context of limited positions and almost unlimited applicants, all of whom knew each other. One woman, hired together with her sister when the Riverton warehouse first opened, expressed this view:

> Well, Mark Jackson is the guy who, he was my neighbor, and he quit farming, and he went in there and I heard he got this job [as local manager], and so, kinda inside track. Say, "Hey, Mark, ya know, I'd like ta do this." And so that's how ya got hired. As far, I think it was more word a' mouth.

Her sister agreed:

> We got called because Mark knew us. I mean, there were hundreds of applications, and we're sisters and we both get called. But his older sister and I did a lot together in Stevens Point. She lived up there when I was up there at that time. And he's younger than me. And he called me up and said, "Do you wanna do it?" And he knew we grew up on a farm, he just said, "I think all the farm girls are good workers." So we went into it. We got all these screws and they trained us, you know, for one hour there and hauled all this stuff home, . . . and we were doing screws.

The sense of a personal connection as important to the selection process was also clear in the comments of some homeworkers in Prairie Hills.

Well, I've known Chuck Mueller [the manager]. We used to do a lot of excavating work for him and his dad. Also done some shop work for him. Uh, the other fellows that worked in the warehouse, we've done a lot of work for them. I mean, they's all friends. It was really no big decision to be made. They offered us a job, and we took it.

Another family, after having passed through rough times economically, found themselves with a contract before they even applied.

Well, Chuck is interrelated to my husband as an uncle through marriage. Just so happened that we was out to the welding shop and thought we'd just stop over and see the facilities, and, you know, 'cause we knew that Chuck had the job, and we brung home a gluing machine. We were never interviewed for the job or anything. . . . We didn't fill out the application till the day we was hired.

Quite a few people did fill out a formal written application and have an interview before they were given contracts. In the first few months of selecting workers, the company sent personnel people to help Chuck and Mark interview in their communities, stressing that "we need really good people at first to get this thing off the ground." Both men understood this in the context of a small-town community: having the operation start out well was an important part of managing public relations locally. Good, reliable workers, at least in the beginning, were the people trusted by and known personally to the local managers. Moreover, the TMC manager pointed out that Chuck and Mark were hired partly on the basis of their local ties and relations, resources important to an out-of-state firm.

The formal process of application differed in the two communities. In Riverton, applications for all local private-sector jobs were handled centrally through though Job Service. Most people who became contractors had applied through this office, which had about 500 applications on file just for home assembly positions. Job Service itself did not screen applicants but simply forwarded all paperwork to the manager. As positions became available through attrition or creation, Mark Jackson said he found himself selecting workers on the basis of their persistence in contacting him and expressing their need for the job. One contractor described such an incident:

You know, there's a lot of people that are looking for jobs. I know that Mark gets a lot of calls every day, and I know that people ac-

tually come right in and ask him. My father-in-law just found out
that he was out of his part-time job last week, and I know he was
going out today to talk to Mark about, um, possibly, ya know, being that he was ta hire more, if he was interested and keep him in
mind. Which, Mark, I think, is more apt ta choose them people
than ta actually go ta the file, 'cause he knows they're good
people that are interested, if they come and actually say, ya know,
"I'm interested in working, I really need the work."

Another factor that affected local hiring in the early stages and
that was discussed publicly centered on a particular issue: For whom
were the jobs intended? Through the Riverton Job Service and the local paper, the home-contractor positions were publicized as jobs for
farm families, specifically farm wives. This limitation caused some
friction as the townspeople saw themselves contributing through
taxes to the creation of these jobs and felt unjustly excluded from the
benefits. Homeworkers living within the city limits described the reaction:

Oh, everyone was mad, . . . because the town people couldn't
apply for it. It was let out that only farmers that, uh, qualified
could have the job. But it's not so, not anymore. They let anybody
do it. But they were really mad about that.

I think they brought this corporation into Riverton for farmers. It
was particularly designed for farmers' wives, and even at first, ya
know, I think one a yer qualifications in order ta even work there
was to be a farmer's wife. . . . I really think that it's something
that it was offered through the Job Service for low-income people,
um, for farmers that were having a hard time making ends meet,
because of the milk prices and because of the drought, this last
summer.

If the requirement was economic need, then residence should not
have been used as a criterion, some people argued. The anger of the
townspeople led TMC and local officials to speak of hiring town and
farm people who needed the work. Although the company wanted to
employ people who needed the work, they also screened carefully to
make sure that home assembly would not provide the only source of
income in the worker's household. At the outset, both farm and town
residents were hired as contractors and a few of their observations reveal their different perspectives:

Yeah, it was supposed ta be for farm wives, is what they said first, and then, uh, the first people they all hired was town people, which kinda made a lotta people mad, 'cause I put in an application [as a farm wife] and didn't get hired right away, and a bunch of town people did.

When we first started, see, I live in town. Now, when I went down and applied, I went to Job Service, and they said to me at the time that, 'cause it asked when they put on your application, do you live on a farm? And I said no, so they put, they said, well, this is mainly for farm people, they said, to try and get them more money. So I didn't think I had a chance. Well, then, Mark acourse called me the next week and I was hired in the first group.

Oh yes, they talked about it in town, about the plant coming in and how it'd be good for . . . the farmers that were havin' a rough time of it, but then afterwards Mark says, "Well no, it isn't for just the farmers. It's for anybody that has a hard time tryin' ta find a job, or wants ta do a job at home.

In Prairie Hills the hiring process was seen differently by the workers. Applications were handled through the local bank, whose administrator was also president of the Development Commission. The farm-town controversy did not emerge because the amount of space needed to do the bolt assembly made farm families more likely candidates for the work, and since a truck or van was required to handle the weight and bulk of the average kit, farm operators met this requirement more often than did townsfolk. Two concerns regarding the hiring process did emerge in Prairie Hills, however: the role of the local bank in the selection process of the manager, Chuck Mueller, and the impression that farm viability was important in determining who would be hired.

Fred is an older, disabled man who glues grommets and washers together in a corner of his garage for TMC. Like many workers, he voiced strong feelings about the bank's role in local hiring processes:

Well, in every town, there's always someone of more influence than other people, and the bank out here, like banks in most communities, has the influence, and if you owe money ta the bank, you got a better chance a gettin' a job than if ya don't owe money ta the bank. . . . I think they have their finger in the control who gets jobs out there and who don't.

The bank's the one that told the city, ya know, "Hey, we put this building up. We can get this industry ta come ta town, and they'll help a lotta people out in this community. They'll get jobs and . . ." They don't tell them "they'll be helpin' us out, because we got a lotta people out there that aren't gonna get their notes paid if we don't help 'em out." And so they was lookin' out for their own interest. . . . I don't know the whole inside story on that, but that's almost disgusting. That's almost disgusting, some a the stuff that's goin' on, but what can you do about it? . . . The manager up here is a displaced farmer. The bank sold him out, or he was forced ta sell out.

Robin, Fred's neighbor, also glues grommets and washers and, in a quiet and matter-of-fact way, agreed with Fred's observations: "I know that the manager up here got the job because somebody through the bank told him about it, and they wanted him ta have it. And at that time, he was just pretty much going under."

The bank served as the local job center, a role that underscored the perception that those people whose farms were less viable were being given preference for these jobs. Lucy, a middle-aged woman hired to assemble bolts early on, recalled a conversation with another contractor:

One lady said to me, well, something about, well, "Is your farm gonna be sold? Or, are you guys, when is your bankruptcy coming up?" We said, "What?" And she said, "Well, all of us are, and were recommended by the bank because we're totally broke." . . . And I did notice right away, that the way they were talking, it was all farmers that were hurting really bad.

Dorothy applied for an assembly contract with her husband and remembers the early application process in which many people were under the impression that their farm's financial status affected their job possibilities.

We also heard that the first few that, when they applied or got called in for an interview, that they wanted to see your financial statement, you know. . . . We just heard, you know. And our friends said, "No way, we're not gonna show it." Well, we wouldn't show ours either. That would make you think that people who are really in need are gonna get the jobs. Well, that sounds good, too. But they never did anything like that with us.

Neither the company nor the city development officials wanted the perception that these jobs were created for the needy in an agricultural community. In Riverton, the farm-town issue was a variation on this idea, in this case, for dairy farmers. In both communities, the managers and local officials stressed that the company was only looking for "good workers" and that other characteristics, such as need or personal connection, were immaterial.

Once hired as a contractor, the applying household was trained. In Riverton training was short and simple: Mark Jackson would take homeworkers around the warehouse to show them the different types of washers and bolts, the size of a kit to be done in a week, and the press and table that the company provided. Then the trainees would sit at the press and punch bolts for a while to learn how the process worked. After about an hour, workers were sent home with a full kit. Mark had learned from experience to forewarn new contractors that the early weeks were often frustrating because the kit could take an inexperienced worker from fifty to sixty hours to complete. After achieving a comfortable rhythm with the press, however, a worker could expect to complete a kit in thirty to forty hours.

Training for home contractors in Prairie Hills was more involved and varied for groups of contractors hired at different times. According to the workers, the first two groups of contractors had longer periods of training, largely because the company was still figuring out how to handle the work. There was not enough work available then to send a kit home with each new contractor, so the workers assembled bolts in the warehouse for up to two weeks as part of their training. Later groups of workers were trained in a matter of several hours spread over a day or two. In all cases, training involved not only the assembly work but also learning the various tasks necessary to complete a kit, such as packing, labeling, and taping the boxes. Elise remembered her training period as taking place over two days:

> We assembled and packed. Learned labeling. You had to do several, there's about twenty different types of these suspension parts that we assemble, and you had to do them. So there was different things about each one of them that you had to learn. I think you could have figured it out on your own, cause you have a blueprint to look at. But it was nice to feel more comfortable with it.
>
> They went through a tape to show us how the car plant manufacturer used the pieces, and had some discussion. We assem-

bled that night and then we came back the following night and assembled again, and that was the extent of the training.

The training itself was not demanding, but one detail stood out in the minds of the contractors: quality control. Above all the company emphasized the quality of the completed kit, and there were set "error rates" above which work was declared unacceptable and for which one was not paid.

> [The manager] taught you how to put boxes together and label 'em and then put these together and make sure that you don't have mistakes, you know, checking them and make sure they're checked, because if you make too many. They check these boxes in [the warehouse], not all of them, but they'll check so many out of the whole kit. If there's too many mistakes, they can call you in, you gotta go through the whole thing. Which I don't wanna do.

Like Mark, Chuck Mueller had learned to forewarn new workers that the first several weeks were the hardest; the kit often took about twenty hours longer than the thirty to forty hours per week reported by more experienced contractors. Although most contractors felt the work was self-explanatory, they often acknowledged that the value of training was to "build up speed and comfort" with the work. The start-up time was longer for Prairie Hills workers because the work was more complicated, and it varied enough from week to week that the contractor was given a blueprint to follow with each kit.

Payment for training was worked out on a kind of collective piecerate basis: Several contracting households attended a training session during which they assembled so many parts, the total rate of which was then divided equally among the households. The amount was small enough that most workers had trouble remembering if indeed they had been paid for training. Fred did remember that in order to be paid for training, workers had to fill out "papers that went to this here retraining program and stuff. They was down there, and we had ta sign some forms and stuff, so I assume that some a the money come from there." The company had received federal funds for retraining displaced agricultural workers, which covered the training of some of the home assembly workers.

Once a household had a contract and training and was sent home with a kit, the next step was to set up a work area. Many people were tremendously creative in their use of surplus space or in reclaiming previously used space. Some people liked to set up their work inside their homes where it would be easily accessible, doing "a bit here and there" during the week. Others preferred to keep it out of sight, using basements, sheds, garages, or converted chicken coops, partly because they did not want to be reminded constantly of the remaining work and partly because it was messy, bulky, and rather unattractive.

On many occasions the interview took place in or near the work area, either in the home or in an outside building; other times, the work area was not readily observable during the interview, but the worker would show me through the work space during or after the interview. Thus it was possible to see almost every work area and to observe firsthand the basis for workers' central concerns about adequate heat, light, space, proximity to living areas, and convenience for loading and unloading heavy parts.

Riverton homeworkers had a little more choice in where they could set up a work space; since their press and table were fairly easily moved the work space did not need to be permanent. Most Riverton workers set up their work area within the home, either in or off the kitchen or in the basement; a few had work spaces in sheds or other farm-related buildings. The bolts and washers were greasy, and the grease was easily spread so that many workers wanted to keep the operation away from the main living area lest more housework be generated. Riverton homeworkers voiced a range of considerations regarding their work spaces:

> At the other house we lived in I had a small bedroom that was downstairs, and it was nice just ta have it all outta the way, and I didn't hafta worry about when somebody came, ya know, all these boxes strung all over and stuff, whereas now my back porch has all my boxes and stuff in it. . . . My original idea was ta have it in the laundry room in the bathroom, which is in here, but it just didn't work. I was too secluded and couldn't keep an eye on the kids, ya know, at the same time, whereas here [the kitchen] I can peek to the living room and see what the kids are doing. . . . Even in the evenings when my husband is home and they're watching TV, I can be out here punching bolts and still feel that I'm with the family. If I was stuck back there it makes quite a bit a difference.

> If it wasn't right there in front of me, then it was out of my mind, I wouldn't keep at it as much as I would have to. . . . We consid-

ered puttin' it downstairs, but, ya know, I thought, "Well, if it was down there, then you wouldn't get at it." If it were here in front of the TV, then it's right there handy.

It works out pretty good, being in the laundry room. I mean it's heated there. I even have a little TV there. Then, when the laundry's done, why I can just jump up and wash my hands, till they get all chapped. And take 'em out, you know. It's in the center of the house. You don't feel like you're isolated, like some of 'em have it out in the garage and stuff like that. Or down in the basement. Which is nice, cause you're out of the way and you don't have the boxes and stuff sitting around. This way you're still in the center of living, yet.

It's very hard to sit back there by yourself and work. It's very lonely. . . . So that part I don't care about, is sitting back there all by myself. You kinda feel sometimes like it's punishment, you hafta be back there workin' when everybody else is out here, ya know, watching TV and talking.

Yeah, I could use a better light right now. We're working on that. We hate to put one up permanent now, 'cause we move [the press], so I hate ta go punch holes in the ceiling or anything.

For several homeworkers, the location of the work was actually a family concern. Family members sometimes objected to the constant banging noise of the press, which interfered with sleeping or with evening entertainment; others disliked the functional appearance of the press and table. Yet a choice that was convenient for the family as a whole was not always good for the worker. Family members, notably husbands, were influential in determining where and under what conditions assemblers worked at home. One woman worked in the back storeroom of her house because her husband and children objected to the noise of the work and the appearance. The room was cold in winter and hot in summer, making her dread each working hour:

If I had my choice, I'd have it in the living room, where I could watch movies and watch TV, but my husband can't stand it in the living room, 'cause we have a lot of people that come here through the day, and he doesn't think it's a nice sight in there. Last summer it was so hot that I couldn't work back there, so he finally let me move it to the living room, and I much prefer it in the living room. But he just does not like the looks of it sitting in the living room, so he bought me a TV to put back there, but it's hard to sit back there by yourself and work. . . . But you hafta keep the family happy.

Homeworkers in Prairie Hills had less choice about work spaces than their Riverton counterparts. The assembly kits in Prairie Hills typically contained sixty to ninety boxes, each weighing about fifty pounds. Most assemblers used a long table set over bins containing the various parts as their worktable. Not provided by the company, this table usually was homemade by the worker, with average dimensions of about two feet by five feet. Thus it was not a particularly movable setup, and often a house did not have too many spaces where a table and kit would fit. Workers who glued or did the nut assembly shared this problem; their machinery was bulky and the glue was messy, so their work space often settled into one spot. Most homeworkers in Prairie Hills set up work spaces in outlying buildings and garages on their property. Nonetheless, a great deal of variation and creativity surfaced as people adapted spaces for working, especially in Prairie Hills. Some workers used rudimentary shops, converting sheds or coops no longer in use on the farm. Often, these spaces would be equipped with small gas or space heaters, an assortment of small lights, a radio, and usually a cordless phone.

The interviews in Prairie Hills took place during the winter months and afforded me the opportunity to experience the adequacy of available heat in some work areas. One setting remains etched in my memory: I am sitting on a somewhat rickety stool in an old shed across from an older gentleman who is well dressed for the frigid February weather. Harry is a farmer in his sixties, his face worn and leathery; he sits on two boxes of the grommets he is gluing and is wearing heavy boots, thermal snowpants, a pile jacket, gloves, and a knit cap with an attached mask (which he did not use during the interview). There is some sort of small heater that goes on and off, providing brief and noisy bursts of heat that quickly dissipate into the cold air. As our conversation progresses, his answers and my questions get shorter and shorter and are punctuated by our chattering teeth. Harry's setup is typical of those workers who limit investments in their work spaces, who prefer to use the income earned for farm or living expenses.

Other work spaces were more comfortable and better equipped than the surroundings that one might find inside a factory. A few workers sectioned off portions of their garages, put in paneling and carpeting, equipped the area with heating and cooling, and installed the almost indispensable and ubiquitous television, radio, and telephone. Another advantage of such a work space was its proximity to the house, yet the dirt and grease did not spill over into the living environment. Other workers redecorated unused farm buildings, equipping them with the comforts of home. A couple of workers had small spaces set aside in their basements, the disadvantage being the inconvenience of stairs for loading and unloading kits.

Robin, a young woman who lives in town and works part-time as an administrative assistant, has her glue machine and the kit of 11,000 to 13,000 rubber grommets and washers set up in a corner of her basement. Fortunately, the basement has a ground-level entry with a few steps, which facilitates handling the kit.

> It's okay, except we don't have a lotta heat down there, so Will [her husband] has had to open up one a the vents in the furnace ducts ta give us heat. And then I run a little heater under my table the whole time I'm down there working. Um, it's never been too bad until this last week. . . . In fact, it was so cold last weekend that when I came upstairs, my hands were just, um, I don't know what I wanna say, they were chapped. They were just so sore. And they had been just so dry all week. But basically it works out okay. I keep my mess down there. I don't like it up here. I don't want that glue smell in my house up here. And, ya know, the rubbers have a smell, so it works out okay, and it works out good for unloading, because we back the pickup up ta the steps, and we unload it.

During the winter, adequate heat was a major concern for many workers. Although basements were convenient locations for many people, most basements were not finished rooms and did not provide well-insulated and draught-free working environments. Jill, a young woman with two children still at home during the day, had been assembling bolts in her basement, but after working there through several recent cold spells, she and her daughters had caught bad colds: "We did it in the basement. But the wood burning stove down there, it's just not a big enough stove to heat the whole area, and it gets cold down there. And the girls were catching cold, and I was catching cold all the time. . . . I really don't like doing it up here, but I can't be cold and sick, too."

Like the assemblers in Riverton, the Prairie Hills workers were concerned that their work space not cut them off from "what was going on around here." Since many people worked in outlying buildings, cordless telephones were quite common, and many workers arranged their place so that they could see arriving visitors or children getting off the bus. One woman liked working in the garage even though a nicer shop was on their property because the garage was only two steps away from the entrance to the kitchen; she could "just hop over and tend the wash or put a roast in" with minimal interruption to her assembly work. She did not even need a phone since she could hear the kitchen phone.

Just as workers were on their own to develop a work space, they were also free to adapt the assembly process to suit themselves as long as the end product remained the same. Riverton homeworkers, faced with weekly totals of 20,000 to 30,000 bolts and washers, quickly learned ways to alter the work process. Most people put their energies into developing speed based on shortcuts, but a few ventured attempts at automating the bolt press. One couple was extremely productive together and dedicated to the work. Harlan, a retired farmer in his sixties, had creatively automated one press so that after he loaded it, the press would punch the bolt and pop it out into a bin of assembled parts. Harlan claimed that although automation did save a little time, the real value was in the saved energy: He did not have to exert the force to punch the bolt and could manage to fit an extra kit in each week. Other workers opted for more primitive, nonautomated methods to make the work easier; they simply hammered the bolt and washer together, finding this method less cumbersome than the heavy press.

The first group of homeworkers in Prairie Hills contributed a great deal of mechanical know-how to the assembly work. When the company started up in Prairie Hills, the production engineers had developed a rather slow and primitive way of assembling the bolts: The worker was to hold the bolt in one hand and put on the pieces, one at a time. After a few weeks of assembling 5,400 bolts per week, the homeworkers came up with their own variation, much to the delight of the engineers. Lucy and Phil were among the first workers hired, and Phil developed the "bolt board," a piece of wood or metal that held many bolts upright and allowed the worker to slide the pieces on, assembly-line style. Instead of doing one bolt at a time, a worker could move down the line and complete enough to fill one box. The company was pleased because it felt the board made checking easier for the worker, ensuring higher quality production for TMC. Among the workers, the bolt board was adapted according to available space and to the number of people who would be assembling bolts. Other workers adapted old farm machinery no longer needed on the farm: Carrie and her husband converted an automated hay conveyor on which she placed her assembled bolts, which were then rolled down into the box. She prefers this method because she can work sitting down instead of standing and walking along the bolt board. Since it is the end result that matters to the company and that determines the pay, the worker has an incentive to figure out the quickest and most convenient way to produce high quality work, making the process somewhat individualized.

The organization of the homework process is as particular to households as is the development of work spaces. How the work is completed each week depends on the participant, the schedule of activities, and a host of other considerations that varies among households and among household members. Generally, each contracting household has one person, not necessarily the person named on the contract, who takes responsibility for completing the work. The responsible person actually may do most of the work or may delegate the work, making sure it gets done. When the responsible person is an adult woman, the assembly work is accomplished along with housework, child care, and sometimes another outside paid job. Most of the adult males responsible for homework combined it with farming and tended to delegate more of it to other persons.

In most households the homework is shared although to what extent varies tremendously. When the adult woman is responsible for the work, it is largely children who share the tasks, either through household chores or the assembly work itself. Some children are paid a nominal amount by the parent, a kind of allowance. Older children are usually paid more; since they tend to do more assembly work regularly the family may treat it as an outside job for wages. Generally, children in homeworking families in both communities put in very few hours, perhaps accounting for 5 to 10 percent of the assembly work done in their families. Alice described her children's participation:

> The kids hate it. They just really hate the job, but, um, they help out when I'm running behind, or when they have extra time off, or when they're home. Uh, there are maybe three weeks that go by, and they never touch it, and then there may be times go by, ya know, this weekend, I think. My daughter helped me for, let's see, two hours on Thursday night finishing up last week's kit. I

think it took her two hours. She had ta do two boxes, and it took her that long, and then she helped me yesterday for an hour and a half.

Another worker who was well known for completing her work in record time explained how she managed:

All the children work, um at certain times of the year. Right now, the two oldest ones don't. They're not here enough to, to help do it. Because they have practice after school and they don't get home till late. But the two youngest ones and my husband and I have been doing them. But when the kids aren't busy, they all help.

Another arrangement involved assistance from retired parents or other older family members; participating in the homework on a minimal but regular basis afforded the chance to visit and to be useful simultaneously. Thus about 10 percent of the assembly work was accomplished by older people who were related to the contractors. Three Riverton homeworkers who were related to each other received help regularly from an older relative.

My aunt comes over like one day a week and helps. She probably puts in like six hours a week. She helps me and Rita and Lil, so she like puts in one day a week with each of us. . . . On the day of my nephew's birthday, my aunt, my brother-in-law, and my sister set there, and they put 'em together, and I got two presses, and they put 'em together as fast as they could, and me and my aunt were hittin' 'em, and I think we did three boxes in an hour. That was really good.

Sometimes, if a relative or family member was not available to help, the main contractor in the household would further subcontract the work to a friend or neighbor. Some of the workers actually had started out as subcontractors; when an opening became available, they had the advantage of experience and were able to get their own contract. In some cases, the person helping the contractor did not want to invest the time or energy in completing an entire kit each week and was satisfied to subcontract on a part-time basis. One farm operator in Prairie Hills was helped seasonally by a neighbor:

Uh, the neighbor lady has been doing some of them for me, like through the busy times, spring and harvest. So, those times, why, I put in, I've been doing two-thirds of them. And I probably put in oh, twenty-five to thirty hours, and she probably puts in another ten or fifteen. And that's kinda the way it works.

Gradually, that situation changed, because the neighbor lady wanted more than seasonal income:

Lately, she's been doing 'em, helping me every week. She kinda wanted a little guaranteed money. So this winter she's been doing a third of them every week. And, we'll probably keep that arrangement right on through the summer.

Robin began to subcontract her work out to a friend: "I have had her come in here three Sunday nights in a row and help me, or Sunday afternoons, I guess, we worked until about seven. And I did it strictly because, for awhile I was feeling just really drained, like I wasn't gonna be able ta ever finish 'em."

In spite of many homeworkers describing their assembly work as shared, further probing revealed that in most households, one adult was completing the kit for the most part. In Riverton, all but one of the contractors were women or women assembling with some help from their husbands. The home contractors of Prairie Hills were mostly women, but there was more male involvement in the work, partly because the kit was so heavy to load and unload. The pieces to assemble were not as small as those in Riverton, either; many men expressed the opinion that women, with their "small, dexterous" hands, were much faster at assembling the screws than were men. A few men explicitly called the homework in Riverton "women's work."

Homework as women's work was added to women's other tasks. The major difficulty expressed by women contractors was about keeping up with housework and children while completing the kit. The women on farms often described how they fit farmwork into their schedules and were aware that husbands and children rarely crossed over into housework. As Irene put it, "I do my parts and he comes home, and he cleans up. We have supper. He sits in his easy chair and I do parts. It's my job and I do it." Lucy agreed: "It doesn't bother him to be in here all day long, down watching his screen and his computer stuff, and having me out there and doing bolts."

Although more work in the home did not always mean all the work was shared, most contractors believed that at least the potential for helping one another was there. Van and Myra operate a large hog farm, and we chatted in their work space, a shed. Although Van admitted he did not help with housework, he put the homework in a different perspective:

> I think I'm helping her. Now see, she was gonna have a job in town, which would have been eight hours a day, five days a week. It would have been forty hours. I couldn't have helped her in there. I can here [with the bolts]. Now I'm not maybe necessarily doing more help in the house than I ever did before or anything like that, but I do help do this, so I'm still helping her.

Van's position was fairly typical of most homeworkers' husbands; they may not help with the housework, but when needed they will pitch in with the assembly work.

Probably the most difficult question for homeworkers to answer concerned the number of hours they spent per week on the assembly work. Those people who tended to do the work in blocks of time and who worked alone had the least difficulty estimating hours; such a homeworker was rare indeed among those interviewed. Other homeworkers had small amounts of help that varied from week to week, and they interspersed assembly work with housework, farmwork, and other tasks. These workers, by far the largest group, tried to estimate their own hours, the hours of those who helped, and the time spent on other tasks.

> I don't know, I never really sat down and figured it out in hours, because it's, it's broke up because of feeding the kids, and stuff, and I have little things. I'll stop pressing ta take the clothes outta the dryer ta fold 'em or whatever, ya know, so I've never really considered it as far as hours that I've put in. . . . I guess if I thought of it that way, I'd be depressed.

Another homeworker agreed on the difficulty of estimating time:

> That is so hard ta tell, because sometimes you go fast, sometimes you go slow, and I'm settin' there workin' at it and get up and do the wash, set and do it a little bit longer, get up and fix dinner, sit down and do it and decide, oh, the floor needs vacuuming. Now that the kids are bigger, I figure like thirty-five to forty hours.

All workers gave their best guess on the time it took them to complete a kit, trying to average in the hours worked by any helpers. A few workers found it confusing to count their hours separately from the hours of those helping them at the same time; it seemed to these workers that three people working two hours completed only two hours worth of work rather than approximating six hours of work by one person.

> I never even stopped to figure it up. I'd say it takes about an hour a box, and there's sixty boxes. So, you could count, for one person, sixty hours, probably to do a kit. But see, since we have so many people working, it's hard for me. I've never really stopped to figure it up, and maybe a third of that.

Another factor affecting the workers' time estimates is the type of work; different pieces varied in the amount of time needed for assembly. In Riverton, there were three-piece kits and two-piece kits; the former required the worker to handle more pieces while ending up with the same number of finished pieces as the latter and thus increased the overall assembly time. In Prairie Hills, the different bolt assemblies varied in the amount of time required by the average worker. Kits that had fewer pieces on the bolt or did not have the final top screw took much less time than the more involved kits, which could easily take fifteen hours longer. Commenting on a kit of greater difficulty, one Prairie Hills worker said that they "put in another ten to fifteen hours and we figured we made about one dollar an hour on them. They're just harder."

Kits varied also in the quality of pieces included, which affected hours spent completing the work. If the pieces were of a lesser quality and the threads of the bolts were poorly formed or did not fit easily on the washers, the workers found assembly time increased noticeably, usually about five hours total. Not only did the time increase, but the effort required to force together pieces made inaccurately was also greater. A former homeworker in Riverton figured that her pay "when I got pretty good, it was like $5.00 an hour. But then when you got rotten parts, you're talking down to $2.50 an hour, that's not worth it whatsoever." Bad parts occurred frequently enough that she quit working for the company.

Oftentimes, workers would count only the hours it took them to assemble the parts, reasoning that they were paid for assembly time and excluding the required ancillary tasks involved. All kits required the contractors to make boxes, tape the boxes, put labels on them, stamp the labels with their name and worker number, pack the boxes a certain way, and then load finished work onto a vehicle and transport it back to the warehouse. These tasks took time that workers often did not count until specifically asked to do so.

> Yeah, I think I know what you're getting at. I guess when I first started this job, they said one person can do this job in thirty to forty hours a week. And I do count the hours that someone helps me. . . . But I have found it almost impossible ta get the job done in thirty hours, and you hafta count the time that you go ta pick it up, your transportation time, your unloading time, your load-up time, and so on. Um, you hafta prepare all the boxes, so when you take all that inta consideration, it's a full-time job. It's a forty-hour-a-week job.

When variations are taken into consideration, Riverton homeworkers reported spending twenty-five to forty-five hours per week assembling screws, the most common estimate being about thirty-five hours. Average hourly pay figured by these workers came to $3.35 or so. A retired couple in Riverton described their earnings:

> I would probably say minimum wage. You know, really not too much over that. It all varies. We don't have as many screws, or if they're easier to assemble, it don't take us, you know, quite as long, and you might make a little bit more than that. But when you consider both of our hours, we're lucky, I would say, to make the minimum wage.

Homeworkers in Prairie Hills reported working thirty-five to fifty hours, with forty-two hours weekly about average; their hourly pay averaged between four and five dollars.

In both communities there are exceptional workers at either end of the speed/earnings continuum. A few women in Riverton reported completing kits in twenty to twenty-five hours, estimating earnings closer to about $4.00 an hour; on the other hand, a few Riverton households reported working well over forty hours each week with an hourly wage of about $2.50. As one of the latter workers said, "You'd be better off ta look at the check at the end, and don't figure it by the hour." Exceptionally high hourly earnings for Prairie Hills workers were usually reported by contractors who glued grommets and washers; they had the lowest overall weekly hours invested (an average of fifteen), and they estimated earning about eight to nine dollars per hour. There were a few workers in Prairie Hills whose reported hourly earnings fell below minimum wage: Pay was based on a rate per piece finished; handling more components did not necessarily translate into more money if the end result contained the same number of pieces as a simpler kit. In Prairie Hills, the piecerate for certain kits was lower if the contractor handled fewer pieces, but it did not increase for greater numbers of pieces.

> Like the kit I'm doing now pays two and three-quarter cents per bolt, and in my opinion, it's just as hard as the rest of 'em [that pay more]. You've only got thirty boxes, but there's 180 to a box. Ya gotta remember that ya got one grommet up, two grommets down. . . . How they figure it is on how many pieces you're handling, see. And they will lower it because you're handling less pieces, but if you're handling more, they haven't raised that one. . . . They don't up that one for handling the extra piece, but they take money away for handling one less piece. Which I don't think is quite fair. . . . And the boxes, they give you a bigger box. You gotta put a divider in. They don't pay ya for puttin' the box together. I think they oughta, for puttin' their boxes together and takin' the time ta do it, they oughta pay a little extra for doin' that. . . . But they don't pay ya anything other than just the bolt assembly.

In Riverton, workers earned less for a three-piece kit than for a two-piece kit even though they handled more pieces completing the former and had to make, label, and stamp the boxes. The workers objected to the inequities of the piecerate system because it did not compensate them for effort or extra time in the case of more complex assemblies.

Pay could also vary if the kit did not contain adequate parts to assemble an entire kit. The average kit in Prairie Hills contained about 5,500 assembled bolts, providing the warehouse had supplied the worker with the correct number of bolts, grommets, washers, and spacers. The contractor was paid for what she completely assembled, and her paycheck would reflect the variations in supplied parts. All spare parts were to be returned to the company each week.

The workload among the homeworkers also varied. In Riverton, contractors were expected to complete one full kit each week but were allowed to do more than that if they desired, which served as an incentive. Harlan, the retired farmer who had automated his press, worked diligently with his wife Louise, and together they managed to assemble about four kits each week; the average Riverton homeworker did the one required kit per week, sometimes increasing that to three in two weeks, with help.

The workload in Riverton was changed by the company in order to increase inventory; at the time of interviewing, the size of the kit was up by 20 percent. Workers were not given a choice about this; each contractor was required to complete one kit per week, regardless of fluctuations in the size of the kit. The piecerate for the larger kit did not change, so the pay increased proportionately with the size of the kit.

Assemblers in Prairie Hills did not have the same options regard-ing their workload. All bolt assemblers and other homeworkers were limited to one kit per week in order to "spread the work around the community." This ceiling on the amount of work allowed robbed the piecerate of any monetary incentive it might have offered the worker. No matter how quickly a worker could complete a kit, the pay would be the same. Most contractors were very clear on this distinction:

> But you're not really workin' piecerate on this. I mean, they just pay ya so much. . . . Basically, it's so much a kit. They pay ya so much apiece, but it's not really piecerate work. There's no incen-tive work to it. Incentive is you do as many as you can in eight hours, ya know, we'll pay you X amount for eight hours' work for that day. The next day ya come and you might do less, you might do more, but you get paid for what you do. This is not really piecework. . . . It's not really incentive or a piecework type basis.

In this case, the company controlled the quantity of work and thus the weekly earnings of the contractors. Under a true piecerate system, at least theoretically, the quantity is unlimited, and earnings are driven by the ambition of the worker to produce.

If the workers in both communities were to speak up about their discontent concerning the pay, they would be quick to point out that the company does not reward them monetarily for length of service: "I wouldn't mind it, uh, truly wouldn't mind it if, maybe since this company's been goin' now about three years, maybe it wouldn't hurt if we had a raise. Other people's getting raises. Senators are gonna try to get their big raise. Maybe it wouldn't hurt if we got a little bit of one." This was a point of contention especially for those contractors who had started working when the company first opened its doors; their earnings were the same as those of a contractor taking home her first kit three years later:

I think after, maybe, we sort of feel like you deserve a raise after so many years, maybe, you know. They have a tendency to just let you keep going like you are as long as you're willing to do that. Then they'll let you do it, you know. . . . I feel like we deserve a little recognition or something like that. Incentive . . . to continue doing it well, I guess.

As one former homeworker asked, "Would you keep a job where you didn't get a raise in over two years?" This point was not merely a material one to the workers but also a psychological one. They were proud of their high-quality work and their loyalty to the company and wanted TMC to recognize them in a manner more lasting than an annual appreciation supper, or a box of nuts at Christmastime. TMC often told the local managers and the homeworkers that they were very pleased with the quality of the work. At the appreciation suppers in Prairie Hills, homeworkers were informed about how profitable home-based production was for TMC; the workers reasoned that the company should therefore increase their compensation and materially show the company's appreciation for their work.

When asked about the advantages of home assembly work, contractors indicated a high level of satisfaction with the opportunity to work at home. Most workers first cited the expenses of commuting, clothes, meals, and babysitting that they were able to avoid by working at home.

Commuting to and from a job is a major issue to consider, especially for those workers who live ten or more miles from town. Some open-country roads are unpaved or paved only with gravel, some are poorly lit, and many are not cleared of snow promptly during winter weather. And daily commuting takes time, lengthening the workday and increasing job-related costs. Harlan and Louise figure that working at home translates into a better wage for them as contractors:

Our son drives prob'ly sixty miles to work. Now, he can't deduct his mileage for driving, so he's got sixty miles a day, jeepers, criminy, you know, they figure it costs, what, twenty, twenty-two cents a mile to drive your own car. Well, look at right there, so there's twelve dollars a day right there they figure it costs him just to drive, and you can't deduct that. Besides if he works, say, eight hours, it's thirty miles down there, it'd take him prob'ly forty-five minutes, well, he's got an hour and a half extra that he's not gettin' paid to work. So, when you figure it all out, why maybe we're just as well off here than he is down there. He might be making more [per hour], but when he figures everything out. . . .

Time is saved as well as money, and some workers see it as reinvested in home assembly. Kim lives in open country, so commuting would be time-consuming:

You don't have to drive to work. I keep telling myself, when I go to work every morning at 8:00 [to do bolts]. When I get out there I keep telling myself, I didn't have to spend an hour getting ready and I didn't have to spend an hour driving to work. And I won't have to spend an hour driving home from work. That's three hours that day that I can work free, because I would be spending that time just getting to my job and getting ready for a job. I think that's an advantage. You're here with your children. That's gotta be an advantage.

Meals and clothes were figured as savings, too. Working at home meant eating more cheaply, and workers did not need a special wardrobe as they might have for a job in town. One farm woman, Myra, described how she made the decision to work at home:

And so then I had to decide whether I wanted to work there, or [at home]. And there was times I would try to help him sort some hogs, and I didn't want to get too dirty, then I had to shower and I had to be at the job in town by noon. Well, that would really rush me, and I thought, this way, if we pick a day we wanna sort hogs, you know, I know now, if I still stink, I can come in and do bolts. You can't go to town work, in, you know, a store, so I thought, well that would be better. I wouldn't have gas money going to town. I wouldn't have to buy clothes, new clothes, because you've gotta dress appropriate if you're working in town. And, down here, nobody's gonna see you in blue jeans and sweat pants, whatever. So, that helped me, kinda, to decide.

For families with young and school-age children, the benefits derived from not needing a babysitter were more than monetary although the cost savings were appreciable. In families where more than one child would need daycare, babysitting costs were estimated to be equal to at least half of their projected income, seriously undermining the economic benefits of working outside the home. Moreover, many homeworkers expressed strong beliefs about the impor-

tance of staying home with children or about being home when the
children came in from school. Marilyn, a middle-aged woman with
two school-age children, explained how home assembly work fit in
with her values:

> I have a definite priority, that children are over any job, you know.
> The home is over any job. A very old-fashioned type of value sys-
> tem. . . . I feel that it's a very important part of development of
> children to have the stability of the mother at home. To be a
> mother and a wife, you know, and so, my priorities lie there. And
> this works in with my priorities, yet gives us extra money.

Many homeworkers expressed similar priorities, with remarks such as
"I don't want my children raised by a babysitter," or "I want to be here
to see my child's first steps, not just to hear about it from the babysitter." Such comments were commonly voiced by women contractors;
men who did homework tended to view this advantage in terms of
appreciating that "women can be home for their kids."

Flexibility is one of the biggest advantages to home contractors; it
is a catch-all category used to describe many aspects of homeworking.
Workers spoke often about setting their own hours and work pace,
not having to deal with supervision and developing their own style of
work. The assembly work was similar to factory production but without some of the problems associated with that setting. Fred, who also
works at a local food-processing plant, compared homework to his job
at the factory:

> Well, there's the free time, ya know, you work at your own pace,
> your own time. It isn't like assembly line, like over there where I
> work, in Derryville, there's assembly line stuff, and if you can't
> keep up with the assembly line, they say "Sorry, we can't use
> you." [At home], you can be slow as a mud turtle, and they won't
> fire you as long as you turn back a product that they want,
> whether it takes you all week to do it or not, that doesn't make
> any difference. You do it in ten hours, it doesn't matter ta them,
> as long as they're satisfied with the product ya bring back. So that
> is the main advantage, that you do it at your own time and you
> don't have any time clock ta punch in and out, ya know, so ta
> speak.

Freedom to set some of their working conditions meant a great deal to
most workers who often combine the assembly work with other

chores and tasks. For women, the latitude to determine their own schedules meant that the work could be woven in with housework, child care, babysitting, and farm chores; for men, assembly work could be combined with farm chores or off-farm work. The flexibility of homeworking also allows for multiple job-holding.

Most workers found more advantages to the homeworking situation than disadvantages, but as a group they were critical of various aspects. Almost all the workers agreed that the work was monotonous and that forty hours or so per week of repetitive assembly work could become burdensome; televisions and radios were popular in their efforts to counteract boredom. Elaine, a Riverton homeworker, described a remedy for the tedium of the work:

> You're better off if you can get daydreamin' about something, if you can set there and not think about what you're doin', but think about somethin' else, or be totally involved in the TV or somethin', is the only way you can stand to do it. Because I've set there sometimes and think, "Oh, I hate this," and you just set there, and every piece is just like pain. But if you get yourself thinking of somethin' else, 'cause sometimes like I'll be off in a dreamworld and I'll be settin' there workin', and . . . ya look in the box and it's half full. But if you set there and think about what you're doin', it's painful.

To Lucy, a contractor in Prairie Hills, the problem went beyond boredom; she found the mindlessness of the work, the lack of stimulation, and the absence of challenge burdensome. In her case, entertainment in the work area was no solution, and dreaming served only to remind her of what she would prefer to do. Lucy articulated the conflict that a number of the women experienced: The combination of limited job options and rigid sex-role definitions that kept her out of the job market resulted in homeworking as her only choice.

> The whole time I am doing it, because I'm thinking about so many other different things I would want to be doing, and to tell you the truth, as soon as I can find an office job, this will be gone. But I've been out of the business, the work force, for many years, and it's gonna be hard. I was a bookkeeper, secretary. I love office work. And I've always missed it. My husband never wanted me to work outside the home. But now, he has said, he won't fight it. Put it that way. And I'm gonna find something.

Those other workers probably think I'm just an old stick in the mud, or think I need to do something better. It's not that I, I think I need to do something better. It's inside me that it doesn't work. I'm glad for those women that it does help them, and if they don't mind doing it, all the power to 'em! But I guess I'm not the right type. . . . I need something more . . . would you call it a challenge, or you have to use your mind a little bit. 'Cause you don't use your mind at all, and I find if I'm out there too many hours, all of a sudden, I'll stop and I'll think now, did I do this, 'cause my mind is totally on something else. And I'll just get goofy, almost.

Many contractors tried to find ways to make the time pass quickly; however, the problems with the weight of the materials were not so easily resolved, and all the workers cited that as a major disadvantage. Both groups of contractors are predominantly women, and most of the couples who work together are retired, so the task of unloading and loading materials is a twice-weekly challenge. Some farm families had access to equipment, such as a forklift, to unload materials from the back of a pickup, but most contractors unloaded the kits manually. Prairie Hills workers have to deal with a 500-pound box of steel bolts, so most assembly workers dip into the big box and take out only what they can carry into their work space at one time, making many trips to unload the bolts. Even the smaller boxes of materials weigh fifty to sixty pounds, and usually there are sixty of those to load and unload. One farm woman described her method:

The heavy boxes, I mean, during the summer, spring, and fall, when he's out in the field, and there sets a 500-pound box on the pickup, and I can't get the sucker off. So I have to take a little box out there and dip it out into that, and unloading it is terrible. And loading it, 'cause the boxes range from forty-one to sixty pounds. I'm strong enough to do it, but I can tell when I've done it by myself, because the next day the back is [out]. A woman isn't built for that. The back isn't built for that kind of stuff. And it takes a toll. And I've noticed that a lot. It has taken a toll.

Male contractors also considered the weight of the materials a disadvantage. Workers who had to climb stairs in the process of loading and unloading were more vocal about the cumbersome weight of the kits, complaining because neither the time nor the effort were covered by the piecerate system.

Transporting kits to and from the warehouse is the worker's responsibility. The company prefers that the kits be transported in a pickup or van, and in Prairie Hills the size of the kit requires the use of a small truck. One aspect of learning the ropes of this work is figuring out how to secure the kit in the truck so that it stays intact. Many workers had experienced taking a turn too sharply and having the contents of the truck topple out onto the highway, leaving the worker to reassemble and rebox the spilled parts; thus some workers saw the responsibility of transportation as a disadvantage.

Injuries were common experiences among the homeworkers. In Riverton, most workers had caught their thumbs or fingers in the bolt press; although a minor injury, it keeps them away from the press for a few days. More lasting problems were cited, however, such as soreness and stiffness in the back, neck, and shoulders and swollen hands and wrists. Workers in Prairie Hills would tape their fingers because they "were raw, just raw, and they would bleed from just screwing those little things on." The top nut, which fastened all the pieces on the bolt, was rough, and the threads often did not match the bolt's; the effort required to secure the nut on 5,400 bolts took its toll. Riverton workers had similar complaints about certain low-quality pieces that were rough and hard to handle; the difficulty added more worktime.

All workers saw the pay as a disadvantage of the job. They had various suggestions for the company, such as increasing the piecerate for those contractors with longer service, giving incentive pay for work that TMC requested earlier than the due date, and increasing the piecerate for kits in which one handled more pieces.

Women workers thought that isolation was a disadvantage, describing it in terms of their work space and how it separated them from family activities. Yet they viewed isolation as a disadvantage inherent in homeworking. Myra, a home assembler near Prairie Hills, did not recommend the job to a friend because of this factor:

> I had a girlfriend whose husband told her, "Get this job." He's a trucker and he's gone all the time, like two months at a time. And I told her, "Don't do it. You would be in that shed working all day. Your son goes to school. You go home at night. Your husband's not there to talk to. There you'd sit by yourself again. The next day you're out in that shed all by yourself. If you're going to get a job, go get one anywhere you can talk to people." And I didn't recommend it to her, you know.

Contractors saw both the advantages and the disadvantages of having the work at home. On the one hand, it was convenient and accessible; on the other, many workers did not feel as though they ever had a day off since they completed a kit it was returned and another loaded up and brought home. The presence of the work in the home meant for some contractors that the "workplace was never left," as Rita Kelly pointed out:

> The disadvantage is, if you go out to work, you work, and when it's time to go home, you leave it, and you go home. This is here all the time, and you never get done. You get one kit done, you go get another one, and you start on it. And then too, you know, you have so many other things to do, so you're always getting up from it, whereas if I worked in a factory doing this, I'd sit there and I'd do it. . . . If you take time off, you think you should be working, because you should get the kit in by a certain time. It's just the advantage to goin' to work is when you leave it and come home, you leave it, and you don't hafta think about it till the next day. This is here. Some nights ya think, "Oh, maybe I better stay up late tonight and work," and ya know, it's hard to ever get set in a schedule.

Irregularity and insecurity are features of homeworking that many workers disliked. With the former, two practices in particular affected the workload and thus the pay. First, because of the warehouse irregularities, a contractor could never be sure if she had enough parts to complete a kit each week. In this situation, the worker has a few choices: She can make an extra trip to town and pick up the needed pieces, she can wait until she brings the completed kit back in and then assemble the remaining parts in the warehouse, or she can turn in an incomplete kit. In the first case the contractor will earn the full check but will have made an extra trip. If she takes the extra time in the warehouse to assemble the parts, at least she avoids the extra trip and still earns the full check. The third choice simply involves foregoing the full check. It irritates the workers that they must expend the extra effort to receive the full check when the fault is in the warehouse: "You know, you run out of stuff. OK, whose responsibility is it to get the stuff here? I mean, I've already made my trip to town."

As for the insecurity of homeworking, the workload is affected by the availability of work: There are no guarantees on the quantity. The company guarantees forty weeks' worth of kits to assemble per year, but there is no advance notice to the workers when any stoppage will occur, as one older contractor pointed out: "Another disadvantage, though, is you take your kit and expect ta get another kit, and they don't have the stuff on hand ta send it out with ya, so ya come home.

Then when they get it, they call ya, and then ya gotta drive back in and get it, and they don't pay ya mileage or anything like that." This sense of insecurity and the way the company handled it created some negative feelings among workers. Ray and Tricia, who farm outside Prairie Hills and have been home assemblers for two years, discussed work insecurity:

> Well, it's the irritation of people, big business using people, because sometimes you had a kit. When you started out it was a part-time job. Just like thirty-eight to forty hours, forty weeks a year, is what they originally told us. Then after a while, they said, well, it's gonna be about full time. All you can do. Then two weeks later, you don't have a kit. And it's the frustration I guess, of not knowing. You know, sometimes you depend upon, and I know we're warned. Don't depend on these. Don't depend upon the check. But you know, so you think every week you're going to have a kit. And then, all of a sudden, you never know until you drive in that day whether or not you're going to have a kit the next week.

As the workers see the job, no one single disadvantage outweighed the advantages but taken together, the disadvantages chipped away at the positive aspects of working at home. Some workers declared themselves satisfied overall with the job opportunity and evaluated the advantages for them as having greater weight; others saw the disadvantages as conditions under the control of the company that could be improved, making the job opportunity more attractive.

The company offered no benefits when it first opened shop in Prairie Hills, but toward the end of the first year, Social Security was deducted by TMC at the matching employee rate. Benefits, such as health insurance, workers' compensation, unemployment compensation, or other formal stipulations governing the worker or the work were absent from the contract for workers in both communities.

Industrial homework is woven throughout the day, affecting the organization and accomplishment of other tasks and activities. Because of its flexibility, it is like a sponge, soaking up any and all available time. Homeworking brings people together, parents and children or neighbors, redefining some as coworkers, others as supervisors. The relationship between the homeworkers and the company itself and the meanings of various aspects of homeworking will be explored next.

4

Integrating Home and
Informal-Sector Work

Light-assembly homeworking in Prairie Hills and Riverton has the characteristics of informal labor-capital relations. Defining these jobs specifically as informal are those aspects that are not governed by institutional or contractual regulations but that have come to be considered normative features of this type of worker-management relationship.[1] These include the lack of security inherent in a weekly contract over which the worker has no control, the lack of the company's contribution to social benefits, the responsibility the worker takes for payment of taxes and social benefits and for the development and use of a private work space, the worker's lack of control over regularity and quantity of work, and the company's lack of coverage for work-related injuries and health insurance. The influence of these informal work relations can be seen in the lives of the homeworkers.

This set of labor-capital relations is encouraged by the specific context and conditions of the rural labor-market areas and the agricultural economy. A combination of factors that define the downturn in the agricultural economy, such as the decline in the values of land and farm products and high farm indebtedness, resulted in local economies unable to absorb the growing numbers of people seeking wage employment. In areas highly dependent upon agriculture, local businesses suffered from the reduced cash flow in the retail market. The primary resource this type of community can market to an outside industry is its willing, and often cheap, labor supply. Married women in rural areas constitute a large segment of this labor supply, many of whom are newly seeking wage labor or have been laid off from local industries recently closed. To a large extent the rural work-seeking population in the 1980s was formed by the increased need for household income, the decreased security of farming income, and the insecurity and limitations of local employment options; this was the context in which informal labor relations developed in Riverton and Prairie Hills.

The values and priorities of homeworkers and their articulation and acceptance of particular sex roles support informal work relations as a desired opportunity. A household's need to increase the cash flow must be balanced with the needs of children to be nurtured and the requirements of both adults and children to care physically and emotionally for one another. As women encountered the need to help out financially, they often sought work that would allow them to continue meeting basic family requirements. Both women and men saw homeworking as positive insofar as it allowed women to earn wages without neglecting those domestic tasks defined as feminine. Male homeworkers in these two communities had histories of physical disabilities, interrupted employment and prolonged unemployment or underemployment, age discrimination in the job market, and job loss resulting from the recent decline in the agricultural economy. Homeworking for them was most often combined with other forms of wage labor and was seen as consonant with acceptable roles for men: Homeworking did not prevent them from engaging in other wage employment, their obligation as breadwinners.

Interview data suggest that it is not necessarily only economic marginality that brings workers into informal labor relations. In these two communities the combination of age, sex, class, education, job skills and history, and local labor-market conditions resulted in the formation of workers needing or wanting to accept home-based work contracts. Just as different factors contribute to the formation of groups of workers engaging in homework, the worker's experiences of homework vary according to the organization of production imposed by the company. Homework means that paid work is set in the context of individual households with their particular divisions of labor. Thus various characteristics of the worker and of the household context interact with informal labor relations to shape the conditions of wage work performed in the home.

An analysis of those aspects of rural industrial homeworking that constitute informal work relations reveals certain implications about the experiences and the working conditions of the contractors.

Themes including the labor contract, flexibility, supplemental income, control over the workload, and other working conditions will be explored in the context of worker-management relations, and the assembly homework will be examined in comparison to job options in each local labor-market area and as a household response to internal and external conditions.

THE LABOR CONTRACT

Each worker signs a general contract with TMC at the beginning of employment that broadly covers basic regulations. The company then sends out piecework on a weekly contract to a household, specifying the nature and quantity of the work; the contractor picking up the work signs for the workload and takes it home.

Only one application for a contract is permitted per household. When Harlan and Louise went in to apply, they learned that the company "wouldn't take two applications for one place, from one family, 'cause I went in with him, and he filled out the application, so it's in his name." Harlan quickly added, "I get all the money, though." Several members of the household may contribute labor, but only one member is named as contractor, and the paychecks are made out to that individual. Responsibility for timely completion and quality control also rests with the contractor.

The general contract specifies TMC's responsibilities to include the provision of parts and the equipment needed for the assembly work, the maintenance of accounting for work completed and returned, the payment for work meeting or exceeding the quality standards set by TMC, and the right to inspect individual work spaces. The quality standard understood by the workers was a 2 percent error rate, greater than which was deemed unacceptable by the company. In return, the worker agrees to be responsible for pickup and delivery of all parts in a vehicle providing sufficient protection of the materials, assembly of the parts according to the specifications of TMC, keeping the delivery schedule set by the company, and development and use of an appropriate work space located in the worker's residence. The contract ends with the statement, "as an independent contractor, Contractor shall not be eligible for any Company employee benefits."

A separate agreement regulates the lease of machinery. The company agrees to provide the machinery necessary to perform the assembly work, to provide free of charge any needed upkeep or repair on the machinery, and to repossess the machinery upon termination of the work contract. An official fee is charged for the lease, which workers said was one dollar, but no one could remember paying it or having it deducted; apparently it was a mere formality on paper. The agreement specifies that workers may not remove the machinery from their residences without written permission from the company nor make any modifications "in order to improve performance" without said permission in writing. In reality, workers did move equipment from one place to another and even more frequently modified the machinery to "improve performance" without written permission. The attitude of the local managers, as well as that of TMC, was that the end product was what mattered and that as long as the quality standards were met or exceeded, the process of production was a private matter.

The application form for a position as a contractor clearly defines the applicant's entire household as potential workers. The applicant is asked about the number of hours members of the applying household have available for this kind of work and about the number of workers. Estimates of potential working hours on the applications reviewed in Riverton were often higher than full-time, ranging from forty to eighty hours, and usually were based on more than one worker in the household. Since the quantity of work in Prairie Hills is limited, the question of hours per household was unnecessary, but the applicant was required to specify the number of potential workers.

FLEXIBILITY

From the perspective of the company, the organization of home-based production is flexible, allowing TMC to vary the quality and quantity of inventory as needed at no extra cost. The workers themselves often cited flexibility as the main advantage of homeworking since it allowed an autonomy in setting hours, an ability to share the work within and between households, and the potential to accomplish other tasks along with the work. The assembly work has a pervasive effect once it enters the household: Time, the nature of work, people, and space become flexible through the interaction of paid and unpaid labor in the home.

Workers often discussed flexibility as the autonomy to set their own hours. The assembly work must be completed within a week but within that week the worker sets the schedule in accordance with other tasks and chores. Even the weekly deadline was somewhat flexible, as workers often spoke about the local managers as "being real good" about reasonable extensions of time as long as requests for them did not become regular.

Norma, a Riverton homeworker, cited flexibility as one main advantage of the work but described various aspects of it:

> Well, it's up to us. I mean, that's the bottom line. You either work on it. We know the amount of screws we gotta get done. We know the amount of time it takes, and if we wanna bring it down to the wire, well, it's us that's gonna have to work our little butts off. I mean, if we were real, real smart, and put, you know, say five to six hours in every single day, you know, and got a real routine set up here, but then there's no flexibility. You know, that's no good, either.

Norma's neighbors, Janice and Ken, complete at least one kit each week, and Ken has a full-time, off-farm job. Janice agreed with Norma: "I think, too, if it just comes up to that you do want somethin' that you wanna go to, you go. It's not like I can't. It's that you can, but you know you're gonna hafta make up the time." Ella, an older woman whose husband would "not touch those bolts with a ten-foot pole," recognized the limits of time on the flexibility of work in general:

> It just depends, you know. You have to realize that if you're gonna take the time to do something else, then you're gonna work, work the bolts in someplace else, is all. I mean, you know you can only do so much else, because the bolts have to be done and that's it.

The reality that "the bolts have to be done" tends to govern a worker's schedule so that other activities become a trade-off in terms of the time needed to complete a kit. Mollie, a young woman with six young children who assembles bolts in Riverton, understands this juggling:

> Your kit has to be done. Sometimes I'll take a day off, and I'll do the sort of things around the house that I know won't get done unless I just plain say "tomorrow I'll just hafta punch bolts all day long in order to make up for the day before that I just had ta take time to do other things.

Most workers consider flexibility as an advantage because they see it as a matter of their choice; they can put off the assembly work and do something else, recognizing that later they will have to make up for it.

Even with this job, and you know that you have to get so many boxes done per day to get your quota filled. The nice thing about it is, if a funeral would happen to come up, or you have to take your kids to the doctor, you can stop what you're doing, and you don't have to call into anybody except yourself. You can pick up and go and come back. You may have to work a couple hours later that night, or you might have to finish up on a Sunday, but it is your option. Where, if you're working for someone else, you can't do that.

Another aspect of flexibility is the absence of boundaries to the work schedule, which means that although workers set the hours, they may also find that there are no off-duty hours. Homework is always there, regardless of other tasks or activities that take time during the day. Peggy, a young homeworker in Riverton, has tried to explain to others that the assembly work is time-consuming when combined with other work though it may not appear so when the hours alone are considered.

It just takes time. That's what I tell most people. I said, "Anybody can do it. It's just whether you wanna sit down and work five hours a day or not." I think most people that I've heard think that you just go home and make a few parts a day, and you're gettin' paid, ya know. They don't realize that you gotta sit down for five hours or so, I would say a good five hours every day. I think a lotta mothers don't realize that that's a long time, in a way, when you still hafta get breakfast, dinner, and supper, and do your laundry and lay 'em down for naps and things. I don't think they realize it's gonna take that much time.

Rita Kelly agrees, noting that even her family seems to think that such flexibility means she can be easily interrupted.

My husband thinks I should get the bolts done somehow, but yet I don't know when he thinks I'm supposed to do it. I haven't figured that out yet, because, no, he doesn't treat it . . . if I'm here, everything else is s'posed to be done too, 'cause I'm home and at night, ya know, if I'm sitting there and the kids want somethin', he thinks I should be with the kids. He doesn't really treat it [as a job]. . . . I kinda wish I could set hours, I'm gonna work from this hour to this hour, and that's the way it's gonna be. I'm not gettin' up. This is my work time, ya know. But none of 'em can understand that if you try to set hours, they can't, ya know. They'll call you away for somethin' and, I have done it before. I said "I'm not leavin'. This is my job. I'm staying here. I'm workin' at this and that's all there is to it." I have done that to 'em before, and I'll sit there in the evening and I won't leave. I just work, and none of 'em like it. They don't like it when I stay back there and work, and they don't like it when I don't help 'em out, but once in a while, ya just hafta do that once in a while so they can see it's a real job. Because I don't know otherwise how, some weeks it is hard to get it done. The week goes and you've done this and that and all, ya don't get it done.

The flexibility of the homework schedule depends upon many aspects of the household: how to set working hours apart from family needs and desires, how to accomplish the work while attending to children and other chores and tasks, and how to get other family members to contribute to the assembly work or to the housework. Rita Kelly points to the difficulty of getting her family to recognize her work hours; informal labor done in the home means the worker is responsible for setting those boundaries ordinarily set by the outside workplace that allow the worker to accomplish tasks relatively uninterrupted by the needs and concerns of family. The formal workplace concretely separates home and work for the worker, but the home-worker is responsible for maintaining that separation. This flexibility leaves Rita the option of responding to family needs when necessary, such as picking up a sick child from school, but it also results in greater conflict and tension over how to set aside adequate working time. Rita also expresses the difficulty of accomplishing work that is not taken seriously; somehow it is "not a real job" because it is done in the home at odd hours of the day and night by Rita and whoever else may be available and willing to help. Thus, because of its flexible organization, homework lacks the form and status of a real job in the view of those people around her.

The lack of formal boundaries between home and paid work allows work to infiltrate many areas of the home. Many women home-workers stated that "being home for my children while I earn money" was an important advantage of the assembly work. Yet most of these homeworkers also believed that working in the home affected their time and ability to care for their children and that their children's needs and presence often determined their own time and ability to work.

The homework itself can bring family members into the work

process, but the needs of children that cannot be met by the working mother may also bring others in to help with unpaid family responsibilities, as Mollie's experience illustrates:

> Oh, the work definitely affects it. There's many times I fix Jenny her bottle and give it to her, and she holds her own bottle and sits in her rocker, whereas she needs to be picked up and held, ya know, and you need to just sit down with her and cuddle her and spend time with her. And a lotta times when my schedule just plain won't allow it, my older kids will. I'll have one of the kids hold her.

Another homeworker talked about taking care of her children: "No, I'd be lying if I said it was easier or the same. It's harder, it's harder. I mean, you just hafta allow for something else, ya know, naturally it takes a little more time away from your family." One man who assembled bolts at home during a period of unemployment commented that one improvement would be to get "a babysitter once in a while so you could do a little more work." Although some of the homeworkers reported using this alternative occasionally, it was seen as defeating part of the purpose of working at home: saving on the costs of child care and being present for one's children. Two former homeworkers commented on the challenge of working on bolts while taking care of young children:

> Um, the bit about, as far as a mother staying home with the kids, so she can be with her kids. That's not gonna work. Cause she actually can't be with her kids when she's doing this. There's no way. I mean, kids have to be in bed at night so she can work and still do it. . . . Well, that's the way it was really broadcast. You know, you can stay home with the kids, you can stay home with the kids. And like I told you, that's not true. Because you can't do it with your kids. They have to be in bed. They cannot be standing there and you're entertaining 'em. . . . That's what [TMC] wants to make it. And it's not. There's no way. They're trying to make it family.

> I wouldn't recommend it for a mother with young kids, not unless she was really strict. . . . Because I don't think you can pay attention to your kids and do this job if, ya know, in the back of your head you thought, I'm gonna be home with my kids, and I'm gonna be the perfect mother and all this stuff, because your

kids are more deprived than if you went outside and someone was watching the kids.

Most homeworkers with young children discovered that the assembly work and child care could be combined although usually not at the same time. And most of these homeworkers clearly viewed their children and family as their first priority, putting the work second, at best. Yet as the weekly deadline approached, the bolts would assume a higher priority, pushing other needs temporarily to the side. Flexibility thus comes to mean that the worker juggles family needs with work requirements and that the juggling changes from day to day. Rita Kelly's situation illustrates that children, housework, and assembly homework form a continuous cycle to which she responds throughout the day and evening.

Gail, a young woman who assembles bolts in Riverton, works part-time in town in the evening and is at home during the day with her daughter and several other children whom she babysits. Her husband does agricultural wage labor and other short-term jobs. Discussing how hard it was for her to balance family needs and homework, Gail described her mix of responsibilities: "It's just left up ta me. Everything left up ta me. It doesn't really affect anybody but me. It just leaves more work for me and more worries." She completed one kit per week, which usually took her thirty-two hours.

So that's pretty hard, ya know, it's pushin', although sometimes I stay up till two in the morning. So in between those day hours and workin' on my bolts, or my laundry, baking, cleaning my house, and watching my kids, I do spend two hours a day with the kids. I have to. Because it's my job. I'm babysittin' for 'em. I feel I need ta give 'em my attention, too, so we read and play and things like that, sing songs, don't we?

Sometimes it seems like I work hours, and I'm never gonna get done, and when I get to the point where I think that I'm gonna be late, I get really nervous and tense, and it's really hard ta handle sometimes. Like sometimes on the weekends, one weekend I had ta work [bolts] because I was gone two days during that week taking my daughter to the doctor, and I was sick, she was sick and then I'd go out and help my husband on the farm. And I had ta fill in the weekend with my bolts, and I had ta have it in on that Monday. And I thought I was gonna be late, and I just got so upset, because I had the feeling of bein' late, and I didn't want them upset with me, so then we were on the outs all weekend. 'Cause every time my husband wanted somethin' I'd go, "Leave me alone. I've gotta get this done." It's like, "Don't bother me." Every time my daughter came ta me, I said, "Take her away from me," and that's really hard. . . . That's about the only bad, ya know, the hard times I've had with the work, has ta do with my family.

Proponents of homework often assert that home-based work can resolve women's conflicts between outside wage labor and attending to family needs, yet the conflict seems to remain unresolved for many of the women homeworkers. Bringing the work into the home adds to their work, extending the workday. The other needs and tasks do not disappear and usually are not considered by the family or the worker to be as flexible as the homework. Gail's experience illustrates how flexibility can come to mean that her needs, especially as a worker, go unattended:

I asked my husband once, okay, I asked him once, ya know, if he could help me out, and he said, "I've got my own work to do." You know, he needs time to relax. I hate ta pressure him, ya know, because he works really hard all day, too. Even though I do go out and help him when he needs me, I don't really think that he could put in the time for me that I do for him, because he hasta be responsible for his job, and he hasta stick to his duties, so, ya know, like what can I do about it?

Families often assume that life at home will continue as usual. Women homeworkers find themselves dealing with the same situation that women who work outside the home face: the double day, or double sets of expectations about work. Women become flexible in this context, and their time becomes flexible to accommodate the work. Women's work space also becomes flexible as families request that they work beyond their vision and hearing. Flexibility goes well beyond the autonomy to set one's own hours; indeed, the extent to which this autonomy exists is somewhat questionable. In many of these households, women homeworkers become flexible to the multiple demands of family, home, and work.

Men who do homework do not usually experience flexibility in the same way. Homework as a job is appreciated because it fits flexibly with farmwork or other remunerative labor, not because it allows them to remain at home with their children or because they can "throw a load of wash" in while doing the bolts. One male homeworker reflected on the advantages of the assembly work: "It works out good in connection with the farm. Because where I'm working here at home, I can work nights or rainy days. I can fit this in with the rest of my schedule." Another male homeworker agreed that this was the main advantage of the assembly work: "Well, I'm at home, and if I get a call, or if they get a call in down at the station, then, you know, she knows I'm at home. She gives me a call, and I can go, if I'm doing bolts, I just shut the machine off, and go make the delivery. I can do bolts and keep the delivery route."

Men homeworkers also tended to set up shop outside the home in outlying buildings on the property, reinforcing their sense of separation between home and work or at least putting distance between work and the activities and needs of the home. Because the definitions of men's primary roles do not include domestic chores or child-rearing, taking on the homework did not create the need to separate work and home; rather, the homework is added to farmwork or other wage labor. The male homeworker has less trouble defining the assembly work on the premises as "a real job" in addition to his other "real jobs."

Men were solely responsible for the assembly work in eight households, which followed the general pattern: Homeworkers were combining the work with other wage labor, with self-employment, or with the operation of the farm. None of these men described themselves as active or equal participants in housework or in child-rearing, nor did any who participated in homeworking as a couple describe greater involvement in the home as their motivation for the work. For male homeworkers, informal labor relations are not embedded in the context of home and family but are an extension of other economic activities.

The division of labor in most of the households in both communities followed a pattern in which men were largely responsible for wage labor or farm operation, if the latter was applicable. In only one household was the man described as actively in charge of cooking, cleaning, and child-rearing in addition to his outside job; his wife was the homeworker. Theirs was not a farming household; indeed in none of the active farm households were males described as equal participants in domestic tasks. In contrast, the women in the farming households often helped with farmwork while still retaining responsibility for major household work and the assembly homework. These general patterns varied little according to the ages of those interviewed, but flexibility varied in quantity as well as in quality for women and men homeworkers. Men who did home assembly work were more likely to subcontract part of the work out to other people or hire labor to help with the farmwork; they did not take on greater domestic or family responsibilities. Thus they dealt with flexible production by hiring help and by maintaining the separation between work and home. Women experienced the flexibility of homework as an activity that absorbed all spaces of free time in between other major responsibilities of child care, housework, farmwork, and outside wage labor. The women's flexibility centered on their ability to cross over into all spheres of labor, but the men's roles were defined so that men could avoid taking on "women's work." In many households, the assembly work was seen also as women's work, and they were solely responsible for it.

Housework, child-rearing, and sometimes assembly homework are not casually defined as women's work. The definition of women's sphere of activity enters the realm of strongly held values and beliefs that order family life and influence activities inside and outside the home. These beliefs are so deeply ingrained that it was commonplace for a woman with only male children to assume that there was no one to help out with the household chores. Or, as one former homeworker said, "I have my 'hired' girls: the washing machine, dryer, and dishwasher are working with me all day long." It was also common for women to speak of household tasks and child-rearing in the possessive: my cleaning, my cooking and baking, being home with my children. Men, too, used language to define the boundaries of these activities: "She doesn't deep clean the way she used to," or "Sometimes I help her with the dishes or the kids." Tanya, a young homeworker with three children, defined housewife as someone "married to the house" and responsible for all the chores. When these tasks were combined with child-rearing and assembly work, conflict sometimes resulted from her sense of overload: "If I have a bad day where I don't get enough bolts and stuff done, I wish he would pitch in more. If he would help with the laundry or whatever, the dishes, make a meal. But we just fight about it and then I have to do it anyways. I might just as well do it." Women would mention housework as a distraction from the tedium of the bolts, but men did not. Janice and Ken share the assembly work but definitely not the housework.

Last night he was gettin' really tired of doin' bolts, and I said, "Well, I'll do the bolts, and you do the dishes." He said, "I'll do the bolts, and you do the dishes." Ya know, he don't do dishes, and so I don't think anything really changes. He would rather do them [bolts] than anything else, and there are times I won't do them 'cause I know I've got these other things to do, and it's just impossible [to do both].

PART-TIME WORK AND SUPPLEMENTARY INCOME

The company advertised these home assembly positions as part-time jobs designed to provide supplementary income, primarily for farm families needing to increase cash flow. Interview data reveal the average number of hours spent working, the workers' motivations for taking on the work, and the ways they report using the income earned from this work. The concepts of supplementary income and part-time work have specific meanings in the workers' experiences, which vary by the household context in which the work takes place. We shall also examine how these concepts can support informal labor-capital relations.

The company and local community officials were explicit about the type of income to be earned through the homeworking. One official referred to the jobs as "secondary jobs for women," and all company managers explicitly said the intention of the assembly work was to provide "supplemental" income; no one, they assured me, was meant to "live off this income" as a main or an only source of income. Their definition of supplemental income is compatible with the notion of pin money, or money earned by women for incidental expenses rather than for the necessities of food, shelter, or clothing. By calling the income supplemental, the company does acknowledge that the low wages and intermittent workload do not provide a living wage; that acknowledgment, however, does not mitigate the circumstances that may leave some contractors with no choice but to live on the income earned by homeworking.

In some ways the concepts of part-time work and supplementary income are inseparable. Part-time work is usually thought to generate supplementary income as opposed to full-time work that should provide a living wage; a worker is not expected to support herself, much less her family, on part-time work. Using the Census Bureau's definition, part-time work is employment that requires fewer than thirty-five hours per week. In the context of the assembly homework, these concepts are rather slippery: For whom is the work part-time and the income supplemental and under what circumstances?

The question regarding hours devoted to homework was one of the most difficult for the workers to answer. Hours vary tremendously from week to week, depending on the kit and on the number of people helping with the work; hours also vary from worker to worker for the same reasons and because of different household and worker characteristics. Older workers tended to work more slowly, often with a partner, putting in more hours per kit than younger workers. In Riverton, the worker could choose to complete more than one kit, and hours would vary according to the quantity of work each week. For the purposes of definition, therefore, hours spent working are those hours reported by the worker as the average amount of weekly worktime.

Riverton contractors, including those workers who chose to complete more than one kit per week, worked an average of about thirty-five hours per week. Prairie Hills workers reported a weekly average of closer to forty-two hours needed in order to complete one kit. By the standard of the Census Bureau, on average, none of these workers is employed on a part-time basis. The company justifies the use of the term part-time by focusing on the household as the worker rather than on the individual contractor. If more than one person contributes to the assembly work, then the workers might be considered part-time. The weekly contract is "part-time work for the household" and not for the individual, a discrepancy that does not go unnoticed by workers such as Liz Schaeffer in Prairie Hills:

Oh, I guess what I always think about is everybody says it's a part-time job, but to most of us, it's definitely not. It's still a full-time job, because it's so time-consuming, and you've got to figure that it takes at least forty hours a week. And that's pretty much a full-time job. You can't think of it as part-time work. You know. If you have a big family, where, you can get five or six people all working on it at the same time, like some of them do, then they can whip a kit in two days and have the rest of their week for everything else. But if you're working on it alone, it's definitely got to be considered a full-time job.

Her neighbor Kim assembles the bolts alone each week and assesses the work as full-time:

It takes five days, five full days. And that's, you don't sit and drink coffee. It takes five full days, and the sixth day you load them and take them back and bring them home again and unload them. And that leaves you one day, and that's if you really keep at it. You can't cook and do the wash and hang it out on the clothes-

line and bring it in and do all your bolts. You can't do it all in five
days. You have to stand at the rail and not leave.

Whether this job is part-time depends on how many people in the
household are doing the work on a regular basis. In farming households, the number of available co-workers varies seasonally as men
and boys are often excused from assembly work in order to operate
the farm. Spring, summer, and fall mean more homeworking hours
for women than in winter in most farm households; winter is the only
season when a woman might count on reliable and regular help with
the assembly work. Yet school-age boys and girls are involved in
sports then, which decreases the hours they might work. In the workers' experience, this job is part-time sporadically and more regularly a
full-time commitment.

Hours of work, even the same kind of work, varied by the number of workers in the household, but TMC considered only hours
worked per household rather than total hours per kit and could then
define the work as part-time. Moreover, the company used the hours
worked per household as normative, often telling new contractors
that "most people can do a kit in about thirty hours." As one worker
replied, "I know they tell us that some people can do it in thirty to
thirty-two hours, but I have yet to talk to anybody who does it in
thirty to thirty-two hours without help. If there's more than one of
you, yes, but one person, it's impossible." Thus, defining hours per
household as the average allowed TMC to call the work part-time and
artificially to lower the average worktime they claimed was necessary
to complete a kit. Homeworkers with sole responsibility for the work
usually took longer than this average to complete the kit and by comparison seemed much slower.

The implications of defining worktime in this manner go beyond
whether a worker is considered slow or fast. It allows the company to
keep the piecerate down so that fast workers seem able to earn four to
five dollars per hour, regardless of how many individuals may be
working. Those contractors who work alone work longer hours and
more days per week, and their hourly pay is comparatively lower. Using "household worktime" as the normative facilitates the underestimation of hours and the overestimation of the hourly wage. Kim and
her husband reflected on the situation:

> You're gonna interview her cousin and she's gonna say, "Oh, I do
> all [the bolts] and do all my family and everything." Well, her
> mother and her mother-in-law and she gets her sister-in-law in

there, and her husband, and she's gonna claim, I do all this myself. She doesn't. . . . These people are just hurting themselves, I
mean. I'm not a believer in unions, but if all these contractors
would get together, there's no reason why they couldn't get another dollar or better. I mean, but they try to brag about how fast
they can do it. And then that hurts themselves.

The workers "brag" about their efficiency in completing a kit, and
TMC uses the underestimation of hours to claim that the average
worker has no trouble earning at least five dollars per hour. As Kim
pointed out, boasting about speed leaves the worker little room to negotiate a higher wage. If contractors work at a slower pace or complete
their kits alone and take longer, then they simply earn a lower hourly
wage. The company treats this circumstance as though it is a choice
determined by the worker, yet it is the worker's household composition and other work commitments that largely determine how many
family members might work for any length of time. Those contractors
who have help with the assembly work boast fewer hours and higher
hourly pay and are touted as "average workers" by TMC in support of
the current piecerate. The notion of part-time household work supports the flexible organization of production to the benefit of the company by maintaining a ceiling on the piecerate and by promoting the
artificial underestimation of total work hours per kit. Defining the
household as the "part-time worker" means that officially about forty
households have contracts, but the actual number of workers may
vary from forty to well over one hundred in each community.

Defining the job as part-time also tends to support the workers'
practice of holding more than one job. Since the assembly homework
can be shared, adults can hold down other jobs outside the home or
on the farm. Homework is flexibly squeezed in around other work,
suggesting to the worker that another job or complete responsibility
for the home and family can be compatible with it. Indeed, most
homeworkers do hold down another major job, giving the outward
appearance that the assembly work is indeed part-time.

Some families were unable to find other jobs, however. Among the
two groups of workers, several families discussed how they lived solely
on the income from homeworking for periods of time ranging from one
to several months. Most of these contractors were farm families, whose
farm income went to the bank to pay debts. "Sometimes, like right now,
um, we're not milking as many cows, and by the time the banks and
everybody takes out their money, we don't get a milk check. So then, my
husband says we gotta punch more bolts, 'cause that's our only in-

come." Among other farm families, farm income went "back into the farm," and income from homeworking and other sidelines contributed to the operation of the household: making house payments and needed repairs, paying grocery, clothing, and utility bills, covering health insurance premiums, and occasionally, helping to make car payments. As one farm homeworker said, "What money I got was used for grocery money. So that's basically what it was for. Grocery money, so it didn't take away from the farm income, so all our income from the farm could go back into the farm. That's why I've always worked, just mostly for the grocery money." Another contractor, whose husband is semiretired from farming, explained why she worked:

> I usually buy the groceries with it. But the reason why I think I do it is because of this high [health] insurance, you know. But whichever way. If it was just used for the insurance, or if it was used for the groceries, I could adequately pay for either one of those. Not both of them, but, you know, one or the other. And we can't be without [insurance], you know. So, this is one of the reasons why. I think if we didn't have this big insurance premium, I might think twice about doing this all the time. So, the bolts help out.

Among town residents the income from homeworking was at times the sole income in a household where one or more adults were unemployed and not receiving unemployment compensation. In some cases unemployment was a regular feature, as in the case of the family where the husband was laid off each year around the holidays; these families depended upon assembly homework to make it through such times. Mollie's husband was laid off seasonally each year, and homeworking income was supplemented by unemployment checks for part of the duration. In tight financial circumstances all income is necessary, regardless of the source.

> And the rent, ya know, for us it's rough 'cause we pay $300 a month here, which includes the electricity, but that's a lotta money all at once for somebody who doesn't have a real large income. Actually, my check more or less goes for bills. . . . Usually by the time his check comes, half of it hasta go in the checking account ta cover the check that you wrote out two days before. Ya know, those beat-it-to-the-bank checks.

One worker with chronic health problems discussed how the assembly income was used: "Well, it goes in the bank and, uh, we try ta get our rent paid. See, I haven't paid this month's rent yet, but I had ta wait until my second paycheck come, and it didn't come until the twenty-eighth." Their rent was overdue one month because the first paycheck had been used to cover health insurance. His wife worked part-time in town and helped with the assembly work. It would be most accurate from the workers' perspectives to describe homeworking income as an occasional sole source of income and more usually as a supplemental source, if, by the latter, it is meant that this income is combined with another source of income.

In some households, the income from homeworking had a designated, special purpose, such as higher education for the children, vacations or recreational expenses, or the building of a second home. Among farming families, farm income was often divided from any other income; typically these families placed a priority on reinvesting that income in the farm when there was money left after paying the bank. Other income, such as that from homework, was expected to support the household; repairs and remodeling were the items most commonly mentioned by several farm-based homeworkers:

Well, last summer we built the bathroom on with the money from the bolts, because we really needed another bathroom. We lived here over ten years, and we never stuck ten cents in the house. And we needed some more room, so we put the windows in upstairs. Which we wouldn't have did, if we wouldn't have had that money, because you hate to take that out of the farm and spend it.

Well, put it this way, I take care of the household bills and stuff like that. That's basically why we went to doing the bolts. It paid for all this remodeling last year. This kitchen and clear out there. Because this kitchen was bad. And that's basically why I went into it. 'Cause if I wanted something in here, I had to find a way to get it!

Then I just use it generally for family living. I don't write a check on his farm account for anything. I keep the house up. I don't pay the light bill. Ya can't touch it anymore. But I pay the phone bill and I pay all the groceries. Last year I had ta get me a new deep freeze, and just anything like that, if you want it, you better save it up and get it, 'cause there's no extra surplus anywhere else.

The concepts of part-time work and supplemental income are accurate only in certain circumstances. The work is part-time if there is more than one worker, and the income is supplemental if there are other sources of income for the household; calling the work part-time and the income supplemental does not make it so on a fixed or permanent basis. The labor relations are embedded in the changing personal and financial circumstances of the members of each household so that these concepts take on a different and dynamic meaning in each situation.

WORKING CONDITIONS

There are four aspects of working conditions for homeworkers that affect pay: control over the quantity and type of work, rush work, rejected work, and factory shutdowns. These factors illustrate the benefits of flexible production for TMC, according to the experiences of the workers.

The quantity of work was controlled differently in each community. In Riverton each contractor was expected to complete a minimum of one kit per week but was allowed to complete more if she showed she was reliable in getting it done. Some families had more than one work station with a press; they were expected to complete more work or the extra work station would be given to someone else. There were several different kinds of small bolts assembled in the Riverton area and the manager usually allowed contractors to choose the type of work each week, depending on inventory and the needs of the larger factory. Workers had their preferences, too; some preferred small bolts with only two pieces because they could handle fewer pieces but produce more assemblies, earning more money.

> I think the two-piece pay a little better, because TMC is figuring on total pieces, and the two-piece is gonna be quicker to put together than a three-piece. See, and they figured that by your total pieces done. You know what I'm saying? But they give you more of 'em, but then they pay ya more, ya see? I said that to the manager one day, and he says, "Well, I make up the rates." I said, "Oh. It'd be nice if it went by how many pieces you get altogether instead of pieces made.

On the piecerate system, the end quantity determines the gross pay, not the number of pieces handled in the assembly process; workers can handle more pieces and yet get paid less, even at a higher piecerate, because the end quantity may be lower. Other workers preferred larger bolts with three pieces because they were easier to handle and family members could preassemble two of the pieces, decreasing the time spent at the press. Yet with this kit the worker produced fewer assemblies, and the rate per kit was lower.

> I like the three-piece, because I have found that the three-piece is the least amount of press time. It's the least amount of time that I hafta be married ta this press, ya know, because it's preassembly time. You can sit in front of the TV in the evenings with the rest of the family and preassemble. The kids can help. You get your two-piece, and it's all a one-person job. As far as I'm concerned, the less time you sit behind that press, ya know, the easier life is.

Workers in Riverton could not always choose the type of work, however, and change was often mentioned as a disadvantage. Switching to another type of work from week to week was often a problem because each type of assembly called for slightly different motions and setups, requiring an adjustment from the worker. Changing the type of work added hours to the work week, especially if the work change was perceived negatively by the worker because of the quality of the pieces; such pieces required more effort and time but were compensated equally with those that were of better quality. Elaine described the difficulties she encountered with pieces of varying quality:

> Yeah, 'cause these that I'm doin' right now aren't real hard, and sometimes the same kit, you can have Buick one time and Buick another time, and if the stamping is smaller inside and they're real hard ta hit, maybe ya gotta hit it a couple times or somethin'. Ya know, it takes longer ta do it. Besides that, you can't stand to do it as long because it's hard to do. But then I probably make like two dollars an hour, somethin' like that.

An older woman, Ella, also had worked with poor quality pieces:

> They gave me this kind that were real hard to put together. And I pounded and I pounded and I pounded. And I'm not kidding. My hand was so sore here that you couldn't hardly touch it. And I put two kits together. . . . The manager got me a long, weighted handle, which helped. I was still pounding my head off. And then finally they found out that the threads were in the wrong place, or something, and I suppose I was trying to pound the part

down over the threads or something. But they were terrible, they really were. Most people woulda quit the first day.

A number of workers did quit for that reason, as one former home-worker explained:

And it was going pretty good, until then I started getting really bad parts. And then I got mad. I thought, this job is bad enough without getting bad parts. And I'd tell them, you know, "These screws are not fitting together right. You have to hit them so hard." And they said, "Oh no, they passed inspection. They're OK." . . . I quit after a month of getting bad parts. Otherwise, I probably would have kinda hung in there, 'cause I did have the system down.

The work was controlled differently in Prairie Hills. Each worker was limited to one kit per week, and the different types of kits were rotated among the workers on a weekly basis; generally, each contractor was on an eight-week rotation with the kits. The kits varied in the ease of assembly, the average amount of time required, and the piecerate. The gross pay ranged from $130 to $216 per kit, and the rotation distributed the possible earnings across the group of contractors. The workers were satisfied with this method, not only because it averaged the earnings among them but also because it distributed the "hard" kits, which were rather universally disliked.

Usually it's already decided for you, unless, I like the small kit. And nobody else likes it, so I tend to get that one quite a bit. It doesn't pay as well, but it doesn't require as many hours. So sometimes I prefer that kit. Usually they try to split the kits around so nobody is stuck with the same kit week after week. And every kit has a pro or a con to it. Some of the grommets have to be pushed on. Some of 'em just fall on easy. Some the washers are cupped, some are flat. Some don't take nuts. Some do. So each kit has a good or a bad part. And so to keep it more fair to everyone, [the manager] pretty much rotates the product. He watches what he's been giving you, and they have it already written up what you're gonna get.

Distributing the kits according to the levels of difficulty is important to the workers. Like the homeworkers in Riverton, many in Prairie Hills would quit if they had to work consistently on the harder kits. Kim explained that the more difficult kits added significant work:

> There's black and white truck bolts, that have the tops treated with something. I'm not sure what. But, when you turn them on, they go on real hard because the stuff that they're treated with fills in the threads of the bolt, and then they don't. They might go on a little ways and then they'll catch. And then they hurt. Those are hard to turn on. . . . And then there's a kit that we get every once in a while. It's black and it's got cupped washers, too, and it has just a regular little nut on the top, and by the time you get all your pieces on, the washer just barely sits on the top, and you have to go and push all that down to get your nut on. And it's unbelievable how much longer it takes to push that down and to put that nut on than it is to just go on and put your nut on and screw it on. . . . I never thought that it would make that much difference before, you know, piecework like that. I never thought little things made such a difference, I thought efficiency experts were crazy. Every little movement extra just means hours at the end of the week.

Some kits had painted parts that would clog the threads of the bolts, making it difficult to screw on the final nut. Other kits had top nuts that were treated with a sandy substance like graphite that chafed the fingers as the worker tried to screw it in place. Kim described it as "the gritty stuff in the top that tears your fingers, that you can't get the tops on, and it really slows you down." Both of these kits required greater time and effort, and all the contractors agreed that they felt underpaid for the extra effort. Workers who easily finished in thirty-five to forty hours on other kits found they had to work about seven to ten hours more on these two kits, without an increase in the piecerate: "Well, like I say, it depends on your kits, too, 'cause there's some of these, that, you can put in another ten to fifteen hours, and only make—we figured we made about one dollar an hour on them. They're just harder." Like their counterparts in Riverton, Prairie Hills contractors noticed that the piecerate did not compensate them for the number of pieces handled but only for the number of units finished; a long bolt with more pieces paid the same rate as a shorter bolt with one or two fewer pieces even though more work was involved. Tricia's husband, Ray, explained the inequities of the piecerate system:

> There is a difference, see. You don't get paid quite for the work that you do on some of the kits. Some are overpaid. Some are un-

derpaid. Well, none of them are overpaid. Some are underpaid more than others are underpaid. Because some of the, it's piece-work, and some of the pieces are, if you have to put a burr on and screw it down on there, takes more time than it does to throw a grommet on. Or throw a washer on. And some of them are paid by the piece, and they aren't really paid, comparing, according to the work you have to do. . . . It's not equitable.

Rejected work—work in which the error rate exceeded the standards of the company—was the responsibility of the contractor. When the contractor brought the work back to the warehouse, a random inspection was performed on at least part of the kit for quality control; kits that did not pass inspection had to be redone on the premises by the worker before the pay would be approved. This did not occur often, and no contractor reported having work rejected more than once. As one contractor said, "Ya do it once, and ya just don't do it again. I had ta come and get them from the warehouse. Ya don't get paid, ya do that on your own." In a few verifiable instances, TMC "let go" contractors whose work was rejected several times, simply by reclaiming the equipment and refusing them a weekly contract.

Rush work occurs when the company wants the completed kit back in less than the usual week given to do it, a situation that occurred more often in Riverton, where for several months, the local manager would call up the contractors and request that any completed work be brought in. The contractors often complied with these requests but expressed mixed feelings about TMC's approach. Often workers said they were glad to comply but after many such requests were irritated that the company did not compensate them for their extra efforts. Harlan and Louise had completed many rush orders for the local warehouse in Riverton:

> Yeah, two days we pulled him out, every day we'd have to take the truck in, load it and take it in with what we had done, well, he'd want 'em that day, and they went out direct. . . . Two days he was behind, or a couple days we cooled him right out. We have fifteen [boxes] one day. The manager come right over with the truck. . . . It pulled him out, he was s'posed to have more, otherwise they'd hafta shut the line down at the factory. I called him the next morning, and he said, "Yeah, would you come in and get [bolts]? I need 'em done the next day." We did 10,200 that day, and had 'em back in there.

Sarah and Dave, an older retired couple, noted the connection between the rush orders and work in the GM factory: "Especially if it's in short supply, like when the platers went on vacation, well, see, they didn't produce anything, see. Well, then when they come back, well then the push is on, see. The company says we want some more, want some more. We feel the push." The homeworkers "feel the push," the ripple effects of just-in-time production implemented at General Motors, reverberating through TMC, and passed along by the local manager. Sarah and Dave's neighbors, Janice and Ken, talked about the extra burden caused by requests for rush orders:

> But then a lotta times, like, just a few months ago, the company come around and wanted ten extra [boxes]. Within two days. . . . Yeah, yeah, they called us different times and wanted to know if we would come in and pick up like ten of the Buicks, ya know, when we were doin' Australians or whatever, and see if we'd bring 'em back in two days, and that was real hard on us, because, ya know, like I say, ya don't put your kids on hold. You don't say, well, we've got these ta get done, ya know. You guys just go in a corner till we're done.
>
> I see that they expect a lot more of ya, even like the weeks when they have called, like I said that one week, it was four times, bring in what you've got done, ya know, no matter how many you've got done, even it it's two or three, bring 'em in. We need ta ship 'em. Ya know, and for us, unless we've got several things ta go ta town for, we don't go ta town. Ya know, we don't run in just because we need a gallon a milk or somethin' like that, ya know. It's just, it's somethin' we don't do, and then that upsets me is when they call and say, "Well, bring in whatever you've got."

Requests for rush work decreased the advantage Janice saw in not having to commute and also diminished the autonomy she wanted to set her work schedule around her family and household needs; temporarily setting the work as a priority above her children was a situation she found untenable. Other workers complained that rush work interfered with their beliefs about not working on Sundays and that TMC requested delivery of rush work even on that day.

Tanya, a contractor who had worked in various capacities for TMC, had raised the issues of compensation for rush work:

> 'Cause if they need something, like, you know, when they needed those Buick parts fast, they really pushed their contrac-

tors. You know, they told them, "We've gotta have these now." And they did it. But there's no reward for the people that did it so fast. The bosses just said, "No. We need parts, and you guys are gonna put 'em out there. That's it."

Several workers thought that rush work should be rewarded financially. A former contractor said she had stopped doing rush orders because of the company's refusal to increase the compensation:

It used to make me mad, too, is, TMC is wrong about this. 'Cause I caught on to them after two weeks. "Pat, can you get this done. We need a rush. Somebody's coming in here tomorrow." Sure, I'd say. 'Cause I liked Mark, and he hired me and I'm like, yeah. Try to get as many boxes as you can up here. So I would stay up another two hours that night, and do some more boxes and get them up there. Well, after two weeks of that, I caught on. I don't get paid any more. Why would I wanna stay up at night to work for you? Because you're my friend? I mean. And I don't know why TMC don't say, hey, there's some money in here for you, but there's not. There's nothing. It took me two weeks.

TMC relies on the use of personal relationships and networks in these rural areas to demand the completion of rush orders. In a more impersonal, anonymous organization of production, the company might have been more forthcoming with material incentives, as this worker suggested. TMC uses intangibles such as personal relationships, the benefits of flexibility, and the responsibilities of child-rearing and the chance to combine them with homework as leverage to generate needed production at the lowest cost possible in ways that obviously and tangibly benefit the company and add to the profit margin. Pat is among those workers who vocalized her preference for tangible benefits and saw them accruing only to the company.

Many workers, however, did not feel able to assert themselves as Pat had done. Because of the insecurity of the weekly contract and the high demand for this kind of work, most contractors complied with the rush orders. Janice said, "I do think that they expect too much that way for the pay, but then it comes down that if you wanna keep the job, you keep doin' it and don't say anything." Two contractors in Prairie Hills concurred:

That's why you never get a pay raise. There are a lot of people around that would like to get on, doing it. I mean, we know a lot of people who would love to do it.

There is enough interest in it, that, if you complain too much, they'll say, well, we've got other people to do it, that want to do it. And they will do it at this price. So you're, like the old saying, you're caught between, in the middle. Lot of people want jobs.

Rush-work orders were tied to the production needs of the factory line at General Motors. When the need for certain parts was high the demand for kits increased, and the contractors were pushed to produce more in less time than was stated in the weekly contract. Conversely, when factory needs decreased, the amount of work put out to the contractors also decreased, sometimes completely shutting down the local warehouse activity for a few weeks or longer. In Prairie Hills, shutdown had occurred several times, and the company would guarantee the contractors only forty weeks of work per year. Usually, contractors received less work in the summer months, and then around December TMC would close down and reduce work again. One contractor described the workload:

When they started they told us we're gonna be running around forty weeks a year, according to car sales. . . . And I think last year we got right around forty kits. You know, Christmastime there's a couple weeks off the end of the month. Thanksgiving there's a week off. And at least every spring there's usually a month when car sales are off.

Fred also remembered the irregularity of the workload:

Well, the first year I started out, well, it was just a year ago, I started in April or May, whatever it was, and I worked. I was gettin' a full kit all the time through April, May, June, July. Then August nothin', September nothin', October I think I done two or three. Then I didn't have anything 'til, maybe November, done one or two, and then I didn't have anything in December.

In the first nine months, Fred had about twenty kits rather than the thirty-eight he had expected from the weekly contract. Another contractor who does the same type of work remembered the period of shutdown, too, which resulted in the size of their kits being reduced because of the surplus that had accumulated:

There was periods when there wasn't. They build up a considerable inventory. Oh, a year-and-a-half ago or so, somethin' like that, we didn't work for about three or four months then. They had ta work that up. Well, we were takin' the full box, which was 20,500 at a time. Well, that just kept building up, and so they got rid of that surplus, and then they cut us down ta 16,000, and this is what we've been getting, nearly a kit a week for quite a while now. There's been a time or two when they couldn't get their supplies or something, but it's been pretty well steady.

When reduced workloads or shutdown occurred in the summer, many farm families appreciated the reprieve even though it diminished their income. Dana explained that factory shutdowns made the income from homeworking seem flexible:

You get used to having about, you know, the $200 a week, but sometimes, like around Christmas, you don't get a kit every week like they take off because the factory's closed, you know, the car makers are closed. So there, you might only get two kits a month, which is like $400 compared to like $800 say. You know, and you miss it, but yet, we're not really. You know, this pays like, we pay in a car payment, different things that you depend on it for, but yet this money is more flexible, too. So, you know, you don't really count on it, like, 'cause it may change. You know, you might not get a kit every week.

The company does not give any advance notice of changes in the workload or of factory shutdowns. Lucy reported that although she appreciated the break from the work in the summer she had more help around the house then and could have completed her assembly work more easily.

One whole summer, I had two kits the whole summer, when I had all the help. But they weren't making the cars in Detroit. So, and I felt sorry for a lot of those people [other homeworkers], because I know some of them, they were depending on that to live on. And they were just, oooooh, almost scared.

Shutdowns affect pay; as many workers said, "No work, 'course that means no money." The irregularity of the work also means that the income is not to be depended upon; not only is the work flexible, so is the income. With shutdowns, rejected work, and rush work TMC avoids the overhead of idle workers, production errors, and the costs involved in changing the type of production and complies with

GM's requirement for just-in-time production. The home contractors cannot control these aspects and end up absorbing these costs. Rush work and shutdowns are clear indicators of the subcontracting chain of production, in which control is mandated from General Motors through TMC to the local managers in the rural warehouses and ultimately over the homeworkers.

HOMEWORKING IN THE CONTEXT OF LOCAL
JOB OPTIONS

An assessment of informal industrial relations in these two communities must include comparison with other work opportunities that the contractors see available to them locally since such job options provide the context for an understanding of how the workers evaluate the assembly work. Material for comparison came from three sources: first, from contractors who had outside jobs in addition to the homework; second, from other contractors who had held local jobs in the recent past; and third, from some family members of homeworkers who were local employers and employees. Each group contributed comparative material on local job options, pay, and working conditions in general.

In Prairie Hills, the average hourly wage (about $4.50) that most contractors estimated they earned was the same as or better than the average wage they could earn at an entry-level position locally. In the long term, assuming incremental raises in pay in a local job, the average wage from the outside job would catch up and eventually pass the wage earned through assembly homeworking, but that could take several years in some local establishments. Liz Schaeffer reported starting at $3.35 per hour in a local office, and three years later she was earning $4.10 per hour; after three years of full-time clerical work, her hourly wage in the office was still below her estimate of her hourly wage from assembly homework. Fred works in a local food-processing factory and earns $3.50 an hour under rather poor working conditions. The employees are not paid overtime beyond an eight-hour day unless they exceed forty hours in a week, which the management is careful to avoid. They are required to stand at the assembly line for the entire shift. Workers have observed the management of this factory harassing workers, often until they reach the point of quitting. After one-and-one-half years at this factory, Fred earns $3.75 per hour, substantially below the $6.00 per hour he estimates he earns as a homeworker.

A local job in Prairie Hills offers relative job and income security and sometimes the possibility of fringe benefits; although the wages from entry-level jobs are usually lower than those from homeworking, the former is regular and dependable. Moreover, the formal work-place offers the worker a minimum of protection against discrimination in hiring, wage levels, and firing that the weekly contract cannot offer. Yet the advantages of homeworking, such as no clock to punch and no mistreatment or harassment in the workplace, were such that many contractors said they would choose to work as full-time assemblers if the homeworking income were more regular and dependable. Elise described her transition from a part-time job in town to assembly homeworking and the pros and cons she and her husband considered along the way:

> And then, I loved the residents there, and I liked who I worked with, but I went to work [early]. My hours was from 6:00 till 2:30, and I had to go at 5:00 in order to get everything done. So I was truly working nine hours, and getting paid for eight. Well, I didn't say much about it, but my husband was very upset. He said, "You're working nine hours, you should get paid for nine hours." Well, the rule of thumb was that you could only get in an eight-hour day. So you wasn't gonna get paid for any more, it didn't make any difference. So with that, and with getting up at four in the morning, and starting out on a morning like this morning [subzero temperatures], there'd be nobody in the world up, from here to town, so you'd just be on your own if your car stalled or anything, there you'd be. And then, I was the part-timer, so I felt that every job that anyone else didn't do, "Well, Elise has time, she's a part-timer." And I thought, you know, I really don't have to be the dirty-job lady.

Elise's husband got a state job in maintenance, which, she said "saved our day, because we truly could not live on this job [homeworking]." His job meant that Elise could leave the job in town and work as a home contractor, which they saw as an advantage.

Riverton's local job market did not offer much competition to the homeworking jobs, either. It was slightly more diversified in that there were several restaurants, and a few of the homeworkers supplemented their wages by working as waitresses; others worked in local clerical positions. Starting wages in clerical and retail work were minimum wage, or $3.35 per hour. Riverton workers, however, were much more likely than their Prairie Hills counterparts to commute to nearby small cities; there were three within a forty-minute drive. Wages were somewhat better than in Riverton on the average because each of these small cities had at least one major factory with starting wages of about six dollars per hour and incentive pay systems. Although higher wages and benefits could be earned by commuting, many people preferred not to because of the expenses, such as extra babysitting costs, wear and tear on a vehicle, and extra time away from home. The local factory in Riverton started workers at minimum wage, which was raised slowly in small increments. Most homeworkers did not rate these options more highly than the homework itself even though the pay per hour was greater. Tanya had had several years of experience in the retail sector in Riverton and had taken a decrease in pay as a homeworker but preferred the working conditions at home over those at the office:

> I like it better at home. It's easier. And there's not as much pressure. Towards the end of my job, there was a lot of pressure. I had worked as a retail checker. I went from a checker, I worked behind the courtesy booth, and from there I went to part-time office worker. And there was a lot of pressure, you know, a lot of pressure. And there's no pressure at home here. Except for some days, if you're in a hurry and trying to get your kit done, you know, by the deadline, you aren't gonna make it, so.

Riverton homeworkers as a group had more young children still at home than did the workers in Prairie Hills and placed greater value on being able to stay at home, regardless of the absolute difference in hourly pay. Gail, a Riverton homeworker who also has two jobs outside the home, compared local job options:

> In Riverton it's really hard ta get a good job, so I think, ya know, it's why we do bolts. Like a lotta mothers wanna stay home with their kids because I feel I would go out and work outside the home and pay a babysitter for my daughter, I would never [earn much]. Right now I feel I could bring in $210 a week. If I went out and worked and paid a babysitter, I wouldn't bring in that much. I'd only prob'ly bring in half of the amount. Like around here, I think a lotta mothers feel like that. People aren't working, it's not gonna pay, so they feel if they do bolts and babysit, that it's a lot better for them. I think this is a real good place for the company to locate. And there are a lotta older people too that find jobs hard ta get for them around here, so they just do bolts.

Like Gail, Mollie assessed the value of homeworking relative to other jobs from her perspective as a mother, which she feels is different from the way men would evaluate the opportunity:

> I have two uncles that at one time were doing the bolts. And to them, the men look at whatcha get in a check. They look at the money side of it, ya know. Ta me, I look at the benefits. Ya know, the money is nice, but when you figure up what you're making an hour, doing bolts, it's just a little bit over $2.00 an hour, which is not very much. But you add on $2.25 an hour for your babysitting, and you add on your wear and tear on your car, your oil, your gas, the hassle in the wintertime especially, ta get the kids out at a particular time, tun around and get 'em fed breakfast, put 'em in snowsuits to drive 'em five minutes inta town and take it all off, the packing of the diaper bag, ooh, the bottle, it would just drive me nuts. And that's the way the guys look at it. And my husband's the same way. He tells me all the time, he says, ya know, "You're a fruitcake for doin' this." But, see, he doesn't look, he's not looking at it from a mother's, from a wife or a mother's point of view. When I figure up what I make an hour, I'm making well over $5.00 an hour staying right here at home, being with my kids, setting my own hours. . . . I think men feel that they're the breadwinners, and you know, the almighty buck is what makes the world go 'round, and that's sad, but it's true. . . . They just can't see it through a woman's eyes.

Mollie evaluated the job beyond the paycheck, placing priority on her ability to "raise my own children and help make ends meet." She had worked outside the home for several years and with the birth of her youngest child no longer felt she could balance her responsibilities. Homeworking was an opportunity Mollie said she "would fight to keep."

In evaluating homework, many of the women were comparing it to past or present outside jobs. Emerging consistently among Riverton women homeworkers was their sense of being penalized by the outside workplace for holding their families as a top priority. Several homeworkers mentioned that workplaces had been very insensitive to absences due to illness during pregnancy or absences to care for seriously ill children. Many women reported quitting jobs to care for family members when the workplace would not permit them to use vacation time or to take a leave of absence. Informal labor relations that allow women to work at home are appreciated as giving women the opportunity to balance income earning with family responsibilities even though homeworking often generated less income. Workers felt that assembly homeworking, unlike outside work, supports women in acknowledging the importance of their family lives by making the work compatible with their values. At one of the annual appreciation suppers, the company expressed its values as "God, family, and work, in that order," wanting to show the workers that both management and labor held these priorities in common. For women who had experienced those values as reversed in the formal workplace, such a statement by the company went a long way in affirming their roles as mothers first, workers last.

HOMEWORK AS JOB AND INCOME SHARING

As a job opportunity, homeworking allows the contractor the autonomy to distribute the work as she chooses in order to complete it on time. Many households incorporate family members into the process, not all of whom are living with the main contractor. Other contractors incorporated neighbors, especially nearby teenagers who needed jobs. Unlike most jobs in the formal workplace, homeworking allows the worker to redistribute work and income as the needs arise. Jane had several older, married children, some of whom had fallen on hard times financially; she described the value of homeworking in her family context:

> We'll probably just keep it, because even if I went back ta work someplace, and I've thought about it at different times, there's always somebody that needs some extra money, whether it's like Tom and Lynn downstairs, ya know or the kids. And then that way they would just, ya know, help out, and we'd just pay 'em for doing it, too, 'cause sometimes things come up where somebody needs extra money. If Tom and Lynn need some extra money, then they'll do some of the boxes. And then I have a daughter, too, that just got laid off, and ya know, she might do a little bit or, ya know, whatever. It really comes in handy.

"It comes in handy" because, as another worker said, "there's always someplace to put the money from the bolts, always some need for it."

In a context of intermittent unemployment and local economic decline, especially in the agricultural communities, there was an expressed need to earn income that would allow a family or a household to "hold on a little longer." Carrie told how homeworking fit in her life at different times. She and her husband first took on the homework contract when they lost their farm; at the same time, her husband started commuting to an outside, full-time job, a new experience for both of them.

> When he first left, we needed the money, the total money coming from the bolts to be able to pay bills and everything, and then that was getting to be quite a responsibility for me alone, all the time, because of trying ta do the crafts to sell and all these other things. That money was helping also. So, we finally got in a position, because of his job situation, that I felt I could ease off just a little bit, so we have a married niece who lives about thirty miles from us and she has two little children and it was going to be nice for her if she could have a little extra money coming in, but yet she didn't feel that she could go leave these children with a babysitter, and get a job and be able ta make enough money. So she has helped us in the last couple of years with it, and we made a decision to give her part of the kit. So that does help me. A few days a week she comes here and works. She does about a third of the kit.

The income and the ability to redistribute the work support the workers' sense of autonomy and flexibility inherent in the job. Homeworking fits well with the ethic of helping out family and friends, not with charity but with an economic sideline. It allows workers to decrease the isolation of working at home by bringing in family or friends to share the work. Many contractors said they would continue homeworking in order to have this financial sideline that could be shared so easily when necessary.

5

Understanding Industrial Homework as Subsidized Development

In examining the creation of industrial homeworking jobs as part of the rural development strategies in Prairie Hills and Riverton, it becomes clear that regional and local state support is based in part on beliefs about women as secondary workers and earners of supplemental income. The material conditions and working experiences of the homeworkers themselves illustrated the ways in which paid work at home is interwoven with unpaid work and often becomes labeled as women's work. These conditions and the social context of wage work at home shape the worker's experience of the job. Included in this work experience are material ways in which homeworkers contribute to the overhead savings reaped by TMC, referred to here as worker subsidies.

INFORMAL LABOR RELATIONS AND WORKER-SUBSIDIZED INDUSTRIAL DEVELOPMENT

Homeworkers subsidize industrial development through specific aspects of their relationship with the company. TMC controls factors such as Social Security, lack of benefits, the training process, and the adjustment period when contractors are working up speed and have a much lower hourly rate of pay; TMC also can demand rush orders

and reject work. By developing their work spaces and by their technological adaptations of the production process, workers further subsidize the company.

TMC's policies about Social Security changed during the first years of
operation. When they started hiring in Prairie Hills, no deductions of
any kind were made from the contractors' paychecks, and all workers
were responsible for contributing Social Security at the self-employed
rate. During the second year of operation, however, the company assembled all the contractors to inform them of the change in policy.
One homeworker recalled that "up until August of last year [1988],
they didn't deduct anything. And then in August, I think it was August, they came and said that they had to start taking Social Security
out, because it wasn't a cottage industry anymore." Another worker
remembered how TMC explained the change in policy:

> Uh, it used ta be, it, a bolt would pay four cents. Uh, they've low-
> ered it to .038 cents, but they did that for the Social Security fac-
> tor. Uh, the way they explained it at the meeting, each person
> would have twenty-six dollars, I believe it was, twenty-six dollars
> of tax ta pay per kit, of Social Security. So they lowered the
> amount of pay to help, so the company wouldn't hafta pick it all
> up. I mean, you're payin' your share, and when it was all ex-
> plained to us, when it come down to it, we are making actually
> one dollar more per kit now, than if we took that twenty-six dol-
> lars out of each kit, and set it aside for Social Security.

Tricia and Ray also remembered the context of TMC's discussion of
Social Security but disagreed that the net amount after the change
was even one dollar higher.

> That's where the company lawyers messed up. They told them
> they were self-employed contractors. Well, we're not self-em-
> ployed contractors. We are, and we're not. Well, we're a cottage
> industry, which has a different labeling, as far as Social Security
> goes. So if you're a cottage industry, which technically we are,
> you have to withhold Social Security. If you're a self-employed
> contractor, which they told us we were all gonna be, you don't
> have to. . . . It's kinda funny. Their corporate lawyer screwed up.
> So actually we make less now, yea. Checkwise we make less.
> Supposedly we're not making less, because they're putting more.
> They're paying Social Security, too. Part of Social Security. The

way it was gonna be afterwards, they would be paying their 7.5 percent, and we'd be paying 7.5 percent, and our check would be more. Our net check after Social Security was taken out, would be more than it was before, when we were self-employed. . . . We've contributed our half, but they haven't contributed their half, as far as Social Security goes.

Actually, TMC lowered the piecerate at least 5 percent to compensate the company for the employer's contribution of 7.5 percent, so that the worker, in effect, was still contributing more than the employee's share. For example, the largest kit originally paid a gross amount of $216.00, and the contractor was responsible for 13 percent self-employment Social Security tax, which came to $28.08, for a net amount of $187.92. When TMC changed the policy to matching 7.5 percent contributions, the gross amount on the same kit was $205.00, and the worker had $15.38 deducted from the check and assumed the company matched it with an equal amount. The decrease in pay was $11.00, so TMC's contribution was $15.38 minus $11.00, for a net contribution of $4.38. The worker was then contributing $26.38, or 12.9 percent tax. The net amount of the kit was $205.00 minus $26.38, or $178.62, about $9.00 less than the original net pay. That difference adds up to about $36.00 per month per worker, multiplied by an average nine-month working year for forty workers. This nets the company approximately $12,960 annually with no corresponding loss in productivity.

Social Security was handled differently for Riverton workers. At first, no deductions were made, and the worker received the gross amount per kit completed. About one year later, according to a local manager, TMC decided to deduct Social Security "just to keep the government off our backs"; however, they deducted Social Security at the self-employed rate from the workers in Riverton. It is unclear how this practice is justified, since self-employed persons are responsible for their own contributions. None of the workers understood why the tax was deducted in this manner. The piecerate was never changed in Riverton, either, but the end result was about equivalent: Riverton workers had 13 percent deducted from their pay, and in Prairie Hills workers were contributing 12.9 percent from their paychecks.

The company contract explicitly states, "Contractor shall not be eligible for any Company employee benefits." TMC covered the warehouse-manager positions with the equivalent of 26 percent of their wages in benefits, but no homeworkers are covered with Worker's Compensation, paid time off, protection from layoffs, disability or unemployment insurance, or health insurance. Thus TMC realizes a yearly savings of $2,080 to $2,340 per homeworker in Prairie Hills, based on what they earned for forty-two weeks of assembly work. As one elderly contractor said, "'Course the thing, like in industry, the fringe benefits that people get today. You know, it's just fabulous. Where with this, we don't get no fringe benefits. We get what we do, and that's it. We don't get any pension or anything. You just work harder!" Although it is difficult to calculate accurately the dollar amount of this subsidy for the company, one cost comparison can be made, according to some of the workers in Prairie Hills. During the process of interviewing and training for these positions, workers were informed of the average hourly cost for having the same work done in a factory in Detroit.

> We were told when we trained that the person that used ta do this job on the line, by the time they figured his environment, his benefits and everything for him, it cost them forty-four dollars an hour ta have him there. Well, then if you put it in perspective and even give us five ta six dollars an hour, there's quite a spread there, and so, ya know, again they aren't beholden to us in any way, because we're just part-time contractors, so ta speak. So that's the risk, I guess, everybody accepts, ya know.

Other workers recalled similar comparisons being made by the company.

> I've never worked in a factory, but they tell me, the cost of keeping an employee in a factory runs around forty-five dollars an hour at General Motors, when they figure all their insurance and their benefits and their total costs of keeping the plant running. So, if we're doing it for four to five [dollars per hour], hey, they're not hurting.

The point here is not that TMC has a profit margin of forty dollars per hour of work but that the difference in labor and overhead costs is great enough to substantiate major savings for the company at the expense of the workers. Taking the work out of Detroit and moving it to Prairie Hills cut the labor and associated costs by 90 percent.

The lack of coverage for work-related injuries also results in a substantial savings in overhead for TMC. A worker whose finger is caught in the press gets no special attention or consideration. Nanette's husband said that when she "smashed" her finger in the press, she "just went and bandaged up her finger and went right back at it again. Ya just keep right on workin' a lotta times." In a factory, he acknowledged, such an injury would have excused the worker from the assembly lines for "at least the rest of the day, with pay."

When health insurance is provided, it is a major cost for labor. The contractors are not covered for health insurance, nor are they defined as a group in order to be eligible for lower rates. This situation was a problem for many households, some of whom were totally without health insurance; other households paid out very high premiums for insurance because they were not members of a defined group. Again, the company saves the expense of the worker, as Marilyn explained:

> It would be economically more feasible for the company to go this route, because they don't have the overhead. They don't have insurance on each employee. They don't have a pension fund. They're not having the, uh, electricity, the cost of the building, and uh, there's a lot of hidden costs in having the employees there assembling. We foot all those costs, you know, our own medical, our own, whatever. You know, TMC's not responsible for anything. So I would say that would be very advantageous for the company, definitely.

The absence of job security coupled with no Unemployment Compensation leaves the worker totally unprotected during times of shutdown or temporary layoff. The frequent experience of intermittent unemployment and income insecurity that brings the worker to home contracting also leaves the worker at higher risk for both conditions because of the nature of the work and the lack of protection. Workers in Prairie Hills reported work stoppages occurring two to three times each year that coincided with slack periods in auto manufacturing. Riverton workers often had less work over the winter holidays or no work at all when transportation of the parts was delayed, the latter occurring several times throughout the winter. Thus these informal jobs only sporadically relieved the conditions they were intended to eliminate for the workers and their families.

The contractors were not paid an hourly wage for their training periods, which ranged from as little as an hour or so in Riverton to several days in Prairie Hills. Riverton workers were not paid at all, and most workers in Prairie Hills remembered their pay was simply a share of the total number of pieces assembled during training. For the latter group, the average hourly pay was less than minimum wage.

The period immediately following training, referred to as the adjustment period, was experienced by all contractors as a period of low pay, during which they said they could not and did not make the minimum wage. This period lasted about one month for most workers, who needed about sixty to seventy hours to complete the kits. Average hourly pay during this period for Riverton workers was about $1.50, and for Prairie Hills workers, about $2.00. As Fred recalled, "I would say, anyone startin' out would prob'ly have a hard time makin' minimum wages. The first month." More work-related injuries occurred during the adjustment period, which also slowed the pace of work.

Workers had to adjust to the assembly work in other ways as well. Many workers mentioned muscular aches and spasms, back trouble, adjusting to standing for long periods of time, and adjusting seat height appropriately for working at presses. Lucy described her first months as a contractor:

> For a long time, I thought, oh, my gosh, I'm having, I must be having heart trouble or something, because my left arm would just ache, and the shoulder. I thought, I'm not going to the doctor. I'm too young. I don't want to know I have troubles like that. Then we had a three-week break [from the bolts]. And it went away. And then, I started thinking about that. Now, it must have something to do with out there. Well, then I realized, my left hand, I'm left-handed. I hold the drill up in the air, going down there like, going down that line of bolts back and forth constantly all day, and I'd never had that kind of strain on one arm before. And that's what was doing it. It was just the aching muscles in the shoulder. . . . Or the joints started aching. I thought, oh, God, here comes arthritis now. Well, it's from grabbing into that stuff [boxes of parts]. And you just get used to it and find different ways to make things comfortable. And then everybody was complaining at first about standing on cement all that time. So you learn what kind of shoes you need to wear so your back doesn't ache and the legs don't ache.

Sore fingers were another common complaint, a result of handling rough-edged pieces or pieces with graphite-like coatings; some workers taped their fingers to lessen the chafing and cracking. Lucy concluded the list of problems: "And calluses and blisters and swollen hands and aching joints, and in the fingers. That was the hardest thing to take, to get used to." The workers were responsible for their own safety and well-being on this job. Hourly pay was definitely affected by injuries and physical adjustments, and the decrease was absorbed by the worker since the company did not compensate any differently during the early period of work. In effect, workers subsidize their own training periods, first in the warehouse and later, for at least one month, with substandard wages while they build up speed and endurance.

Switching parts from week to week meant workers had to make adjustments. Tanya, one of the quicker Riverton contractors, said, "If you get a new part in, it's gonna take you longer to learn how to do it." The company exercised control over which part was put out each week, and frequently the workers faced readjustment as the parts were changed or rotated. Lower hourly pay because of this kind of adjustment meant the workers again absorbed the costs of flexible production.

Rush work and rejected work were other means by which the company passed costs on to the workers. In a formal factory setting, where a worker is truly paid on a piecerate, rush work would result in higher hourly wages as well as greater productivity. When done at home, rush work yields higher productivity without increasing the compensation to the worker. Rejected work in the factory is usually weeded out and repaired, if possible, but both the original worker and the repair worker are paid for their labor. Home contractors are expected to redo the assembly work on their own time and are paid only once per piece completed.

Work spaces and technological adaptations are a significant source of subsidy for TMC. Homeworking reduces the overhead costs of building and maintaining a facility to house the workers and the supplies, eliminates the costs of maintaining occupational safety standards and insurance for work-related injuries, and eliminates any down-time on the line for changing or repairing machinery. The contractors develop and maintain their own work spaces, sometimes investing a few hundred dollars and a few weeks of effort to establish a place that is relatively comfortable and conducive to work. George and Helen described some of the expenses related to developing their work space:

We redone our shed out there this fall. This summer we worked out in that hot weather without any air conditioning, had fans goin'. It was hot out there. It was miserable. . . . We've insulated it and closed it all, ya know, and put a new door on the shed so it'll seal the cold air, and then we'll put an air conditioner in there next year. So it should be comfortable.

As an added bonus to the company, workers are encouraged to adapt the work process to meet their own standards of speed and efficiency, which means they are improving the production process on their own time at no cost to TMC.

Contractors' work spaces were shaped by the availability of space on their property and by the extent to which they wished to invest resources in it. Most Riverton contractors worked in an area of their homes, with a few working in sheds on their property. For contractors working inside their homes, less investment and development generally were necessary to make it an acceptable work space. Contractors working in sheds, garages, basements, and other unfinished spaces, including most of the Prairie Hills workers and a few of the Riverton workers, usually had to put in time, effort, and money to make the space even minimally suitable for work. All workers had to provide light and heat, some of which might be tax deductible, depending on the circumstances; however, some workers provided significant amounts of electricity because their work required the use of one or two air compressors. Other contractors needed to keep one or two fans running during working times because fumes from the use of glue required ventilation. These expenses are covered by the contractors and represent savings in the costs of overhead to TMC.

Technological adaptation was also left up to the contractor, who was motivated by the need or desire to find quicker and easier ways to complete the work. In Riverton a few contractors had automated the work process and said they saved more on effort than on time, but even a savings on effort was worth the expense to them; they had spent their own time and money to redesign the press for automation. Prairie Hills workers did not automate the process but did reorganize the assembly work. At first TMC instructed them to assemble one bolt at a time, holding the long bolt in their hands and adding on the other pieces one by one, a lengthy procedure when they had to complete 5,400 bolts per week. A few creative workers invented a way to stand the bolts upright on a board so that the worker could walk along the board and put on the remaining pieces. Soon almost all the contractors were doing the bolts this way, and the company started training new workers using this procedure as well. TMC's industrial engineers were quite pleased with this contribution by contractors as the change improved quality control at no cost to them. The workers, now trained to assemble the bolts in this new way, would go out and purchase the materials to make their own setup at home, sometimes spending over $100. There was no obligation to do the work exactly that way, but training gives the worker an implicit and strong message that this particular way was approved by the company. Despite the costs, however, many workers did appreciate the autonomy they felt in setting up their work spaces according to their own needs and preferences and in determining their way of performing the work.

A clear pattern emerges of workers subsidizing the informal-sector jobs created in their communities. Behind this notion of subsidy is the real experience of the workers: They are paid minimally by the piece to complete the assembly work yet are not paid at all for the other contributions they make to the production process, nor are they compensated for the major savings in the overhead costs of labor realized by the company. The worker contributes far more than the labor covered by the piecerate when one considers the development of the work space, improvements in the process of production, added labor for rush work and rejected work, disproportionate contributions to Social Security, absorption of lower payrates for training and adjustment periods, and the lack of security and benefits.

When production is moved from the factory to the home, there are definite cost differences, many of which are absorbed by the homeworkers. Perhaps less apparent is that paid work done in the home both supports and is supported by specific sets of domestic relations. Homeworking relies upon a domestic organization that is centered on one adult, usually the woman, who stays at home. The structure of homeworking upholds this pattern of domestic organization and thus supports the model that provides homeworking with its labor supply.

INFORMAL LABOR RELATIONS IN THE CONTEXT OF DOMESTIC LABOR RELATIONS

"She's worth more at home, especially now when she can bring in an extra income from the home," a homeworker's husband explained to me, since as a contractor she can generate a secondary income without incurring the extra costs of child care, transportation, meals, and clothing. The statement is a classic example of economic rationality at the same time that it is an expression of his beliefs about woman's place. Left unspoken are basic assumptions about "her work." She is worth more at home because of her unpaid labor in the tasks of cooking, cleaning, and child-rearing; for her to work outside the home means someone else must be paid to do this work. He reasons that part of her income, then, would go toward paying someone to "help her out" with the children and the housework; homeworking, however, allows his wife to earn money and to carry out those basic responsibilities in the home. Although she teases him about the way he defines tasks as women's work, she agrees with him in the basic assessment that homeworking is a good way for a "woman to contribute" financially. Such an assessment raises the questions we shall explore next: What is women's work and men's work in these households, and how does it affect the worker's experience of homeworking as a job?

The data from interviews with local and state officials suggest that in supporting this kind of work as development, the local state and industry are acting to subsidize particular sets of social and domestic relations. This attitude is quite explicit as development officials speak of developing "jobs for secondary workers, mostly women" and as local officials discuss the importance of job creation that supports their view of the basic values concerning women's and men's roles. It is important to draw out the implications of this kind of job development, which go beyond simple job creation, especially for those people who do the work because homeworking lends economic support to norms and values that define certain spheres of activity in the home as belonging to women by virtue of her sex. This sex-typed work is not taken "seriously" by men as "real work," and homeworking as an extension of this female work is not often seen as "real" work, either. For men, however, homeworking is often an extension of other remunerated labor rather than unpaid "social reproduction" work and as such is seen as part and parcel of "the real work that men do." Thus it is not informal labor relations alone that determine the character of work once it is in the home but the interaction of homework with sex-typed labor that influences the configuration of experiences for the worker: Women and men homeworkers doing the same kind of task at the same piecerate have rather different experiences as workers because the work is integrally linked to their sex-typed responsibilities.

Janice and Ken live out in the country with their four children, two sons and two daughters, three of whom are in grade school during the day. They were relaxed throughout the interview and warmed up to the topics easily although Janice tended to answer most of the questions and to discuss the topics at length. Their toddler, Timmy, ran in and out of the country-decorated kitchen, periodically claiming everyone's attention. Janice talked easily about the conflict she felt between family demands and her job when she worked outside the home and said that to a certain extent the conflict still existed for her as a homeworker. Reviewing her recent work history, she described her last job outside the home:

> I started [at The Shoppe] when they opened up and was there until, what was it, the end of the summer, and then I quit because it was impossible, with the kids ta come home and try, and Ken's mother was watchin' the kids, and Timmy was just so little and everything. I guess I always felt it wasn't fair to him. I'd come home and his grandma would say, "Well, guess what he did today?" And I didn't wanna hear it, 'cause I wasn't there to see it, so I didn't wanna hear it. And I just felt real bad, and even Jake and Patti. Jake was gonna be startin' kindergarten, and he kept sayin', "Who's gonna be there when I get off the bus at noon?" And he was just feelin' so bad, and so I quit there at The Shoppe.

The hours at The Shoppe were long and irregular, and Janice felt her family life suffered as a result: "You know, here the kids were all waitin' at home for me ta come home and make supper." Shortly after Janice quit her job at The Shoppe, she was hired as a home contractor by TMC; Ken helps with the assembly work, and Janice discussed the differences between them as workers and her priorities:

> We can do a box in, what did we figure, just a little over an hour? About an hour and five minutes, we can do a box. And separately, it takes him about maybe an hour and twenty minutes, but it takes me probably an hour and a half, two hours. I'm slower than he is, and plus, with Timmy here, different times, runnin' him to the bathroom or gettin' him a drink, and it seems like days when Ken says, "Make sure you get one box done and maybe two done," then that's the day that he wants Mommy ta hold him and rock him and wants a lot to eat, and "come get me a snack, Mommy," ya know.
>
> Oh, the children, always, and they come first, ya know, even days, like I say, when Timmy's cranky and he's had a cold and, there have been different days, ya know, when Ken says, "Why didn't you get them done?" I says, "Well, because I rocked Timmy today," ya know. I can't see sittin' there doin' bolts if he's

sittin' there cryin', and not feelin' good, and I don't know, the children would be first, and then probably even the housework would be second. It hasta be done and it always does get done. It's just that other things get done first. That's the way I see it. But then, now, see, when Ken's here, he puts it first. I know you would, wouldn't ya? Because he doesn't do the things that I do. I mean, he doesn't give the kids a bath, and like I say, he doesn't get their clothes ready for the next day, and he doesn't make supper, and he doesn't do the dishes, and he doesn't clean the house.

Ken agreed with Janice's assessment of the division of labor: "Generally, when I'm here, there's really nothin' else pressing for me to do really." Janice's sole responsibility for home and children shapes her experience of paid labor whether it is at home or outside the home. When she works outside the home, she is responsible for arranging child care; as a homeworker, paid labor and family care compete for her attention throughout the day. When Ken assembles bolts, he does so without interruption for family needs because "there's really nothing else" demanding his attention.

At one point, Janice was making crafts at home for another manufacturer while Ken tried to keep up with the bolts. That did not work out too well.

Because I started sewing about the time Patti got off the bus, and at 8:00 P.M. when I'd quit sewing, I sent them ta bed, and, ya know, she was feelin' rotten, ya know, "Why don't you ever have any time for us?" and that's all I ever heard is, "Oh, I hate CraftCo. I just hate that, Mom!" And so now, TMC isn't so bad, because they can still talk to me. It's not like, ya know, when I was sewing, there was no way they could talk to me. . . . Gotta keep things in balance at home.

It is clear that Janice's main role is to "keep things in balance at home." She leaves her job when it does not mesh with children's needs, she works at home so she can meet school buses and read to her children at home and at school, and she schedules her assembly work around the needs of an elderly uncle, who "waits for me ta come do his laundry and cookin' and things like that." When she worked outside the home, babysitting was a "major problem for me." She and Ken finally concluded that "there's no way I'm gonna go out and get a job anywhere because we've tried it a lotta times, and it just never works." Working inside the home resolves the problem relatively well for Janice partly because Ken is able to help her with it and partly because she can still manage to keep up with home and family tasks while doing it. Although homeworking allows Janice to balance wage work with home and family care, it also supports the well-defined roles of both Janice and Ken: He can work outside the home full-time without concern for child care or meals or a clean home because she is working full-time inside the home, assembling bolts, cleaning, cooking, and caring for the children.

Mollie is a hardworking, determined woman in her late thirties with six children, four of whom are home during the day with her. Rusty, her husband, works one full-time, seasonal job and has another part-time job, also seasonal; he is most likely to be unemployed during the winter months. Homeworking, said Mollie, has been "the answer to my prayers. I would do anything to help make ends meet, and yet be able to raise my kids. I would fight to keep this job." She has been assembling bolts for two years and completes the kit each week by herself, spending an average of forty hours doing it. Rusty is not home most days until the evening, and Mollie describes her household organization as centered on her own efforts:

Mom pretty much does everything around the house. Rusty's hours are very long. I do all my own cooking and cleaning, and the repairs. I'm kinda handy, like anything that's done with my crafts, or my workbench, that's all me, I do it all. Rusty really doesn't do much because he's not really around that much, and when he comes home in the evenings, he likes ta just sit down and relax. The bolts are my job, and he really has nothing whatsoever to do with it. I do the picking up, I do all the hauling, all the unloading, all the loading. It's just all pretty much, it's my job, and so as far as his involvement even, ya know, with the kit, it's very minimal, very. . . . I pretty much take care of all the budgeting, all the bills I pay. I do the shopping, and I take care of the children. Rusty's not around much on the weekends, either.

Mollie took things "one day at a time" and said she had had to learn simply to accept what she could get done in any given day, which was hard for her, because "for me, there's never enough time in the day. Never. But then it's, at the same time, it's good that there's no more time in the day than there is, because a person would just, I would work myself to death, . . . just to make ends meet." Job and income insecurity motivated Mollie to take on the homeworking, but trying to add the work into "an already full schedule" proved difficult:

There's been days that it's looked pretty bad around here, but then there's other times, like with all the remodeling of the house, I have so many extra things to do other than just the general cooking and cleaning, the wash. When you have a family of eight, I hafta warsh every day. I'm not a Monday warsher. Monday is my biggest day, but even on Sundays usually I hafta run one or two loads. And so just to be able to stay on schedule is very hard. . . . And you find there's a lot of advantages and a lot of disadvantages to working at home. You find out when you work an eight-hour day outside of the home, when your eight hours is done, you're done. When you work in the home, it's usually an all-day job.

Not only are homework and housework an all-day job, but there are no sick days, either: "When I was sick a couple of months ago, ya know, I ended up having ta have three extra days in order ta get my kit in, because Rusty has no interest in the bolts. When I don't feel well, there's really no one ta pick up the slack."

Mollie's sense of roles for women and men is derived from strongly held moral beliefs: "The Lord made men different than women for a reason, and I just feel that my heart is at home with my kids." She describes her married life as "one of adjustment" to these differences between men and women. Men, she explained, cannot even seem to understand why she would stay home and assemble bolts for "$2.50 an hour." Nor do they understand that she feels something close to a moral imperative to maintain home and family and to reinforce the values that her church teaches; men cannot see it from "a mother's perspective." According to her values, a mother's priorities are her children, her home, her husband, and then paid work. The "double day" is not only normative, it is morally mandated for women; Mollie has had "to adjust" to Rusty's lack of participation in the household because help from him would be voluntary rather than morally mandated. In this setting home-based wage labor supports the roles prescribed by church teachings for women, reinforcing Mollie's belief that she can and should work long hours for low pay because she is a woman.

Mollie clearly understood that the combined roles of wife, mother, and worker were demanding, and despite men's perspectives on "hard work," she did not underestimate her efforts:

My work is so demanding. Back in my mom's time, a woman's place was in the home. And they were content ta be there and they were expected ta be no place but there, and this day and age, it's just the opposite. Ya know, the wife and the mother hasta work. It's almost a demand on 'em anymore. . . . And whereas in the olden days, the kids were someone's whole life. Kids were their career, and that's just not the way it is these days. For the majority of mothers, they hafta work and they hafta work a career into being a mother and a wife. . . . I have no choice in our case. And I guess that's why this is so nice because I have big demands as a mother, yet I have demands as trying ta help support a family, make ends meet.

Like Janice, Mollie saw homeworking as a way to "keep things in balance at home." Homeworking provides a meager economic subsidy for "Supermom"; indeed, these women are "worth more at home."

Homeworking clearly supports Janice and Mollie in their particular relationships to their families. The advantages and disadvantages of homework accrue to most workers because they are women; flexibility in paid work means the flexibility to care for home and children, to be responsive and available to family members. Kathleen Christensen discusses the gender base of these advantages as stemming from what she terms the "unspoken contract" of women's lives: "It became clear that their decisions to work at home, the ways in which they structured housework and child care, and the manner in which they handled employers or clients were all tied to the unspoken contracts of their lives—those implicit expectations they have about who they are and what they are supposed to do."[1] Principally, Christensen argues, women are motivated to work at home because they feel responsible for child care and housework, and the unspoken contract of their relationships defined the man as the breadwinner and the woman as the homemaker and mother. In a striking way, many of the women spoke of their image of the "good mother," not just any kind of mother, and of their need to fulfill that role. A good mother stays home with her children, is present and accessible to her children, and defines children and her role as mother as her first priority. Thus, upon the birth of a child, the unspoken contract dictates that the man continue to be the breadwinner and support the family but that she change her roles and priorities and fulfill the position of the good mother.

Most of the women that Christensen interviewed are home-based self-employed workers, and the way they speak of the contract that binds them to home-based work illuminates the motivations and situations of many other homeworkers. For example, many of these workers backed into home-based work in response to their obligations to home and family; consequently they often experience a lack of boundaries around their work, most clearly seen in their use of work space at home, their command of time, and their work identities. The lack of boundaries makes it difficult to renegotiate the terms of the unspoken contract regarding responsibilities for child care and household chores. Many women found it hard to carve out a space of their own within the home that would not be "invaded" by children, spouse, dirty laundry, or other items; in fact, many women set up work spaces that were relatively convenient for doing the laundry, watching the children, or responding to their spouse. Among the TMC homeworkers, having a work space separate from the home was more common in households where men participated in the work; women who were solely responsible almost always worked within the house, rarely if ever occupying a complete room. The lack of boundaries around her paid work also diminishes the credibility a woman has as a worker. Many home-based workers had to explain to friends and neighbors that they were working and could not be interrupted; they had to justify their work whenever people would inquire about their "little business." Paid work in the home became invisible to spouses, friends, and other family members since these people could see the woman only in her primary role of homemaking, which eclipsed all other activities.

As more women worked at home to augment the family income and meet other responsibilities, they learned that the terms of the unspoken contract are not easily renegotiated. One home-based worker observed, "He wants a nontraditional wife but a traditional home, which means he wants me to work, but he also wants me to take care of the house."[2] Working for pay does not mean housework and child rearing are redistributed more equitably; when most of these women work for pay, it entails a balancing act between the various sets of obligations. Many of the homeworkers in the Midwest acknowledged the strength of their beliefs in the roles of women in the home, and their decisions to take on homework are based on an acceptance of those roles. Renegotiating the unspoken contract requires a great deal of strength from the woman: She has to question and rethink her beliefs and values that guide her behavior, her relationships, and her work. Often, women perceive the risks as too great and compromise by "buying" themselves out of certain responsibilities when possible,

paying for a housekeeper or for child care rather than trying to redefine the terms of the contract.

From discussions with various local officials in Prairie Hills and
Riverton it becomes clear that support of female roles as women and
wives, as partners in the unspoken contract, was consciously in-
tended through the creation of these jobs. The chair of the Board of
Development in one community said that his first impression of
TMC's proposal to use homeworkers was not positive:

> [TMC] told us this is what they were going to do. What they
> wanted to do. And when we first, including myself, heard about
> it, we were not real excited over it. 'Cause the idea of somebody
> coming in, not wanting to put employees on the payroll, not pay-
> ing many benefits, not giving any of the workers benefits, was
> kind of a cold feeling.
>
> But when we talked to the women, they thought it was won-
> derful. The farm wives, that don't have to hire babysitters, that
> don't have to leave their homes every day. And they thought it
> was a wonderful opportunity.

The prospective homeworkers thought it was "wonderful" because
TMC had informed the board that each worker would "make around
$200 to $250 per week, which makes it worthwhile for them and
makes it worthwhile for the company. . . . And that was pretty much
for a forty-hour week." This local official continued to explain that
TMC would provide "secondary jobs for farm wives," which was important to the community because they had recently lost a plant that
had employed a few hundred women, a "major source of secondary
income." Another board member gave his views:

> This is a very poor, rural community. And, where second income
> is standard in many, many areas, we're struggling like hell to find
> someplace where we can find a second income. And we have
> struggled like that for a long time. And the first time that factory
> came in here, we were talking about second incomes. We did not
> consider it to be a primary employer, but a secondary employer.
> When TMC came here with a proposal, I don't remember if they
> said twenty or twenty-five people, but it's a home-based type of
> an operation. And it's an assembly operation. . . . They assemble
> things at home. . . . That's an attractive thing to a community, es-
> pecially to a community that does not have a lot of secondary em-
> ployment. . . . At the time TMC told us they can make about five

dollars an hour or one hundred dollars a week on approximately twenty hours of work. And, uh, by this community's standards, those were good wages.

One factory employing mostly women left after a union dispute over wages, and the local Development Board sought to replace those jobs "because it definitely hurts when you lose the secondary income, but not nearly as bad as if it's the primary income." The home assembly jobs were created specifically with married women workers in mind because the wage level was identified as "secondary" or inadequate as the sole support of a person or a family.

> We have not attracted the highest class of employer. That's no condemnation of the people that we have. But we have attracted at this point, secondary employment. Right. That's a low-paying employment, but it's something here in the community. . . . It was another form of employment. It was never mentioned or introduced in this community as being a primary employer. I don't think that that type of labor is a primary employer. I don't know anybody that could live on that. It was intended as a supplemental employment. . . . The intent being that it was not intended to take the place of primary employment.

A primary job in this community, said the official, is farming, and the image of the farmer is definitely male:

> We are a farming community, it's our primary business. The farmer is an expert with so many things. He's an expert at marketing his product. He's an expert purchasing agent. And yet he's a small independent guy. He's an excellent mechanical repairman.

Secondary employment is for "farmers' wives," and that is precisely how the homeworking contracts were advertised around the community: jobs for farmers' wives to help improve the cash flow in farming households. But the realities of homeworkers' experiences are long hours and low pay because, as Mollie said, "I'm trying to fit a full-time job into another full-time job." Creating secondary jobs as part of local development gives public credence to the secondary economic status of women, supporting women's dependence in families; it also reinforces the privilege of men to hold jobs that offer higher pay, status, security, and benefits. Such local development gives official support to the sex-based division of labor in the home and in the labor market.

Still as a job option homeworking is desired by the workers, partly because of its consonance with certain values, and it is in great demand in both communities. Thus it is important as a policy consideration to examine the possibilities of preserving the desired aspects of homeworking while improving upon those conditions cited by the workers as disadvantageous to them. An exploration of homeworking in rural and urban contexts as well as across industrial sectors and national boundaries will help to inform such policy considerations.

6

Homework in a Comparative Context

Interviews with homeworkers provide a rich and detailed source of information regarding their perspectives and experiences. How comparable are the perspectives and working conditions of the Riverton and Prairie Hills homeworkers to those of homeworkers who do garment or clerical work, who work for more than one company, or who live in urban areas or other countries? A broader understanding of the homeworking experience calls for a comparative look at several qualitative studies of homeworkers.

The studies chosen for comparison use qualitative methodologies that present sufficient data in the voices of the homeworkers to allow for discussion of similar themes across the different groups of workers.[1] The first study is based on interviews with fourteen male and twenty-one female home-based informal workers in Silicon Valley, California, who perform clerical, electronics, assembly, and white-collar work related to the information-processing industry.[2] The comparison is broadened by examining different types of homework in an urban area of the United States that are performed under different contractual arrangements. Some of these workers are truly independent contractors who negotiate fees and work activities with various clients or companies; many of these workers, however, depend regularly on one principal client-company, making them pseudoemployees or, as Beverly Lozano calls them "self-employees."[3] Kathleen Christensen's study of home-based workers focuses on women who run businesses from their homes, principally in the area of clerical and computer work.[4] Jamie Dangler studied electronics homeworkers in central New York, most of whom lived in small towns and rural areas and assembled wire coils for various major manufacturers.[5] The Vermont knitters are also rural homeworkers and, unlike many of the other U.S. homeworkers studied here, are the only contractors working in an industry in which homework was previously prohibited but that is now regulated by the FLSA.[6] Cynthia Costello studied insurance-claims homeworkers in Madison, Wisconsin, noting that the employer, Wisconsin Physicians Service (WPS), used homeworking to avoid unionization. The WPS homeworkers are the only contractors, to my knowledge, who are paid on an hourly basis and thus are guaranteed minimum wage for their work.[7] These cases taken together help to broaden the picture of contemporary U.S. homeworkers.

In Great Britain one study included interviews with ninety female homeworkers whose work varied from garment construction and knitting, clerical work, and assembly work to packing and packaging a wide range of goods.[8] In another study fifty homeworkers, one of whom was male, were interviewed in four cities in England, with more than half the respondents living in the London area.[9] These homeworkers represented a variety of job activities that the authors classify into five types: manufacturing, needlework, office and clerical work, babysitting, and other semiprofessional work. This is the only study that includes home-based child care as a type of homework, a category that will not be included for the purposes of this comparison.[10]

Homeworking and other informal economic work have been recognized as important contributions to regional economies in developing nations.[11] Lourdes Benería and Martha Roldán compare and examine a variety of types of homework in low-income urban settlements in Mexico City. They interviewed sixty homeworkers, all of whom were women and seven of whom were single heads of household. These authors found several kinds of work being performed in the home: garment construction; assembly of toys, plastic bags, cartons, and latches; plastic polishing; textile finishing; quality-control inspection of factory work, and packing of sunflower seeds.[12]

Differences among all the homeworkers in these studies help to develop the basis of the comparison. More striking, however, are the several commonalities that emerge from these interviews regarding working conditions, the organization of production, the use of family labor, and the implication of homework for the worker's identity.

WORKING CONDITIONS

The workers interviewed in Silicon Valley and the WPS homeworkers earned income that on the average consistently reached or was above the hourly minimum wage on a regular basis.[13] One of the Vermont knitters who testified at public hearings reported earning five dollars per hour on a good day when there where no problems with children or the knitting; all other days, she claimed, she earned the minimum wage.[14] The Silicon Valley workers earned above minimum, partly because wages are generally higher in the San Francisco Bay Area than in most other parts of the United States, especially compared to the rural areas of the Midwest and New England. But their higher wages are also explained by their labor status: Unlike the homeworkers interviewed in central New York, Vermont, the Midwest, Mexico City, or Great Britain, these workers are mostly independent informal workers based at home who set or negotiate the terms of each contract they accept, including pay. The workers in Silicon Valley and in central New York are involved in various aspects of the high-tech electronics industry, but the pay of the homeworkers lags behind the average pay of the self-employees in California. Thus, the employment status of the worker as well as the type of work and the industrial sector are important factors in examining earnings potential.

For example, the homeworkers in Mexico City averaged earnings each week that were less than one-third the minimum wage, and in Great Britain workers often earned wages that fell below the "low pay standard." The automotive homeworkers in the Midwest averaged hourly earnings from slightly below to slightly above the minimum wage ($3.65 at the time of interview), and electronics homeworkers in central New York found it "hard to make minimum wage." Some of the variation in pay rates is associated with the different types of work being done in the home; garment work, knitting, and various kinds of packing, commonly done in Great Britain and Mexico City, are among the lowest paid jobs for homeworkers. Yet these lower-paid workers often described their pay as "not bad for homework." Some of the pay variation also may be explained by the different contractual agreements.

The workers in these studies were not offered or given access to any fringe benefits as part of their work. In most households the family had no health or life insurance unless they were covered through the employment of another member of the household. In Lozano's study of informal workers, fewer than one-third provided health-insurance coverage for themselves. Homeworkers in Riverton and Prairie Hills were most often covered through one adult's employment, and among those workers who provided their own coverage the earnings from homeworking just covered the cost of the policy. As one Riverton worker pointed out, "That's one of the reasons why I'm doing this, is because our health insurance is so expensive. . . . With Blue Cross–Blue Shield our monthly premium is $350." Another homeworker said her monthly premium was $250, or the equivalent of two-weeks' worth of assembly work. Neither of these two health policies gave the workers 100 percent coverage for major medical care or for office visits. The homeworkers in Mexico City had the least access to health-care coverage because more of these workers lived in households where other adults were unemployed or only sporadically employed, which made them ineligible for health care through Seguro Social. Homeworkers in Great Britain were covered through the National Health system.

Low pay and the lack of health insurance reveal the components of dependency in homework as employment. The pay is not intended to be a living wage but is considered a complement or supplement to other sources of income in the household. The lack of health coverage is certainly motivated by the employer's desire for cost containment but again suggests the assumption that homeworkers will have access to health care through another employed adult. Homework is dependent work, employment that needs to be undertaken in conjunction with formal-sector work; homeworkers thus become dependent workers who must have formal workers in their household in order to earn a living family wage. Indeed, the need for formal employment is emphasized by the fact that a portion of homeworkers studied in the Midwest, California, and Great Britain actually hold full- or part-time formal jobs themselves in addition to their homework.

Instability in homeworking is another aspect that tends to make the worker dependent on other forms of income. The workers interviewed spoke of work stoppages, of factory shutdowns that affected their supply of work, and of varying quantities of work from one week to the next. Home-based informal workers or entrepreneurs also spoke of "lean times" when they might have little or no work; over time, these workers learned to plan for the variations in work. These variations also could result in fluctuating income for homeworkers since the piecerate often changed from one item to the next. One hand-knitter reported, "I earned $8.50 a week on average—occasionally I had thicker wool and earned about $10.20 a week."[15] Piecerate earnings also varied because the type of work changed each week, making it harder for the homeworker to build up speed and accuracy.

Homeworkers find that they are dependent upon the supplier for the flow, quantity, and type of work, a situation that affects their earnings.

Homeworkers understand that the low pay and lack of fringe benefits are directly connected to their home and family responsibilities; that is, working at home is often perceived as a major advantage for which the worker forgoes regular wages and benefits. One homeworker remarked, "With children you can't have the best of everything," and another said, "That is the object of people working at home. I know we're paid a lot less."[16] A white-collar worker in Riverton was more explicit about flexibility as a fringe benefit:

> I have two girls that work for me. One works full-time, and one works part-time. The part-time girl has more flexibility and she takes advantage of it. She left this afternoon at 3:00. You know, I need her help right now, but she had something going on. That's her fringe benefit. That's the fringe benefit I can give her, flexibility. For a young mother, that's the fringe benefit she needs. And I feel that probably [homework] offers some of that as a benefit.

Attending to home and family is seen by the workers and others as a woman's primary responsibility. Being allowed to fulfill that responsibility while earning a wage thus comes to be defined as a fringe benefit in the absence of any material fringe benefits; indeed, it becomes the justification for low wages and no material benefits. It is difficult to think of other jobs or careers in which the fulfillment of one's family duty, however perceived, is a major part of the wage-and-benefit package the employer offers.

ORGANIZATION OF PRODUCTION

Working at home does seem to have the potential of allowing workers to combine a paid job with other responsibilities, at least to a certain extent. Homeworkers often say that autonomy in carrying out tasks without supervision and flexibility in setting their working hours are important advantages to them. Yet in discussing these two topics, homeworkers usually consider both sides of the coin, pointing out the limits and the benefits of autonomy and flexibility.

Autonomy, or freedom from the direct, daily supervision of the formal workplace, motivated the Silicon Valley workers to take up informal-sector activities; thirty-one of thirty-five workers had left formal-sector establishments in order to work informally in their homes.[17] Supervision in formal-sector jobs was often described as "overbearing" or as an impediment to accomplishing the work. These workers were willing to exchange income security and benefits for freedom from supervision and more control over their production. One informal homeworker commented that if there was work she did not want to take, she could refuse it. As Lozano points out, "A bossy client can be referred elsewhere. One's boss cannot be so easily dispatched."[18] Autonomy in this form, however, is largely limited to independent contractors working at home.

The situation of homeworkers in central New York and in Vermont was somewhat unusual in that they could set the amount of work they wished to take during any given time period.[19] These homeworkers did not experience work quotas or externally set work rates and enjoyed the autonomy they had to determine their workload.

Yet the experience of homeworkers in several other studies more closely resembled that of formal-sector employees in that work cannot be refused or the quantity controlled and the supplier is more like a regular boss. WPS required that homeworkers be at home from 4:00 P.M. to 7:00 P.M. Monday through Thursday to receive the bucket of claims that would be delivered; the homeworkers had no control over the quantity of claims or the specific time the claims would arrive. All work from the previous day had to be completed by the next day's delivery, with the exception of Thursday's delivery, which was picked up on Monday.[20] The organization of this work served to maintain the employer's control over the speed and the quantity of work; although it is less supervision than one would have in an office, it hardly bespeaks of independence for the worker.

Homeworkers often said they could not refuse work because they feared the loss of their job: "I take what I can get. It depends on the job. That one was hard, but I've got to stick it out because if you say you don't want it then he might not bring another home job round for me."[21] Perceiving an abundant supply of labor, most homeworkers are reluctant to refuse work or to request higher pay and were quick to point out, "I don't want to lose it. There's always someone to jump in."[22] Another said, "I feel as if there's a lot of people ready to step in. I'd be frightened of losing the job."[23] Sometimes this fear is based on another worker's experience:

I don't ever give it a thought, sort of ringing up and saying I want more money. Because the girl that lost the job before me, she kept bleating on she was worth more money and you're only worth what he wants to give you really. That's how it works really.[24]

Homeworkers in the midwestern communities expressed similar concerns associated with requesting higher piecerates. The knowledge that so many people had applied for the positions as contractors kept many workers silent on the topic of wages.

Autonomy in this setting is limited to a literal interpretation of freedom from supervision; that is, the homeworkers are not supervised as they would be if employed inside a factory. Payment by result and by deadlines, however, is an effective and invisible way of supervising workers. Autonomy becomes the freedom to produce what the supplier will pay for within the time limits set by the company or supplier. Even in the best of situations the autonomy of working at home can come to mean isolation for the worker, a lack of contact with other homeworkers; isolation also may lead to greater control over the homeworker, an important factor in setting pay rates, determining quantities and deadlines, and impeding organization among workers.

If the claims of autonomy and flexibility seem so hollow in the experiences of the homeworkers, why are these aspects continually mentioned as advantages? One possible answer is that in working at home, the potential for autonomy may appear greater to the worker, who sees that as advantageous. As one informal worker in California explained it, "Just the *idea* that you *could* have more freedom gives you a sense of well-being. You have a feeling of freedom, even though it may not be a reality. In this business, at least you feel like you have the possibility."[25] Other homeworkers mentioned the freedom to take a break when they wanted even in a tight schedule or to use the phone. As the homeworker said, just the feeling of freedom seems to improve the work atmosphere for some people.

Having a sense of control over her working life, however thin it may appear to be at times, contributes to a worker's sense of well-being that cannot be underestimated by the outside observer, especially in the case of women who see homework as one possible way of balancing family care with wage work. If autonomy and flexibility are important to the homeworkers as advantages, one alternative might be to reorganize home-based work so that workers do have control over productive work and can balance it with family responsibilities as necessary. The other side of the coin, however, is to think of ways to reorganize family care so that women are not by gender the only people assigned to balance or integrate reproductive work with wage work.

FAMILY LABOR

Some homeworkers balance paid and unpaid work in the home by bringing other members of the family or the neighborhood into the labor process. Both informal independent workers and homeworkers regularly brought other people in, some of whom were paid for their help but not all. One woman in Prairie Hills spoke of another worker's speed with the bolt assembly, a speed that depended on family helpers:

> Now, I know there's women. . . . But acourse they have a lotta kids to help, but I know I hear them say, "Well, I got my kit on Monday and I had it done on Wednesday," ya know. . . . Well, I mean, there again, their kids help a lot. She's got three at home.

Often the helpers in the family are the children, especially when the work is relatively unskilled and repetitive; a British homeworker reported, "My daughter will make up the boxes, and my son will help too with the mottos."[26] Lozano interviewed a woman who assembled circuit boards at home and whose children were integral to the work process: "I trained my kids. They were, oh—five, seven, and nine years old. They would stuff the boards, and I would solder them, and we make $2.50 a board, or some outrageously low rate like that."[27] In many of these studies family and child labor were observed and reported as a common feature of the process. It seems that the less the work paid and the less skill was involved, the more likely children, family, and friends were to participate. Garment work and unskilled manufacturing assembly work paid less than other forms of homework and commonly involved family helpers in the process. Benería and Roldán observed that poorer families were more likely to require children's help in homeworking, perhaps because these families were also more likely to do less skilled and lower paid homework.[28]

Incorporating family and friends into the work process puts the homeworker in the position of supervising other people's work and of acting as a manager of the labor supply available in the household. An assembler in Prairie Hills watched over family helpers as they worked: "I probably do two-thirds of the work, and then my son and my husband probably help on the other third. But I'm out there during that other third, you know." Family labor requires supervision, a role that usually falls to the main homeworker because the work or contract is in her name. One homeworker in Prairie Hills recognized that it was "up to me to make sure that it got done every week."

Family and friends become social and economic resources for homeworkers as they contribute to the labor process. Although demands based on family ties may motivate a woman to work at home, later those ties become the basis for labor participation that successfully supports the continuation of homeworking. Having a strong extended family or close neighborhood ties helps a woman homeworker in achieving that balance between paid and unpaid work that often motivates her to take work home. In this sense, rural homeworking families in the Midwest resemble families in households in Mexico City, Great Britain, Spain, and India in which women supervise the sharing of labor and resources in order to maximize income and to maintain the household.

WORKERS' IDENTITY

For women homeworkers the home is the location for her work responsibilities, both paid and unpaid; as the focus of her energies and efforts each day, it takes on central importance for her as wife, mother, and worker. Because her primary responsibilities are defined as taking care of home and family, her paid work in the home merges with her unpaid duties. Like housework, homework is rarely acknowledged as a "real job" because it is done at home, and families expect the duties of wives and mothers to take higher priority than that of paid work. Through her work and responsibilities, the worker herself becomes centered on the home in such a way that she does not see herself as a worker; she is in the home, working as she has always worked. As one homeworker said, "[It] doesn't feel as though I'm really working 'cause I'm in the house."[29]

Such a strong identification with the home has several implications for women as homeworkers. Homework is not defined as a real job, so it becomes harder for these women to see themselves as workers and consequently to take action as such. One British homeworker said she thought it would be too hard to unionize such a dispersed work force: "Quite honestly, I just think of my family rather than us outworkers as a whole."[30] The lack of a formal workplace where workers can identify with each other, combined with work that lacks the status of a real job, can lead many homeworkers to "think of family" rather than of their coworkers. This focus is sharpened by the incorporation of family members as helpers; homework is so deeply embedded in the context of family that it easily can impede the worker from identifying herself and others as workers. The lack of a common worker identity and the dispersion and isolation of the home work force are effective obstacles in the path of any collective action.

Homeworkers have been unwilling to make demands about the piecerate, for example. Most homeworkers complain about low rates or at least mention that the employer could be paying more; many homeworkers in these studies had not received any increase in pay, regardless of the length of time employed.[31] Two reasons for their reticence were given: either they were reluctant to speak up for an increase for fear of job loss or they were grateful to be able to make any money at all working at home. Often homeworkers would say, "I'm just a housewife, I can't ask for more." One British homeworker said that even her husband got angry over how little she was paid and that "he thinks I'm a fool 'cause I'm frightened to ask for more."[32] An isolated and dispersed work force certainly benefits the employing firms through maintenance of lower labor costs over long periods of time.

Another common implication of being centered in the home is the perception that homework is "not real work" and that the homeworker consequently can still do all the housework. A Riverton homeworker puzzled over her family's ideas of work:

> I don't think the kids ever look at it as a real job. I'm home. I should be able to do all this. I mean, my daughter comes home and if the house is a mess, she says, "Well, how come you couldn't have cleaned this house today?" They don't look at it, whereas if I'd a been gone all day, she wouldn't a wondered why nothin' got done. . . . I mean, if I went out and did [the assembly work], it would be a real job. I'm home, and if you're home, you're s'posed to be, so it's not a real job. I don't know if it's a hobby, but it's just s'posed ta be somethin' I do in my spare time, but I have no spare time, so it hasta be a real job.

Her neighbor, also a homeworker, concurred: "Yea, 'cause when I first worked out of the home, he used to do a lot more. He used to help, like he'd do the dishes, or he'd do the laundry. Every now and then. And now, when I'm home, you know, it's my job." The lack of formal, spatial separation seems to indicate to other family members that homework is not a real job like outside jobs, that it is more like housework. One WPS homeworker said, "My husband doesn't see it as a job because I am home."[33] Homework is firmly entrenched in the same category as housework in the perceptions of most family members, and that category is women's work. Homework physically centers the worker in the home and bolsters others people's beliefs that home is her domain and responsibility.

This comparison of the experiences of various homeworkers highlights the importance of a gender-based division of labor within the home to the continuation of homeworking. It is consistently observed that across different countries, types of work, and labor contracts, women's roles and responsibilities for home and family coupled with the need to earn income are circumstances that favor working at home. Yet these circumstances also seem to support common working conditions that are unfavorable to the homeworker and indirectly to her family: long hours, low pay, fluctuating income, and job insecurity. In short, the need to balance family care and wage work in the home can result in dependence for the homeworker, dependence on another's income and participation in the wage-labor process. It is important to distinguish between women choosing to balance paid and unpaid work and women as workers "choosing" the consequences of low pay and other conditions of homeworking. Their experiences indicate that as workers they tolerate the disadvantages of homework because of the lack of available employment and because of family-care options that allow them to meet or share multiple responsibilities.

A major difference among homeworkers across different countries, however, lies in the realm of public policy regulating home-based employment. The International Labour Office (ILO) issued a report in 1989, detailing member countries' policies that define and regulate homework.[34] Many countries, from industrialized to developing nations, explicitly regulate homework either as part of the general labor codes or as specific types of work within industries or by legislation specifically aimed at homework. The United States regulates homework only in certain industries as part of the general codes under the Fair Labor Standards Act.

In the various ILO member countries, legislative provisions for homeworkers vary a great deal, but these provisions are noticeably more detailed in countries other than the United States. For example, Germany and Uruguay have laws that provide for unemployment support for homeworkers; Argentina, Austria, Germany, Uruguay, France, Ontario, and Cuba provide for paid leave for continuously employed homeworkers. The law in Argentina mandates paid leave if the homeworker works forty-two weeks of the calendar year; interestingly, homeworkers in Prairie Hills and Riverton would be entitled to paid leave if such a law existed in the United States. Austrian law specifies paid annual leave of two-and-one-half days for each month of employment after six months of continuous employment. In Ontario homeworkers are entitled to two weeks paid leave after twelve months of employment.

Within specific industries, some countries have regulated the conditions for homeworking, sometimes through support of industry-wide collective agreements. In Denmark, the garment and textile industries have a collective agreement that provides overtime pay for homeworkers equal to that of factory workers; the watch industry in Switzerland has a similar collective agreement. In the Netherlands and Sweden, the collective agreements provide for Social Security for homeworkers. Other collective agreements specify how employers are to calculate the piecerate and require that they supplement it to defray the costs of overhead. The collective agreement of the garment industry in Belgium mandates a 10 percent supplement to defray overhead costs and a 15 percent supplement if the homeworker provides the materials to do the work. Several collective agreements provide wage supplements for work required on Sundays and public holidays. In Norway, employers are not allowed to give out homework in the garment and textile industries unless all factory workers are employed at full capacity, thus protecting inside workers from competition. In Sweden, collective agreements in the engineering sector mandate that employers cover homeworkers with life insurance, severance pay, and injury and pension policies.

It is not clear from the ILO report the extent to which these laws and provisions for homeworkers are actually enforced. The U.S. laws cited are inconsistently and minimally enforced so it is possible that provisions in the legal codes and collective agreements in other countries may not greatly affect the experience of homeworkers. On the other hand, the presence of public policy and collective agreements with provisions to define homeworkers, to recognize their work, and to set acceptable working conditions is evidence of the extent to which homeworkers are legitimate workers in other countries. Even if enforcement is poor, the policies and agreements recognize the existence and work of homeworkers and offer potential legal recourse to them as workers. Further, the policies of other countries offer alternatives that could be considered in the United States: explicit regulation of working conditions, joint state-industry collective agreements, and industry-wide collective agreements.

In contrast to many of these international examples, the United States has recently concentrated energy on deregulation of homework in the several industries in which it was previously regulated and has allowed the development of homework in a burgeoning number of unregulated industries. Interestingly, it was the case of the Vermont knitters who brought the issue of homework to public attention in 1980 in their struggle to keep their home-knitting jobs, which were threatened by the Department of Labor's enforcement of the ban on producing knitted outerwear in the home.[35] This struggle gave rise to congressional hearings during the 1980s in which lawmakers, manufacturers, and union organizers discussed, sometimes heatedly and almost always with passion, whether the existing bans on homework should be lifted. Conservative lawmakers such as Sen. Orrin Hatch (R.-Utah) strongly believed that the bans should be lifted. Homework, argued the conservatives, was the best-of-all-work-worlds for women with dependent children, especially rural women, who could stay home and care properly for children while earning money. Homeworkers, in the conservative perspective, were educated, English-speaking, self-reliant, married white women who lived in nice homes and who knew and were willing to exercise their rights as workers, as typified by the Vermont knitters. They clearly did not need or want the protection of government; the homework bans were an impediment to their pioneering, hard-working spirit.

Liberal lawmakers, joined by union organizers, relied on the image of the urban immigrant woman who lacked the education to know her rights and the language skills to protect herself. She was most often portrayed as a woman of color, immigrating to the urban United States from a developing or even an underdeveloped nation. In the view of the liberals and the unions her inability to protect herself meant that it was the duty of government to uphold the bans on homework in order to protect defenseless, exploited workers.

Within these hearings and discussions, it is notable that very few homeworkers testified; of those who did, most were rural and white. They represented not only the Vermont knitters but also the situations of other white, middle-class homeworkers: They pleaded for government to lift the bans and save their jobs, arguing that the organization of home-based production would keep afloat many small rural manufacturers, aiding rural-development efforts to maintain the viability of small communities. Thus, decline in the agricultural and manufacturing sectors, economic decline in rural communities, the restructuring of production, and the efforts of a conservative administration to deregulate various aspects of the economy during the 1980s converged to support homeworking as viable employment in rural areas.

In some ways the successful efforts to deregulate homework in previously regulated industries and the unwillingness to regulate the "new" homeworkers could be understood as an unwillingness to recognize homeworkers as workers. The relative lack of policies or collective agreements regulating the conditions of homework in the United States perpetuates the veil of invisibility covering homeworkers. Thus federal policy becomes complicit in separating the private sphere of the household from the public sphere of the market economy, relegating homework to the private sphere where public policy fears to intervene and leaving homeworkers isolated and on their own to establish standards of employment.

This lack of support and recognition for homeworkers through public policy may lead them to consider other alternatives of organization; voluntary groups in other countries offer options that may be useful to consider within the United States. In India, the Self-Employed Women's Association (SEWA) is a registered trade union representing the interests of women employed in home-based work. It covers a wide range of activities including protection of homeworkers who experience disadvantage because of the lack of enforcement of existing protective legislation, sponsorship of cooperatives of homeworking women, extension of credit and loans to rural women homeworkers, education programs, and research and video films on working women in India. SEWA offers the example of cooperatively organizing women for their benefit as workers, thus legitimizing the many roles within market production that women may fill. Such associations are not a substitute for public policies that function to legitimate women's work roles but are a complement to them, organized around the interests of women workers and designed to ensure the intent and enforcement of labor legislation.

These associations, organizations, or cooperatives could work in a number of ways. Homeworkers' organizations could bring together home-based wage earners across industrial sectors, or groups could be organized by specific industries, such as electronics or clerical homeworking, or by geography, with people interested in home-based wage work in a given region in one association. In Missouri, for example, one rural extension worker told me that she was trying to find a way for small textile manufacturers to continue to employ rural women to sew at home; they wanted to work at home, and the manufacturers found it a cost-effective mode of production that increased their business viability.[36] Here was a fertile context for the development of two organizations, a workers' association and a consortium of small manufacturers that would probably be geographically based. The workers' association would decrease the isolation of rural homeworkers and could collectively establish acceptable and consistent working conditions among the homeworkers; the employers' consortium could send work to the association to be distributed to the homeworkers. In a context where homework is a desired option, organizations for workers offer the possibilities of local, worker-based regulation and control over the processes of production.

Industrial homeworking has been examined in the context of state-supported rural development in an effort to understand the ways in which homeworking was incorporated into the development strategy in two midwestern communities. The factors that support industrial homeworking in these rural areas are local economic conditions, principally the decline in agricultural and manufacturing sectors, and the active support of the subnational states in recruiting TMC. At the same time, industrial firms are attempting to remain competitive by restructuring production and relocating employment; one result is the use of industrial homeworking.

The early 1980s brought difficult times economically for small communities that were agriculturally dependent or reliant on manufacturing for employment. The decline in the values of land and of farm products and high farm indebtedness left local economies unable to absorb the increasing numbers of people seeking wage employment. Local businesses suffered from the reduced cash flow in the retail market in small, agriculturally dependent locales. The primary resource such communities often market to an outside industry is its willing, compliant, and often cheap labor supply; married women in rural areas constitute a large segment of this resource. Many of these women are newly seeking wage labor or, along with many unemployed men, have been laid off from local industries now closed. The need to increase household income, the decreased security of farming income, and the insecurity and lack of local employment options are the main factors contributing to the rise in the rural work-seeking population.[37]

At the local level, structural factors such as high unemployment resulting from the decline in agriculture and manufacturing motivated local officials to recruit industries to increase job creation. Local banks supported job creation through provision of low- or no-interest financing; state support included financing, money for job training, loans, and various tax incentives. Local and subnational state development officials initiated and supported the creation of homeworking jobs because they defined development, in part, as any increase in available employment. Financial support and incentives to create homeworking jobs indicate that the local states in Prairie Hills and Riverton absorbed relocation, building, and training costs for TMC.

Yet the increased need for employment and the availability of mobile manufacturing jobs are not enough to make industrial homework an integral part of rural development. In the case of providing secondary jobs for local unemployed women, the local state development process is infused with a particular understanding of how households are organized, who does what work, and how that work is valued. Traditional expectations about women's paid and unpaid work that lead industry and development officials and indeed the workers themselves to speak of homework as a "wonderful opportunity" for women workers are a necessary, though not a sufficient, condition for homeworking to become part of an accepted rural-development strategy. Home-based industrial production depends on traditional, hierarchical gender relations both in the home and in the labor market, and the material conditions of the work itself tend to reinforce and reproduce these same relations.

Local norms and values played a role in the acceptance of homeworking jobs as development. Widespread local perception of women's primary responsibilities as centered on home and family tends to define women as secondary workers who earn supplemental wages; thus homeworking as a secondary job for women fit beautifully with these prevalent notions. The value local people place on women fulfilling those responsibilities within the home assured local officials and industrial managers of a constant labor supply. Women workers themselves hold these values and feel that homeworking, despite the low pay, is one way to balance their paid and unpaid responsibilities.

Interview data provided a household-level view of homeworkers' paid and unpaid working conditions. The low pay, Social Security deductions, contributions to the process of production, and the provision of space and utilities illustrated the ways in which homeworkers absorbed costs normally covered by employers and the public sector. Examining these conditions revealed that the savings realized by the employers in lowered labor and overhead costs are possible because the workers materially subsidize production. The greater profits that General Motors and TMC enjoy thus cost the workers in terms of pay and benefits, space, utilities, transportation, and contributions to the process and organization of production.

Increasing the profitability of production is further possible through the employment of a predominantly female labor force. Circumstances in the home, such as the division of family care and

housework among women and men, the lack of formal spatial separation, and the perception that homework is not a real job, showed that
women and men experience homeworking differently. For women,
homework is integrated with the unpaid, daily tasks of taking care of
children and the home; for men, homework tends to be associated
with their other paid work and is often defined as a second job. Flexible work allows men to juggle work time and leisure time, but for
women the balance is between paid and unpaid work time.[38]

Industrial homework as a development strategy in this context
can be understood as being subsidized in two ways. First, through
the working conditions of this type of employment, the workers
themselves, largely women, are materially subsidizing industrial development. These conditions include variable low pay, lack of social
insurance benefits, low pay for training periods, contributions to re-
fine the work process without remuneration, the company's demands for rush work, and its standards regarding rejected work.
Women workers also tend to subsidize this kind of development
through their unpaid contributions to the household in the form of
housework and child care. Second, this kind of development illustrates the indirect state subsidy of particular sets of domestic relations: The informal-sector homework reinforces and reproduces traditional sex roles, and the local state, through training grants,
building subsidies, and tax incentives, is in effect supporting the
maintenance of domestic and labor-market relations in which
women are defined as low-paid, secondary workers. Thus the need
to understand the importance of gender relations to informal-sector
work and rural development is clear.

The homeworkers in Prairie Hills and Riverton are, as some researchers would call them, "disguised wage laborers" or informal-sector workers. They share aspects of the labor relations of both employees and of self-employed workers. For employees and for
homeworkers there are external controls on the hours, quantity, quality, and regularity of work; yet like self-employed workers, homeworkers are responsible for Social Security and any other social insurances, and the collective personal and productive resources in the
household are used to accomplish the work. Unlike the self-employed, however, the homeworker does not control the means of production or the distribution of the profits. The homeworker who is informally employed essentially assumes the risks of self-employment
with few or none of the benefits; similarly, in comparison to the employee, the homeworker shares the aspects of controlled production
with none of the benefits or job security.

These distinctions in the employment status of homeworkers were clearly delineated during interviews in which the workers described conditions relating to the pay, the quantity, and the regularity of assembly work. The labor status of the workers is key in understanding homework as worker-subsidized development; because the homeworkers are not truly independent contractors, they cannot negotiate the terms of their employment and do not have control over pay, hours, workload, or benefits.

A continuous supply of women workers is necessary to the success of industrial homeworking in these communities. As long as women are considered secondary workers and primary home and family caretakers, the labor supply for homework will continue to exceed the demand. Domestic relations uphold women as ideal candidates for homework, and the organization of informal home production depends on these relations, tending to maintain and reproduce them. In a subtle way women subsidize informal-sector jobs through the acceptance and fulfillment of traditional gender roles in the home. Unpaid domestic labor is woman's first job and is used to justify her low wages in the labor market; this view supports and subsidizes industrial homeworking.

Evaluating industrial homework as part of rural development requires an assessment of how the profits and risks of homeworking are distributed among the various participants. The relationship between the local states and TMC showed that several of the costs of relocation were borne by the local states and development corporations; the company was able to move to Prairie Hills and Riverton without risking any capital investment that could not be pulled out easily in the event of failure. By leasing a building constructed and owned by the local development corporations, for example, the company avoided the risk of land ownership and could move more easily when and if necessary. Other costs absorbed by the local states included taxes, loan financing, construction, utilities, and worker-training subsidies. This pattern of absorbing costs for the industrial firm reveals that the risks of generating new employment locally were not shared but were carried by the local states.

Many of the costs of employment are passed on to the workers insofar as they are paid by piecerate and are not for any other contributions they routinely make to the process of production. The workers benefit from the increased income, but because of their status as independent contractors they forgo the social benefits usually given to employees. In its relationship with the workers, the company profits from efficient production with almost no overhead costs.

In terms of development these two case studies suggest that industrial homework as part of a rural-development strategy in Prairie Hills and Riverton reaps greater benefits for TMC than it does for either the local states or the homeworkers. Although the local states and the workers do benefit from this employment TMC apparently gains disproportionately relative to its contributions since it does not share any of the risks of home-based production. The local states and the homeworkers, on the other hand, contribute disproportionately compared to the benefits they receive.

One could conclude that homework should not be part of rural development because the workers and communities absorb most of the costs and the risks rather than the firms. Yet it is important to consider the ways in which the creation of homeworking jobs could be made more proportionately beneficial to the locales and to the workers. Recommendations to modify the existing organization of production are made in relation to the homeworkers' repeated preference for the opportunity to work at home and their desire to combine various responsibilities. These suggestions are in keeping with many homeworkers' ideas regarding improvements that could greatly enhance their work situation.

Workers most frequently mentioned pay rates and the lack of benefits as two aspects of homeworking that should be changed. Especially in Riverton where the piecerate was low, many workers felt that the company should be paying them more for the hours and effort they put in. And workers who thought that the piecerate was adequate complained that TMC never gave them a raise even after three to four years of employment. The lack of a raise aggravated several workers, who asked, "Would you stay on a job where you never got a raise?" Many workers also mentioned fluctuations in income as a problem, a result of variations in the workload. These aspects of homeworking as well as others could be changed if the workers truly were independent contractors.

First, control of the work contract could be turned over to the homeworkers, allowing them to be independent or self-employed workers. As such, the homeworkers could form a cooperative or an association of self-employed, home-based workers and could negotiate the terms of their contracts. As a formally associated group they could make health insurance and other benefits available at a group rate; collectively, they could bargain with private firms and with the local state to support access to benefits such as health insurance. Associated workers could better determine the quantity and the frequency of their own workloads and would have better control of and knowledge about expected income.

Second, if local states are going to continue to support informal-sector work such as homeworking, then the state should take its role in development more seriously vis-à-vis the workers. Local and sub-national states can help homeworkers gain increased control over their work by supporting increased access to health care and other so-cial-insurance benefits and in actively promoting private-public sector cooperation. In Prairie Hills and Riverton the local states acted to sup-port the industrial firm seeking to relocate; in the future the local state could act in behalf of both parties, supporting capital investment in communities but also strengthening the collective position of workers to negotiate working conditions. For example, the local state could support the workers through cooperative associations that would en-deavor to increase access to health and social benefits, disseminate la-bor-status and business information, and alleviate the isolation cur-rently experienced by many homeworkers.

Local and subnational states could assume a more prominent role in educating current and potential homeworkers about their labor sta-tus and their rights as employees or independent business people. The states must recognize that when they actively support the crea-tion of homeworking jobs, they take on the responsibility of inform-ing workers and communities about the implications of work orga-nized at home. There are laws governing the payment of Social Security and unemployment taxes as well as regulations about em-ployment status, and local officials and homeworkers must be aware of them.

Local and regional states are capable of changing and strengthen-ing their roles in development because of decentralization. Develop-ment is not a federal government activity or program; individual states and local communities are responsible for their economic and community development and have great influence over the process and outcomes. Since local norms and values clearly are important to the development process in each community, subnational states, as part of their program, could disseminate information on alternative approaches to structuring home-based work, including cooperatives, associations, or other collectives supporting self-employed workers.

Subnational states should take the initiative in educating local de-velopment officials and county employment agencies about the ef-fects of sex-based stereotypes such as classifying women as secondary workers. The state could assist county and local officials in setting up the mechanisms and support for women to enter non-traditional jobs and occupations. For example, during a visit to a local factory, a young female worker who had advanced to skilled machine work said she thought more women did not follow her into this better paid work because it was seen as men's work and it was hard for women to cross over from the lower paying, female-dominated work. Supporting women's entry into nontraditional jobs would serve to increase their labor-market options and would slowly break down persistent notions of women as secondary workers. A benefit for the local community is that women working as plumbers and electricians, for example, could help fill some of the skilled-trade positions that currently may be difficult to fill.[39]

Integral to the regional and local states' efforts to increase female employment in nontraditional areas are the local, county, and regional job centers, employment training, and required work programs, offices that usually act as a liaison between local private employers and those people seeking work. Often, these programs have particular mandates to serve special populations of job seekers: the long-term unemployed, the hard-to-employ, dislocated workers and homemakers, and low-income persons, especially women with dependent children. Subnational and local states need to work with these programs to decrease pervasive stereotypes of women as secondary workers who need to earn only supplemental income. These attitudes can be influential in job and employment counseling and can continue to channel women into unskilled, low-paying, dead-end jobs that contribute to the persistence of the stereotypes. Social workers in these agencies can be educated to assist in changing job counseling so that it encourages and supports women in seeking nontraditional work; they can also help employers in recruiting and retaining women in those jobs currently dominated by men. Women workers need consistent support to enter nontraditional jobs and occupations, especially in rural areas; by developing support groups for women workers, social workers can educate them about their rights as workers and increase their awareness of sexual harassment and discrimination in the workplace. This kind of support and education is needed especially in small rural cities and towns that traditionally hold strong, negative attitudes toward working mothers and wives.

These recommendations are designed to increase women's options in the local labor market so that industrial homeworking will be one of several choices available rather than the only one. The development process itself could be open to a greater cross section of the local community; more people need to be involved in activities that affect them so directly. As locales increase participation in development, the process itself can serve to educate the community about men's and women's roles and their effects on employment opportunities. Educational efforts can be geared toward increasing information about existing options in development and about various strategies to broaden occupational opportunities. Development then can be based on the choices made by representative segments of the community rather than on the choices of one or two individuals negotiating with private firms.

THEORETICAL IMPLICATIONS

The cases of Prairie Hills and Riverton point to the need to redefine the meaning of development. Is development an activity that simply produces economic and quantifiable outcomes that can be measured by a given standard? Rather than relying on this economic approach, a kind of ledgerbook accounting, we should perceive and redefine development to fit the experiences of people living through it, the home-workers in each of these communities. Development could then be understood as "the many dimensions of human development, the educational, psychological, sexual, involving also community ties and human relations in addition to economic factors."[40] This working definition can propel us from the narrower view and can include factors such as participation in the process and decision-making, clarifying the different ways groups in a community experience new forms of development.[41]

Industrial homework as part of rural development also lends support to existing criticism of linear modernization theories of development.[42] These theories often posit that as economic development progresses, women's roles expand and increase, resulting in greater gender equality. Yet the form and organization of industrial homework depend upon gender-related differentiation at the household level; rather than expanding women's roles, homework solidifies the definition of women as primary home and family caretakers and as secondary workers. Prairie Hills and Riverton can be added to the list of places in which development does not necessarily mean progress toward equality, for women or for workers.[43]

Finally, we can understand that homeworking does not necessarily provide workers with the means to escape the harsh realities of market relationships or of formal workplaces. Homeworking provides no explicit division between relationships in the private and the public spheres or neat separations of productive and reproductive work; indeed those relationships once held to exist in the public sphere of the market now exist and are woven into the fabric of the private sphere. Homeworking enables the family to reproduce in the household the external market relationships of the dominant society, and to varying extents it allows household relations to shape the organization of production in the market. Such aspects include supervision of family members in wage labor, tension over hours and workload, and sex-based division of both productive and reproductive labor. Homeworking means that the private realm of the home is no longer separate (if it ever was) from the marketplace and that the private-public dualism is conceptually incorrect in analyzing this type of work. The theoretical division of public and private social relations was an analytic convenience that emerged from the examination of predominantly male market relations and was then imposed by researchers on all types of remunerative work. This fragmented framework did not grow from any examination of homework, long thought as obsolete, and indeed it does much damage as the notion of separate spheres supports and reinforces public policy in ignoring the needs and experiences of homeworkers. Continued research based on the experiences of homeworkers, their employers, and the macrostructural conditions supporting homework can help push theory beyond dualisms to a more complete framework for an understanding of these complex relationships.

Notes

INTRODUCTION

1. Pat Wagner, a rural sociologist, first, told me about homeworking in the community of Riverton, Wisconsin.

2. Alejandro Portes, "On the Sociology of National Development: Theories and Issues," *American Journal of Sociology* 82:1 (1976): 55–85.

CHAPTER ONE. INDUSTRIAL HOMEWORK AS RURAL DEVELOPMENT

1. Cited in Christopher Clark, *The Roots of Rural Capitalism* (Ithaca, N.Y.: Cornell University Press, 1990), p. 188.

2. See Mary Blewett, *Men, Women, and Work* (Urbana: University of Illinois Press, 1988), p. 29.

3. Property tax is paid indirectly through the lease payments to the local development corporation.

4. Barry Bluestone and Bennett Harrison, *The Deindustrialization of America* (New York: Basic Books, 1982); Michael J. Piore and Charles F. Sabel, *The Second Industrial Divide* (New York: Basic Books, 1984).

5. Throughout the book, I refer to three levels of the state. References to the national state indicate the programs and policies under the control of the federal government; the subnational state refers to the level of governmental programs and policies under the authority of individual states within the Union, such as Alaska; by the local state I mean the level of governmental activity within the community or municipality.

6. See Glenna Colclough, "Uneven Development and Racial Composition in the Deep South: 1970–1980," *Rural Sociology* 55 (Spring 1988): 73–86.

7. Alejandro Portes, "On the Sociology of National Development: Theories and Issues," *American Journal of Sociology* 82:1 (July 1976): 55–85.

8. See ibid.

9. See Lourdes Benería and Martha Roldán, *Crossroads of Gender, Race, and Class: Industrial Homeworking in Mexico* (Chicago: University of Chicago Press, 1987); Martha Roldán, "Industrial Outworking, Struggles for the Reproduction of Working-class Families and Gender Subordination," in N. Redclift and E. Mingione, eds., *Beyond Employment: Household, Gender, and Subsistence* (Oxford: Basil Blackwell, 1985, pp. 248–85); and Susan Tiano, "The Public-Private Dichotomy: Theoretical Perspectives on 'Women in Development,'" *Social Science Journal* 21 (1984): 11–27.

10. Lourdes Benería and Catherine Stimpson, *Women, Households, and the Economy* (New Brunswick, N.J.: Rutgers University Press, 1987); Tiano, "Public-Private Dichotomy."

11. Manuel Castells and Alejandro Portes, "World Underneath: The Origins, Dynamics, and Effects of the Informal Economy" (Paper presented at the Conference on the Comparative Study of the Informal Sector, Harpers Ferry, West Virginia, October 2–6, 1986).

12. See Saskia Sassen-Koob, "The Dynamics of Growth in Post-Industrial New York City" (Paper presented at the Workshop on the Dual City, New York City, 1986); Naomi Katz and David S. Kemnitzer, "Fast Forward: The Internationalization of Silicon Valley," in June Nash and María Patricia Fernández-Kelly, eds., *Women, Men, and the International Division of Labor* (Albany: State University of New York Press, 1983), pp. 332–45; Benería and Roldán, *Crossroads of Gender, Race, and Class*; Alejandro Portes and Lauren Benton, "Industrial Development and Labor Absorption: A Reinterpretation," *Population and Development Review* 10:4 (1984): 589–611; Cynthia Truelove, "The Informal Sector Revisited: The Case of the talleres rurales mini-maquilas in Colombia," in Richard Tardan, ed., *Crises in the Caribbean Basin* (Beverly Hills, Calif.: Sage, 1987), pp. 48–63; María Patricia Fernández-Kelly, *For We Are Sold, I and My People: Women and Industry in Mexico's Frontier* (Albany: State University of New York Press, 1983); and Castells and Portes, "World Underneath."

13. Julie A. Matthaei, *An Economic History of Women in America* (New York: Schocken Books, 1982); Christine Stansell, *City of Women: Sex and Class in New York, 1789–1860* (Chicago: University of Illinois Press, 1987).

14. R. W. Malcolmson, "Ways of Getting a Living in Eighteenth-Century England," in R. E. Pahl, ed., *On Work: Historical, Comparative, and Theoretical Approaches* (London: Basil Blackwell, 1988), pp. 48–60.

15. Clark, *Roots of Rural Capitalism*.

16. See Clark, *The Roots of Rural Capitalism*; Edith Abbott, *Women in Industry* (New York: D. Appleton and Company, 1924); Thomas Dublin, "Women and Outwork in a Nineteenth-Century New England Town," in S. Hahn and J. Prude, eds., *The Countryside in the Age of Capitalist Transformation* (Chapel Hill: University of North Carolina Press, 1985), pp. 51–70; and Blewett, *Men, Women, and Work.*

17. See Dublin, "Women and Outwork."

18. See Abbott, *Women in Industry.*

19. See Clark, *Roots of Rural Capitalism*; Blewett, *Men, Women, and Work.*

20. Blewett, *Men, Women, and Work.*

21. See Stansell, *City of Women,* and Matthaei, *Economic History of Women in America.*

22. See Alice Kessler-Harris, *Out to Work: A History of Wage-earning Women in the United States* (New York: Oxford University Press, 1982); Stansell, *City of Women.*

23. Eileen Boris, "Regulating Industrial Homework: The Triumph of 'Sacred Motherhood,'" *Journal of American History* 71:4 (1987): 745–63; Laura C. Johnson and Robert E. Johnson, *The Seam Allowance* (Toronto: Women's Educational Press, 1982); Cynthia Costello, *Home-based Work: Implications for Working Women* (Washington, D.C.: Women's Research and Education Institute, 1987).

24. See Stansell, *City of Women;* Kessler-Harris, *Out to Work.*

25. Eileen Boris, "Homework and Women's Rights: The Case of the Vermont Knitters, 1980–1985," *Signs: Journal of Women in Culture and Society* 13:1 (1987): 98–120.

26. Jamie Faracellia Dangler, "Electronic Subassemblers in Central New York: Nontraditional Homeworkers in a Nontraditional Homework Industry," in Eileen Boris and Cynthia R. Daniels, eds., *Homework: Historical and Contemporary Perspectives of Paid Labor at Home* (Urbana and Chicago: University of Illinois Press, 1989), pp. 147–64, and Boris, "Regulating Industrial Homework."

27. See, for example, House, Hearings before the Subcommittee on Labor Standards of the Committee on Education and Labor, "The Re-emergence of Sweatshops and the Enforcement of Wage and Hour Standards," 97th Cong., 1st and 2d sess., 1982; Senate, Hearings before the Subcommittee on Labor of the Committee on Labor and Human Resources, "Amending the Fair Labor Standards Act to Include Industrial Homework," February 9, 1984, 98th Cong., 2d sess.

28. Dangler, "Electronic Subassemblers."

29. Ibid.; Christina Gringeri, "Inscribing Gender in Rural Development: Industrial Homework in Two Midwestern Communities," *Rural Sociology* 58:1 (1993) 30–52.

30. Betty Beach, "The Family Context of Home Shoe Work," in Boris and Daniels, eds., *Homework,* pp. 130–46. For a full discussion of shoe homeworking in rural Maine, see Betty Beach, *Integrating Work and Family Life* (Albany: State University of New York, 1989).

31. Kathleen Christensen, "Home-based Clerical Work: No Simple Truth, No Single Reality," in Boris and Daniels, eds., *Homework,* pp. 183–97.

32. Beverly Lozano, *The Invisible Work Force* (New York: Free Press, 1989).

33. Cynthia B. Costello, "The Clerical Homework Program at the Wisconsin Physicians Service Insurance Corporation," in Boris and Daniels, eds., *Homework,* pp. 198–214.

34. Dangler, "Electronic Subassemblers."

35. I am intentionally distinguishing between those people who are employed and work in their homes and those who are self-employed and work from their homes. See Robert E. Kraut, "Homework: What Is It and Who Does It?" in Kathleen E. Christensen, ed., *The New Era of Home-Based Work* (Boulder, Colo.: Westview Press, 1988), pp. 30–48, for a clear discussion of these distinctions and their importance in making estimates of the prevalence of homeworking.

36. See Hilary Silver, "The Demand for Homework: Evidence from the

U.S. Census," in Boris and Daniels, eds., *Homework,* pp. 103–29; Kraut, "Homework"; and Christensen, *New Era of Home-based Work.*

37. Kraut, "Homework"; Christensen, *New Era of Home-based Work;* and Silver, "Demand for Homework."

38. Silver, "The Demand for Homework."

39. Christensen, *New Era of Home-based Work,* p. 79.

40. Dangler, "Electronic Subassemblers."

41. Castells and Portes, "World Underneath."

42. James M. Rubenstein, *The Changing U.S. Auto Industry: A Geographical Analysis* (New York: Routledge, 1992).

43. Castells and Portes, "World Underneath."

44. The Department of Labor defines industrial homework as "the production by any person in or about a home, apartment, tenement, or room in a residential establishment of goods for an employer who suffers or permits such production, regardless of the source (whether obtained from an employer or elsewhere) of the materials used by the homeworker in such production" (Subpart A-General [530.1 "d"] of Regulations, Part 530: Employment of Homeworkers in Certain Industries, Code of Federal Regulations, Revised November 1988 [printed in 1991], cited in María Patricia Fernández-Kelly and Anna M. García, "Informalization at the Core: Hispanic Women, Homework, and the Advanced Capitalist State," in A. Portes, M. Castello, and L. Benton, eds., *The Informal Economy: Studies in Advanced and Less Developed Countries* (Baltimore: Johns Hopkins University Press, 1989).

45. Piore and Sabel, *Second Industrial Divide.*

46. See Lauren Benton, "Homework and Industrial Development: Gender Roles and Restructuring in the Spanish Shoe Industry," *World Development* 17:2 (1989): 255–66; Lauren Benton, "Decentralized Industry and the Limits to State Planning: National Pacts and Local Alliances in Spain," *Urban Anthropology* 17:4 (1988): 279–300; Bluestone and Harrison, *Deindustrialization of America.*

47. See Sassen-Koob, "Dynamics of Growth"; Fernández-Kelly, *For We are Sold;* Castells and Portes, "World Underneath"; Portes and Benton, "Industrial Development and Labor Absorption"; and Portes et al., eds., *Informal Economy.*

48. See Sassen-Koob, "Dynamics of Growth"; Katz and Kemnitzer, "Fast Forward"; Dangler, "Electronic Subassemblers"; Castells and Portes, "World Underneath"; and Benería and Roldán, *Crossroads of Gender, Race, and Class.*

49. Castells and Portes, "World Underneath," p. 10; Katz and Kemnitzer, "Fast Forward," p. 340.

50. Lozano, *Invisible Work Force,* p. 95.

51. Saskia Sassen-Koob, "New York City: Economic Restructuring and Immigration," *Development and Change* 17 (1986): 85–119.

52. *Conditions of Work Digest: Home Work* 8:2 (Geneva: International Labour Office, 1989).

53. Castells and Portes, "World Underneath."

54. Sassen-Koob, "New York City."

55. Castells and Portes, "World Underneath."

56. Ibid., p. 20.

57. Ibid.; Sassen-Koob, "New York City."

58. Fernández-Kelly, *For We are Sold.*

59. Carla Lipsig-Mummé, "The Renaissance of Homeworking in Developed Economies," *Relationes industrielles* 38:3 (1983): 545–66; Sheila Allen, "Production and Reproduction: The Lives of Women Homeworkers," *Sociological Review* 31:4 (1983): 649–65; and Sheila Allen, "Domestic Production and Organizing for Change," *Economic and Industrial Democracy* 3 (1982): 381–411.

60. Portes and Benton, "Industrial Development and Labor Absorption," p. 605.

61. Alex Stepick, "Miami's Two Informal Sectors," in Portes, Castells, and Benton, eds., *Informal Economy*.

62. Fernández-Kelly and García, "Informalization at the Core," pp. 247–64.

63. Castells and Portes, "World Underneath," p. 16.

64. The testimony and reports in the following congressional hearings bring out these interesting issues from a variety of perspectives: Senate, "Amending the Fair Labor Standards Act to Include Industrial Homework" (February 9, 1984); House, "The Re-emergence of Sweatshops and the Enforcement of Wage and Hour Standards" (1982); House, "The Pros and Cons of Home-based Clerical Work" (February 26, 1986), 99th Cong., 2d sess.; and House, "Oversight Hearings on the Department of Labor's Proposal to Lift the Ban on Industrial Homework," (1987), 99th Cong., 2d sess.

65. J. Norman Reid and Richard W. Long, "Rural Policy Objectives: Defining Problems and Choosing Approaches," in David L. Brown et al., eds., *Rural Economic Development in the 1980s: Prospects for the Future*, USDA Economic Research Service Report no. 69, 1988, pp. 201–20.

66. Peggy J. Ross and Stuart A. Rosenfeld, "Human Resource Policies and Economic Development," in Brown et al., eds., *Rural Economic Development*.

67. Ibid.

68. Heather MacFarlane, "Dropped Stitches: Federal Regulations of Industrial Homework in the 1980s," *Albany Law Review* 50 (1985): 107–56.

69. Ibid.

70. Donald Elisburg, "Legalities," *Telematics and Informatics* 2:2 (1985): 181–85.

71. Kathleen E. Christensen, "Women and Home-based Work," *Social Policy* 5 (Winter 1985): 54–57.

72. See Portes and Benton, "Industrial Development and Labor Absorption"; Castells and Portes, "World Underneath"; Sassen-Koob, "Dynamics of Growth."

73. From IRS Circular E, "Employers' Tax Guide," cited in Fernández-Kelly and García, "Informalization at the Core," p. 256.

74. David L. Brown and Kenneth L. Deavers, "Rural Change and the Rural Economic Agenda for the 1980s," in Brown et al., eds., *Rural Economic Development*, pp. 1–28.

75. David A. McGranahan, John C. Hession, Fred K. Hines, and Max F. Jordan, *Social and Economic Characteristics of the Population in Metro and Nonmetro Counties, 1970–1980*, Report no. 58 (Washington, D.C.: USDA Economic Research Service, 1986); Gene Summers, Francine Horton, and Christina Gringeri, "Rural Labour Markets in the United States," in T. Marsden, S. Whatmore, and P. Lowe, eds., *Rural Restructuring: Global Processes and Local Responses* (London: David Fulton Publishers, 1990), pp. 129–64.

76. McGranahan et al., *Social and Economic Characteristics*; David A. Mc-

Granahan, "Rural Workers in the National Economy," in Brown et al., eds., *Rural Economic Development*, pp. 49–76.
77. Brown and Deavers, "Rural Change."
78. Ibid.
79. McGranahan et al., *Social and Economic Characteristics*.
80. Leonard E. Bloomquist, "Performance of the Rural Manufacturing Sector," in Brown et al., eds., *Rural Economic Development*.
81. McGranahan et al., *Social and Economic Characteristics*, p. 40.
82. See Rubenstein, *Changing U.S. Auto Industry*.
83. Bloomquist, "Performance of the Rural Manufacturing Sector."
84. See Summers, Horton, and Gringeri, "Rural Labour Markets."
85. Brown and Deavers, "Rural Change," p. 13.
86. Benería and Roldán, *Crossroads of Gender, Race, and Class.*

CHAPTER TWO. RESTRUCTURED PRODUCTION

1. See Mark Friedberger, *Farm Families and Change in Twentieth-Century America* (Lexington: University of Kentucky Press, 1988).
2. See Janet M. Fitchen, *Endangered Spaces, Enduring Places: Change, Identity, and Survival in Rural America* (Boulder, Colo.: Westview Press, 1991).
3. For an excellent description of the farm crisis in the Midwest and of the various groups of people involved, see Friedberger, *Farm Families.*
4. Ibid., p. 203.
5. See Peter Eisinger, *The Rise of the Entrepreneurial State* (Madison: University of Wisconsin Press, 1988).
6. U.S. Census of Population, 1980.
7. See Friedberger, *Farm Families.*
8. See Osha Gray Davidson, *Broken Heartland: The Rise of America's Rural Ghetto* (New York: Free Press, 1990), for a discussion of the farm crisis and its effects on farm operators, families, and communities in the Midwest.
9. Data taken from *Iowa's Counties: Selected Population Trends, Vital Statistics, and Socioeconomic Data*, compiled by Willis Goudy and Sandra Charvat Burke, Census Services, Ames, Iowa State University, 1992.
10. Statement made by a TMC manager during the course of a five-hour meeting, in which managers were broadly delineating to me how the cottage industry concept came about and was established in Prairie Hills.
11. U.S. Census of Population, 1980.
12. These data were obtained from various Wisconsin agencies. Unemployment rates were provided by the Department of Industry, Labor and Human Relations; AFDC, AFDC-UP, and food-stamp rates were provided by the Department of Health and Human Services; and the free school-lunch recipiency rates were provided by the Food and Nutrition Services at the Department of Public Instruction.
13. See James M. Rubenstein, *The Changing U.S. Auto Industry* (London: Routledge, 1992).
14. Ibid.
15. The UAW has refused to give me specific information about the negotiations regarding GM's use of homeworkers. When asked, UAW officials told me that the use of homeworkers was "GM's business, not ours." A Wisconsin UAW official in the Janesville area, where there were many GM workers, said that the

Detroit UAW negotiated with GM to allow the homework if no directly related factory jobs were lost to layoffs. The UAW did negotiate with GM, however, in the latter part of the 1980s over the extent of outsourcing in general, in an effort to control GM's use of outsourcing and to protect the existing factory jobs.

16. Iowa did not subsidize the costs of assembly machinery as requested in the proposal.

17. This may be because the home-contracting positions had gained a reputation for being "welfare work," in the words of one TMC manager. In Prairie Hills there was a strong sense that the work was for "bankrupt" farmers. Possibly, TMC wished to avoid the reputation that went along with using JTPA eligibility criteria. The training subsidies were so small that the effort may not have seemed worthwhile to them.

18. See Eisinger, *Rise of the Entrepreneurial State.*

19. There is a certain irony to this statement about unemployment. Indeed there is less unemployment paid because TMC defines the workers as independent contractors and therefore does not pay state or federal unemployment taxes. And fewer people will receive unemployment from this pool of workers because their classification as independent contractors renders them ineligible for payment when there is no assembly work available.

20. Eisinger, *Rise of the Entrepreneurial State.*

21. For a good discussion of the role of the state, see Martin Carnoy, *The State and Political Theory* (Princeton, N.J.: Princeton University Press, 1984). See Simon Duncan and Mark Goodwin, *The Local State and Uneven Development* (London: Polity Press, 1988), for an empirical study of the role of the local state in the area of development.

CHAPTER THREE. HOMEWORKERS IN THE
HEARTLAND

1. Liz is referring to the contrast in her family's economic circumstances since the recent agricultural crisis that started in the early 1980s.

CHAPTER FOUR. INTEGRATING HOME AND
INFORMAL-SECTOR WORK

1. Alejandro Portes and Lauren Benton, "Industrial Development and Labor Absorption: A Reinterpretation," *Population and Development Review* 10:4 (1984): 589–611; Manuel Castells and Alejandro Portes, "World Underneath: The Origins, Dynamics, and Effects of the Informal Economy" (Paper presented at the Conference on the Comparative Study of the Informal Sector, Harpers Ferry, West Virginia, October 2–6,1986).

CHAPTER FIVE. UNDERSTANDING INDUSTRIAL
HOMEWORK AS SUBSIDIZED DEVELOPMENT

1. Kathleen Christensen, *Women and Homebased Work: The Unspoken Contract* (New York: Holt, 1988).

2. Ibid., p. 137.

CHAPTER SIX. HOMEWORK IN A COMPARATIVE
CONTEXT

1. These studies add comparison across three countries and various types of homework but by no means cover the entire range of work that is done in the home for wages, the many countries in which homeworkers are found, or the variety of contracts under which people perform that work.

2. Beverly Lozano, *The Invisible Workforce* (New York: Free Press, 1989).

3. Unfortunately, Lozano is unclear about how many of the thirty-five workers are truly independent, possibly because their status is not fixed but may vary between "waged employee" and independent contractor from one contract to another. Yet most of the workers perceived themselves, albeit with some confusion, as being self-employed; see ibid., chart on p. 10, for distinction among labor types and discussion on pp. 37–38 regarding independent contractors.

4. Kathleen E. Christensen, ed., *The New Era of Home-based Work* (Boulder, Colo.: Westview Press, 1988).

5. Jamie Faracellia Dangler, "Electronic Subassemblers in Central New York: Nontraditional Homeworkers in a Nontraditional Homework Industry," in Eileen Boris and Cynthia R. Daniels, eds., *Homework: Historical and Contemporary Perspectives on Paid Labor at Home* (Urbana and Chicago: University of Illinois Press, 1989), pp. 147–64. See also Jamie Faricellia Dangler, "Paid Work in the Home" (Ph.D diss., State University of New York, Binghamton, 1991).

6. Eileen Boris, "Regulating Industrial Homework: The Triumph of 'Sacred Motherhood,'" *Journal of American History* 71:4 (1987): 745–63, and Boris and Daniels, eds., *Homework*.

7. Cynthia B. Costello, "The Clerical Homework Program at the Wisconsin Physicians Service Insurance Corporation," in Boris and Daniels, eds., *Homework*, pp. 198–214; Cynthia B. Costello, *We're Worth It! Women and Collective Action in the Insurance Workplace* (Urbana and Chicago: University of Illinois Press, 1991).

8. Sheila Allen and Carol Wolkowitz, *Homeworking: Myths and Realities* (London: Macmillan, 1987).

9. Arnold Cragg and Tim Dawson, *Qualitative Research among Homeworkers* (London: Low Pay Unit, 1981).

10. Babysitting is often excluded as homework because it is usually an informal agreement between two individuals stipulating the cost and conditions of child care rather than as a contract between two business people or between an individual and a business. Babysitting is seen as the provision of a personal service to another person rather than a service for that person's business (see Allen and Wolkowitz, *Homeworking*, for a discussion of this matter). It is considered as part of the informal economic sector, however, much the same as bartering.

11. Cynthia Truelove, "The Informal Sector Revisited: The Case of the talleres rurales mini-maquilas in Colombia," in Richard Tardan, ed., *Crises in the Caribbean Basin* (Beverly Hills, Calif.: Sage, 1987), pp. 48–63; Martha Roldán, "Industrial Outworking, Struggles for the Reproduction of Working-

class Families and Gender Subordination," in E. Mingione and N. Redclift, eds., *Beyond Employment: Household, Gender, and Subsistence* (Oxford: Basil Blackwell, 1985); Lauren Benton, "Informal Sector Growth as a Development Strategy: Industrial Restructuring in Spain" (Paper presented at the Conference on the Comparative Study of the Informal Sector, October 2–6, 1986, Harpers Ferry, West Virginia).

12. Lourdes Benería and Martha Roldán, *Crossroads of Gender, Race, and Class: Industrial Homeworking in Mexico* (Chicago: University of Chicago Press, 1987).

13. Lozano, *Invisible Workforce*; Costello, "Clerical Homework Program" and *We're Worth It*.

14. Boris, "Regulating Industrial Homework."

15. Allen and Wolkowitz, *Homeworking*, p. 117.

16. Cragg and Dawson, *Qualitative Research*, p. 28.

17. Lozano, *Invisible Workforce*.

18. Ibid., p. 113.

19. Dangler, "Electronic Subassemblers" and "Paid Work in the Home"; Boris, "Regulating Industrial Homework."

20. Costello, *We're Worth It*.

21. Homeworker interviewed in Cragg and Dawson, *Qualitative Research*, p. 18.

22. Ibid., p. 26.

23. Ibid.

24. Ibid.

25. Lozano, *Invisible Workforce*, p. 95 (emphasis in original).

26. Cragg and Dawson, *Qualitative Research*, p. 13.

27. Lozano, *Invisible Workforce*, p. 117. As this respondent's children grew older, they brought friends into the labor process, and the respondent became a supervisor of several youths working in her garage.

28. Benería and Roldán, *Crossroads of Gender, Race, and Class*.

29. Cragg and Dawson, *Qualitative Research*, p. 14.

30. Ibid., p. 26.

31. In Prairie Hills some of the assemblers had been working for over three years without a raise at the time of the interview. Cragg and Dawson report that at least 20 percent of their sample had had "no increase in their rate of pay for two years or more; one was working at the same rate at which she had started seven years ago" (ibid., p. 21).

32. Allen and Wolkowitz, *Homeworking*, p. 130.

33. Costello, *We're Worth It*.

34. See *Conditions of Work Digest: Home Work* 8:2 (Geneva: International Labour Office, 1989). The entire issue is dedicated to homework.

35. See Boris, "Regulating Industrial Homework"; Boris and Daniels, eds., *Homework*.

36. Personal communication with Sharon Stevens, University of Missouri–Columbia, October 7, 1993.

37. Gene F. Summers, Francine Horton, and Christina Gringeri, "Rural Labour Markets in the United States," in Terry Marsden, Sarah Whatmore, and Philip Lowe, eds., *Rural Restructuring: Global Processes and Local Responses* (London: David Fulton Publishers, 1989), pp. 129–64.

38. Lozano, *Invisible Workforce*.

39. The mayor of Riverton mentioned in an interview that small communities are having difficulty filling skilled-trade positions because apprentices often stay in the urban areas where income is higher. By training local women for these positions, communities would reap dual benefits by meeting the needs locally for this trade and through advanced employment for women.

40. Benería and Roldán, *Crossroads of Gender, Race, and Class,* p. 170.

41. See Elizabeth Moen, Elise Boulding, Jane Lillydahl, and Risa Palm, *Women and the Social Costs of Economic Development: Two Colorado Case Studies* (Boulder, Colo.: Westview Press, 1981) for a good discussion of the effects of boomtown expansion on different groups of women in two fairly small communities.

42. Ibid.; Alejandro Portes, "On the Sociology of National Development: Theories and Issues," *American Journal of Sociology* 82 (1976): 55–85.

43. See Moen et al., *Women and Social Costs;* Benería and Roldán, *Crossroads of Gender, Race, and Class;* and Allen and Wolkowitz, *Homeworking.*

Selected Bibliography

Abbott, Edith. *Women in Industry*. New York: D. Appleton and Company, 1924.

Adams, Jane. "The Decoupling of Farm and Household: Differential Consequences of Capitalist Development on Southern Illinois and Third World Family Farms." *Comparative Studies in Society and History*, 3 (1988): 453–83.

Albrecht, Sandra L. "Industrial Home Work in the United States: Historical Dimensions and Contemporary Perspectives." *Economic and Industrial Democracy* 3 (1982): 413–30.

Allen, Sheila. "Domestic Production and Organizing for Change." *Economic and Industrial Democracy* 3 (1982): 381–411.

―――. "Production and Reproduction: The Lives of Women Homeworkers." *Sociological Review* 31:4 (1983): 649–65.

Allen, Sheila, and Carol Wolkowitz. *Homeworking: Myths and Realities*. London: Macmillan, 1987.

Beach, Betty. "The Family Context of Home Shoe Work." In Eileen Boris and Cynthia Daniels, eds., *Homework: Historical and Contemporary Perspectives on Paid Labor at Home*, Urbana and Chicago: University of Illinois Press, 1989.

―――. *Integrating Work and Family Life*. Albany: State University of New York, 1989.

Benería, L., and Martha Roldán. *Crossroads of Gender, Race and Class: Industrial Homeworking in Mexico*. Chicago: University of Chicago Press, 1987.

Benería, L., and Gita Sen. "Accumulation, Reproduction, and Women's Role in Economic Development: Boserup Revisited." *Signs* 7:2 (Winter 1981): 279–98.

Benería, L., and Catherine Stimpson, eds. *Women, Households, and the Economy*. New Brunswick, N.J.: Rutgers University Press, 1987.

Bentley, Susan, and Carolyn Sachs. *Farm Women in the United States: An Up-*

dated Literature Review and Annotated Bibliography. Department of Agricultural Economics and Rural Sociology, Pennsylvania State University, 1984.

Benton, Lauren A. "Decentralized Industry and the Limits to State Planning: National Pacts and Local Alliances in Spain." *Urban Anthropology* 17:4 (Winter 1988): 279–300.

————. "Homework and Industrial Development: Gender Roles and Restructuring in the Spanish Shoe Industry." *World Development* 17:2 (1989): 255–66.

————. "Informal Sector Growth as a Development Strategy: Industrial Restructuring in Spain." Paper presented at the Conference on the Comparative Study of the Informal Sector, Harpers Ferry, West Virginia, October 2–6, 1986.

Bergmann, Barbara R. *The Economic Emergence of Women.* New York: Basic Books, 1986.

Blewett, Mary. *Men, Women, and Work.* Urbana: University of Illinois Press, 1988.

Bloomquist, Leonard E. "Performance of the Rural Manufacturing Sector." In David L. Brown et al., eds., *Rural Economic Development in the 1980s.* Washington, D.C.: USDA, 1988.

Bluestone, Barry, and Bennett Harrison. *The Deindustrialization of America.* New York: Basic Books, 1982.

Bokemeier, Janet, and Lorraine Garkovich. "Assessing the Influence of Farm Women's Self-Identity on Task Allocation and Decision Making." *Rural Sociology* 52:1 (1987): 13–36.

Bokemeier, Janet, Carolyn Sachs, and Verna Keith. "Labor Force Participation of Metropolitan, Nonmetropolitan, and Farm Women: A Comparative Study." *Rural Sociology* 48:4 (1983): 515–39.

Boris, Eileen. "Homework and Women's Rights: The Case of the Vermont Knitters, 1980–1985. *Signs: Journal of Women in Culture and Society* 13:1 (1987): 98–120.

————. "Regulating Industrial Homework: The Triumph of 'Sacred Motherhood.'" *Journal of American History* 71:4 (1987): 745–63.

————. " 'Right to Work' as a 'Women's Right': The Debate over the Vermont Knitters, 1980–1985." Institute for Legal Studies Working Paper, University of Wisconsin, Madison, 1986.

Boris, Eileen, and Cynthia Daniels, eds. *Homework: Historical and Contemporary Perspectives on Paid Labor at Home.* Urbana and Chicago: University of Illinois Press, 1989.

Boulding, Elise. "The Labor of U.S. Farm Women: A Knowledge Gap." *Sociology of Work and Occupations* 7:3 (1980): 261–90.

Brown, David L., and Kenneth L. Deavers. "Rural Change and the Rural Economic Policy Agenda for the 1980s." In David L. Brown et al., eds., *Rural Economic Development in the 1980s.* Washington, D.C.: USDA, 1988.

Brown, David L., J. Norman Reid, Herman Bluestone, David A. McGranahan, and Sara M. Mazie, eds. *Rural Economic Development in the 1980s: Prospects for the Future.* Report no. 69. Washington, D.C.: USDA, Economic Research Service, 1988.

Bultena, Gordon, Paul Lasley, and Jack Geller. "The Farm Crisis: Patterns and Impacts of Financial Distress among Iowa Farm Families." *Rural Sociology* 51:4 (1986): 436–48.

Buttel, Frederick H., and Gilbert W. Gillespie, Jr. "The Sexual Division of Farm Household Labor: An Exploratory Study of the Structure of On-Farm and Off-Farm Labor Allocation among Farm Men and Women." *Rural Sociology* 49:2 (1984): 183–209.

Castells, Manuel, and Alejandro Portes. "World Underneath: The Origins, Dynamics, and Effects of the Informal Economy." Paper presented at the Conference on the Comparative Study of the Informal Sector: Harpers Ferry, West Virginia, October 2–6, 1986.

Christensen, Kathleen E. "Home-Based Clerical Work: No Simple Truth, No Single Reality." In Eileen Boris and Cynthia Daniels, eds., *Homework: Historical and Contemporary Perspectives on Paid Labor at Home*. Urbana and Chicago: University of Illinois Press, 1989.

——. "Women and Home-Based Work." *Social Policy* 15 (Winter 1985): 54–57.

——. *Women and Homebased Work: The Unspoken Contract*. New York: Holt, 1988.

——, ed. *The New Era of Home-Based Work*. Boulder, Colo.: Westview Press, 1988.

Clark, Christopher. *The Roots of Rural Capitalism*. Ithaca, N.Y.: Cornell University Press, 1990.

Colclough, Glenna. "Uneven Development and Racial Composition in the Deep South: 1970–1980." *Rural Sociology* 55 (Spring 1988): 73–86.

Conditions of Work Digest: Home Work 8:2. Geneva: International Labour Office, 1989.

Costello, Cynthia B. "The Clerical Homework Program at the Wisconsin Physicians Service Insurance Corporation." In Eileen Boris and Cynthia Daniels, eds., *Homework: Historical and Contemporary Perspectives on Paid Labor at Home*. Chicago and Urbana: University of Illinois Press, 1989.

——. *Home-Based Work: Implications for Working Women*. Washington, D.C.: Women's Research and Education Institute, Congressional Caucus for Women's Issues, 1987.

——. "The Office Homework Program at the Wisconsin Physicians Service Insurance Company." In Cynthia Costello, ed., *"On the Front": Women's Work in the Insurance Industry*. Forthcoming.

——. *We're Worth It! Women and Collective Action in the Insurance Workplace*. Urbana and Chicago: University of Illinois Press, 1991.

Coughenour, C. Milton, and Louis Swanson. "Work Statuses and Occupations of Men and Women in Farm Families and the Structure of Farms." *Rural Sociology* 48:1 (1983): 23–43.

Cragg, Arnold, and Tim Dawson. *Qualitative Research among Homeworkers*. London: Low Pay Unit, 1981.

Dangler, Jamie Faracellia. "Electronic Subassemblers in Central New York: Nontraditional Homeworkers in a Nontraditional Homework Industry." In Eileen Boris and Cynthia Daniels, eds., *Homework: Historical and Contemporary Perspectives on Paid Labor at Home*. Urbana and Chicago: University of Illinois Press, 1989.

——. "Paid Work in the Home." Ph.D dissertation, State University of New York, Binghamton, 1991.

Davidson, Osha Gray. *Broken Heartland: The Rise of America's Rural Ghetto*. New York: Free Press, 1990.

Dublin, Thomas. "Women and Outwork in a Nineteenth-Century New England Town." In S. Hahn and J. Prude, eds., *The Countryside in the Age of Capitalist Transformation*. Chapel Hill: University of North Carolina Press, 1985.

Duncan, Simon, and Mark Goodwin. *The Local State and Uneven Development*. London: Polity Press, 1988.

Eisinger, Peter. *The Rise of the Entrepreneurial State*. Madison: University of Wisconsin Press, 1988.

Elisburg, Donald. "Legalities." *Telematics and Informatics* 2:2 (1985): 181–85.

Fassinger, Polly A., and Harry K. Schwarzweller. "Work Patterns of Farm Wives in Mid-Michigan." East Lansing: Michigan State University Agricultural Experiment Station Research Report 425, January 1982.

Fernández-Kelly, María Patricia. *For We Are Sold, I and My People: Women and Industry in Mexico's Frontier*. Albany: State University of New York, 1983.

Fernández-Kelly, María Patricia, and Anna M. García. "Informalization at the Core: Hispanic Women, Home Work, and the Advanced Capitalist State." In A. Portes, M. Castells, and L. Benton, eds., *The Informal Economy: Studies in Advanced and Less Developed Countries*. Baltimore: Johns Hopkins University Press, 1989.

Fink, Deborah. "Farming in Open Country, Iowa: Women and the Changing Farm Economy." In Michael Chibnik, ed., *Farm Work and Fieldwork*. Ithaca, N.Y.: Cornell University Press, 1987.

————. *Open Country, Iowa: Rural Women, Tradition, and Change*. Albany: State University of New York Press, 1986.

Fitchen, Janet M. *Endangered Spaces, Enduring Places: Change, Identity, and Survival in Rural America*. Boulder, Colo.: Westview Press, 1991.

Folbre, Nancy. "The Pauperization of Motherhood: Patriarchy and Public Policy in the United States." *Review of Radical Political Economics* 16:4 (1984): 72–88.

Friedberger, Mark. *Farm Families and Change in Twentieth-Century America*. Lexington: University of Kentucky Press, 1988.

Gereffi, Gary. *The Pharmaceutical Industry and Dependency in the Third World*. Princeton, N.J.: Princeton University Press, 1983.

Gerson, Judith M. "Clerical Work at Home or in the Office: The Difference It Makes." In Kathleen Christensen, ed., *The New Era of Home-Based Work*. Boulder, Colo.: Westview Press, 1988.

Greenwood, Robert. "The Local State and Economic Development in Peripheral Regions." Dissertation proposal, University of Warwick, 1988.

Gringeri, Christina. "Inscribing Gender in Rural Development: Industrial Homework in Two Midwestern Communities." *Rural Sociology* 58:1 (1993): 30–52.

Haney, Wava Gillespie. "Farm Family and the Role of Women." In Gene Summers, ed., *Technology and Sociology in Rural Areas*. Boulder, Colo.: Westview Press, 1983.

Harrison, Bennett, and Barry Bluestone. *The Great U-Turn: Corporate Restructuring and the Polarizing of America*. New York: Basic Books, 1988.

Johnson, Laura C., and Robert E. Johnson. *The Seam Allowance*. Toronto: Women's Educational Press, 1982.

Joyce, Lynda M., and Samuel M. Leadley. *An Assessment of Research Needs of Women in the Rural United States: Literature Review and Annotated Bibliography*. University Park: Pennsylvania State University, 1977.

Kanter, Hannah, Sarah Lefanu, Shaila Shah, and Carole Spedding, eds. *Sweeping Statements*. London: Women's Press, 1984.

Katz, Naomi, and David S. Kemnitzer. "Fast Forward: The Internationalization of Silicon Valley." In June Nash and María Patricia Fernández-Kelly, eds., *Women, Men, and the International Division of Labor.* Albany: State University of New York, 1983.

Kessler-Harris, Alice. *Out to Work: A History of Wage-earning Women in the United States.* New York: Oxford University Press, 1982.

Kraut, Robert E. "Homework: What Is It and Who Does It?" In Kathleen E. Christensen, ed., *The New Era of Home-based Work.* Boulder, Colo.: Westview Press, 1988.

Leidner, Robin. "Home Work: A Study in the Interaction of Work and Family Organization." In *Research in the Sociology of Work,* vol. 4, *High Tech Work,* ed. Ida Harper Simpson and Richard L. Simpson. Greenwich, Conn.: JAI Press, 1987.

Lever, Alison. "Capital, Gender, and Skill: Women Homeworkers in Rural Spain." *Feminist Review* 30 (Autumn 1988): 3–24.

Lipsig-Mummé, Carla. "The Renaissance of Homeworking in Developed Economies." *Relationes industrielles* 38:3 (1983): 545–66.

Lozano, Beverly. *The Invisible Work Force.* New York: Free Press, 1989.

Luxton, Meg. *More Than a Labour of Love: Three Generations of Women's Work in the Home.* Toronto: Women's Educational Press, 1980.

MacFarlane, Heather. "Dropped Stitches: Federal Regulations of Industrial Homework in the 1980s." *Albany Law Review* 50 (1985): 107–56.

McGranahan, David A. "Rural Workers in the National Economy." In David L. Brown et al., eds., *Rural Economic Development in the 1980s.* Washington, D.C.: USDA, Economic Research Service, 1988.

McGranahan, David A., John C. Hession, Fred K. Hines, and Max F. Jordan. *Social and Economic Characteristics of the Population in Metro and Nonmetro Counties, 1970–1980.* Rural Development Research Report no. 58. Washington, DC: USDA, Economic Research Service, 1986.

Malcolmson, R. W. "Ways of Getting a Living in Eighteenth-Century England." In R. E. Pahl, ed., *On Work: Historical, Comparative and Theoretical Approaches.* London: Basil Blackwell, 1988.

Mann, Susan, Linda Briskin, Bruce Curtis, Wally Seccombe, Emily Blumenfeld, and Bonnie Fox, eds. *Hidden in the Household: Women's Domestic Labour under Capitalism.* Toronto: Women's Educational Press, 1980.

Matthaei, Julie A. *An Economic History of Women in America.* New York: Schocken Books, 1982.

Moen, Elizabeth, Elise Boulding, Jane Lillydahl, and Risa Palm. *Women and the Social Costs of Economic Development: Two Colorado Case Studies.* Boulder, Colo.: Westview Press, 1981.

Nash, June, and María Patricia Fernández-Kelly, eds. *Women, Men, and the International Division of Labor.* Albany: State University of New York, 1983.

Olson, Margrethe H., and Sophia B. Primps. "Working at Home with Computers: Work and Nonwork Issues." *Journal of Social Issues* 40:3 (1984): 97–112.

Piore, Michael J. "Perspectives on Labor Market Flexibility." *Industrial Relations* 25:2 (Spring 1986): 144–66.

Piore, Michael J., and Charles F. Sabel. *The Second Industrial Divide.* New York: Basic Books, 1984.

Portes, Alejandro. "On the Sociology of National Development: Theories and Issues." *American Journal of Sociology* 82:1 (July 1976): 55–85.

Portes, Alejandro, and Lauren Benton. "Industrial Development and Labor Absorption: A Reinterpretation." *Population and Development Review* 10:4 (December 1984): 589–611.

Portes, Alejandro, Manuel Castells, and Lauren Benton, eds. *The Informal Economy: Studies in Advanced and Less Developed Countries.* Baltimore: Johns Hopkins University Press, 1989.

Portes, Alejandro, and Saskia Sassen-Koob. "Making It Underground: Comparative Material on the Informal Sector in Western Market Economies." *American Journal of Sociology* 93:1 (July 1987): 30–61.

Redclift, Nanneke, and Enzo Mingione, eds. *Beyond Employment: Household, Gender, and Subsistence.* Oxford: Basil Blackwell, 1985.

Reid, J. Norman, and Richard W. Long. "Rural Policy Objectives: Defining Problems and Choosing Approaches." In David L. Brown et al., eds., *Rural Economic Development in the 1980s.* Washington, D.C.: USDA, Economic Research Service, 1988.

Reimer, Bill. "Women as Farm Labor." *Rural Sociology* 51:2 (1986): 143–55.

Roldán, Martha. "Industrial Outworking, Struggles for the Reproduction of Working-class Families and Gender Subordination." In Nanneke Redclift and Enzo Mingione, eds., *Beyond Employment: Household, Gender and Subsistence.* Oxford: Basil Blackwell, 1985.

Rosenfeld, Rachel Ann. *Farm Women: Work, Farm, and Family in the United States.* Chapel Hill: University of North Carolina Press, 1985.

Ross, Peggy J., and Stuart A. Rosenfeld. "Human Resource Policies and Economic Development." In David L. Brown et al., eds., *Rural Economic Development in the 1980s.* Washington, D.C.: USDA, Economic Research Service, 1988.

Rubenstein, James M. *The Changing U.S. Auto Industry: A Geographical Analysis.* New York: Routledge, 1992.

Sabel, Charles F. "The Re-Emergence of Regional Economies." December 1987.

Sachs, Carolyn. *The Invisible Farmers: Women in Agricultural Production.* Totowa, N.J.: Rowman and Allanheld, 1983.

Sassen-Koob, Saskia. "The Dynamics of Growth in Post-Industrial New York City." Paper presented at the Workshop on the Dual City, New York City, 1986.

———. "New York City: Economic Restructuring and Immigration." *Development and Change* 17 (1986): 85–119.

Silver, Hilary. "The Demand for Homework: Evidence from the U.S. Census." In Eileen Boris and Cynthia Daniels, eds., *Homework: Historical and Contemporary Perspectives on Paid Labor at Home.* Urbana and Chicago: University of Illinois Press, 1989.

———. "Growth and Informalization at the Core: A Preliminary Report on New York City." Paper presented at the Symposium on the Informal Sector, Johns Hopkins University, 1984.

———. "New York City: Economic Restructuring and Immigration." *Development and Change* 17 (1986): 85–119.

Smith, Joan. "The Paradox of Women's Poverty: Wage-earning Women and Economic Transformation." *Signs: Journal of Women in Culture and Society* 10 (Winter 1984): 291–310.

Stansell, Christine. *City of Women: Sex and Class in New York, 1789–1860.* Chicago: University of Illinois Press, 1987.

Stein, Leon, ed. *Out of the Sweatshop*. New York: New York Times Book Company, 1977.

Stepick, Alex. "Miami's Two Informal Sectors." In Alejandro Portes, Manuel Castells, and Lauren Benton, eds., *The Informal Economy: Studies in Advanced and Less Developed Countries*. Baltimore: Johns Hopkins University Press, 1989.

Summers, Gene F. "Rural Community Development." *Annual Review of Sociology* 12 (1986): 347–71.

Summers, Gene F., and Kristi Branch. "Economic Development and Community Social Change." *Annual Review of Sociology*, 1984: 141–66.

Summers, Gene F., Sharon D. Evans, Frank Clemente, E. M. Beck, and Jon Minkoff. *Industrial Invasion of Nonmetropolitan America*. New York: Praeger Publishers, 1976.

Summers, Gene F., Francine Horton, and Christina Gringeri. "Rural Labour Markets in the United States." In Terry Marsden, Sarah Whatmore, and Philip Lowe, eds., *Rural Restructuring: Global Processes and Local Responses*. London: David Fulton Publishers, 1989.

Tiano, Susan. "The Public-Private Dichotomy: Theoretical Perspectives on 'Women in Development.'" *Social Science Journal* 21 (1984): 11–27.

Truelove, Cynthia. "The Informal Sector Revisited: The Case of the talleres rurales mini-maquilas in Colombia." In Richard Tardan, ed., *Crises in the Caribbean Basin*. Beverly Hills, Calif.: Sage, 1987.

U.S. Congress. House. "Fair Labor Standards Act Amendments." 97th Cong., 2d sess., 1982.

———. "Home-Based Clerical Workers: Are They Victims of Exploitation?" 99th Cong., 2d sess., 16 July 1986.

———."Oversight Hearings on the Department of Labor's Proposal to Lift the Ban on Industrial Homework." 99th Cong., 2d sess., 1987.

———. "The Pros and Cons of Home-Based Clerical Work." 99th Cong., 2d sess., 1986.

U.S. Congress. House. Subcommittee on Labor Standards. *The Reemergence of Sweatshops and the Enforcement of Wage and Hour Standards*. Washington, D.C.: Government Printing Office, 1982.

U.S. Congress. Senate. Committee on Labor and Human Resources. "Amending the Fair Labor Standards Act to Include Industrial Homework." 98th Cong., 2d sess., 1984.

U.S. Department of Labor. Employment Standards Administration. "Statement of International Ladies' Garment Workers' Union in Opposition to the Removal of Restrictions on Industrial Homework." July 1, 1981.

Valenzuela, J. Samuel, and Arturo Valenzuela. "Modernization and Dependency: Alternative Perspectives in the Study of Latin American Underdevelopment." In Heraldo Munoz, ed., *From Dependency to Development: Strategies to Overcome Underdevelopment and Inequality*. Boulder, Colo.: Westview Press, 1981.

Ybarra, Josep-Antoni. "Informalization in the Valencian Economy: A Model for Underdevelopment." Paper presented at the Conference on the Informal Sector, Harpers Ferry, West Virginia, 1984.

Index